Olga —
Great to
meet you in
SanFran —
Yours in
Careuns!

Stuart MacC
10/96

THE COMPUTER TRAINING HANDBOOK

STRATEGIES FOR HELPING PEOPLE TO LEARN TECHNOLOGY

SECOND EDITION

ELLIOTT MASIE

Quantity Sales

Most Lakewood books are available at special quantity discounts when purchased in bulk by companies, organizations, and special-interest groups. Custom imprinting or excerpting can also be done to fit special needs. For details, contact Lakewood Books.

■   ■   ■

LAKEWOOD BOOKS
50 South Ninth Street
Minneapolis, MN 55402
(800) 328-4329 or (612) 333-0471
Fax (612) 333-6526

Publisher: Philip Jones
Editorial Coordinator: Becky Wilkinson
Copyeditor: Pam Christian
Book Designer and Typesetter: Corey Sevett
Cover Designer: Cynthia Busch

The first edition of The Computer Training Handbook *was published by Tools for Training, Inc. It was coauthored by Rebekah Wolman. All computer systems and programs mentioned in this book are trademarked by their respective developers and distributors.*

10 9 8 7 6 5 4 3 2 1

Lakewood publishes TRAINING Magazine, The Human Side of Business; The Training Directors' Forum Newsletter; Creative Training Techniques Newsletter; The Service Edge Newsletter; Total Quality Newsletter; Potentials In Marketing Magazine; Presentations Magazine, *and other business periodicals and books. James P. Secord, president; Mary Hanson, Philip G. Jones, Linda Klemstein, Michael C. Miller, Jerry C. Noack, vice presidents.*

ISBN 0-943210-37-2

The Computer Training Handbook

Dedication v

Foreword vi

The Future of Computer Training and Learning 1

CHAPTER 1   About the Book 11

CHAPTER 2   About Computer Training 20

CHAPTER 3   A First Look at Adult Learning. 26

CHAPTER 4   The Masie Model of Indexing 30

CHAPTER 5   Learner Resistance 40

CHAPTER 6   Procedural and Navigational Users 47

CHAPTER 7   Learners' Thinking Styles
            (and Other Learning Differences) 51

CHAPTER 8   Needs Assessment 66

CHAPTER 9   Objectives, Targets, and Goals. 78

CHAPTER 10 Vocabulary, Concepts, and Procedures 85

CHAPTER 11 The Sagamore Design Model. 95

Techniques and Technologies Introduction 104

CHAPTER 12 Classroom Environment. 106

CHAPTER 13 Classroom Management 110

CHAPTER 14 Cooperative Learning. 114

CHAPTER 15 In-Class Reading 122

CHAPTER 16 Lecture. 126

CHAPTER 17 On-the-Job Learning and Training 137

CHAPTER 18 Rebooting Learners 143

CHAPTER 19 Self-Study 148

CHAPTER 20   Simulation.................................. 152

CHAPTER 21   Audio Learning............................. 156

CHAPTER 22   On-line and Internet-Based Learning 162

CHAPTER 23   Cheat Sheets............................... 168

CHAPTER 24   Computer-Based Training.................... 171

CHAPTER 25   Flipcharts, Blackboards, and Whiteboards 177

CHAPTER 26   Handouts.................................. 180

CHAPTER 27   Interactive Video 183

CHAPTER 28   Large-Screen Projection 188

CHAPTER 29   Classroom Networking and Mirroring 196

CHAPTER 30   Overhead Projectors........................ 199

CHAPTER 31   Slides 202

CHAPTER 32   Video Teleconferencing 204

CHAPTER 33   User Groups 208

CHAPTER 34   Video Learning 211

CHAPTER 35   Performance-Support Systems 216

CHAPTER 36   Evaluation................................ 219

CHAPTER 37   Managing Computer Training 238

CHAPTER 38   The Computer-Training Staff 243

CHAPTER 39   The Cost of Learning 254

CHAPTER 40   Marketing the Training Function.............. 260

CHAPTER 41   Purchasing Training 264

CHAPTER 42   Documentation and Training................. 273

CHAPTER 43   Support 284

CHAPTER 44   Ten Simple Thoughts About Computer Training . . 297

Dedication

The second edition of *The Computer Training Handbook* is dedicated to:

■ The nameless trainers who have spent hundreds of thousands of hours teaching people to use good, bad, and ugly technology.

■ Joel Goodman, a friend, colleague, and mentor. Joel has pioneered the use of humor in learning. I have learned about both from him.

■ The staff of The MASIE Institute, who helped launch my endeavors in this field and have provided years of support. Thanks to Nancy Brown, Mitch Edelstein, Leslie Smith, Fiona Holland, and the rest of the gang.

■ Pearl Louie and Ben Wax, for developing the structure and direction of The MASIE Center and providing a pathway to new models for professional learning.

■ Philip Jones of Lakewood Publications, for the faith and vision to see a broader audience for this publication and other projects.

■ The computer-training profession, for creating a new and exciting industry.

Note: The first edition of *The Computer Training Handbook* was co-authored by Rebekah Wolman. Special thanks to Rebekah for her efforts in launching this publication.

Foreword

This is a book about *influence* — how to get it, how to use it, how to make it serve both your company and your career. By influence, I mean the difference you're able to make in one of the biggest challenges facing your business, or any business, today — helping employees develop the skills, the knowledge, the *confidence* they need to be productive in today's wired, information-saturated, computer-dominated workplace. I use the word "influence" for several reasons.

Organizations have been providing computer training for a long time. You're reading this book because you want to do it better — or want to do it without a protracted learning curve. Luckily, no one is better able to assist you with this task than Elliott Masie, president of The MASIE Center, founder of The Computer Training Support Conference, and one of the true pioneers of computer training.

But computer training is only part of a much bigger story. Information technology, in all its digital forms, is driving many of the changes we're seeing in our organizations. Just think about how different things are now than they were five years ago or even two years ago. Computers are helping people work smarter, faster, and more productively. Or at least they should be. They have created new ways to staff and organize, new ways to manufacture products and deliver services. And despite everything information technology has done so far, bigger and more dramatic changes are still to come.

Things are happening so fast, in fact, that years from now, people may look back at the 1990s as a critical decade in the history of learning — the decade when most employees in the workplace started relying on information technology to do their jobs, when the activities of many businesses, even entire industries, migrated to computers and information technology. Meanwhile, at home and in the schools, the '90s may be the decade when interactive multimedia become the dominant form of entertainment, education, and information delivery.

Because of these trends, the 1990s may be dubbed the Decade of the Computer. More appropriately for readers of this book, we're probably in the middle of the Decade of Computer Training. Thus, you're in a position to make a difference like never before. But this difference is more than a matter of training. As Elliott Masie reveals here, it's also a matter of:

- Increasing the awareness of computer training's role
- Packaging and marketing the message within your organization that computer training is essential
- Ensuring that training fits employees' needs
- Ensuring that training justifies itself in terms of return on investment and productivity improvement

As you read the second edition of *The Computer Training Handbook,* you'll learn simple principles and common-sense guidelines that will help you accomplish the preceding tasks and more. The book may even inspire you to make some surprising creative leaps. In the end, you'll feel an increased sense of influence, since you'll be in a better position to help your organization meet one of its most critical challenges.

Who is this book for? It makes little difference if you're a training-and-development specialist, an information-systems specialist, a line manager, or a supervisor. You may have a strong technical background, or you may be an instructional designer, a classroom trainer, or a resident software "expert" who people turn to for help because your patient, caring attitude makes you a natural teacher.

One of the primary reasons titles matter less and less these days has to do with the convergence of training and technology. Trainers are learning (finally!) that computer technology is a natural enhancement to training — that technology, in fact, may be the *only* way to deliver many types of training in a workplace where the need for rapid skill development is greater than ever, but the training time available is dwindling.

Technical and information-systems personnel, on the other hand, are discovering that they've got the background, experience, and knowledge to play an important — sometimes central — role in evaluating, planning, structuring, and implementing the information-technology solutions their organizations need to help employees constantly learn and develop new skills.

In the end, no matter who you are or what organizational function you perform, you'll find this book invaluable. If you're a trainer, it will help you understand how computers and information technology support learning needs and teach you the practical skills for delivering cost-effective, responsive computer training that meets real business objectives. If you're a technologist or information-systems person, the book will assist you in discovering how to make technology work to meet learning needs and in developing skills for effectively applying proven principles of adult learning.

The audience for this book explains a lot about why Lakewood Publications is publishing it. Through its books, magazines, newsletters, and conferences, Lakewood has served the nation's training and human-resource-development community for more than two decades. Now, because we are seeing such a strong convergence of technology and training, many people who have felt firmly rooted in one area or the other are recognizing the need to have one foot planted in each. It's simple. Training needs technology more than ever before. Likewise, technology, if it is to have any impact at all, depends on training to an extent never before necessary.

No one does a better job of combining these two worlds than Elliott Masie. As a trainer, Masie understands the politics, economics, and practical realities of running a training function. As an expert on learning and technology, Masie has both vision and a no-nonsense, practical perspective. He'll manage to excite you about technology's potential for your job and organization but keep you thinking realistically about what will work now and why.

Robert W. Pike, CSP
President
Creative Training Techniques International, Inc.
Minneapolis, Minnesota

The Future of Computer Training and Learning

Technology and Learning: Competency, Trends, and Opportunities

**By Elliott Masie, president
The MASIE Center**

The incredible rate of change in the world of technology creates an even greater rate of change in the field of computer training. Each change to a person's workplace technology results in a direct need to learn more. Think about this rate of change. For every 100 pages of magazine articles about new technology, there are 100 unwritten pages of stories about the struggle of workers to cope with these unending changes to their workplace environment. Every release of a new software package, every upgrade to a suite, every migration to a new form of database access, every expansion of networking capacity, every consideration of a new operating system, and every shift from mainframe to desktop focus yields a need for workers to learn new skills, procedures, and even attitudes.

Some of these workers will be fortunate enough to attend a formal training course at their company. Some will be handed a manual or computer-based-training disk to assist them in learning. Many will use the help desk as a personal — and very expensive — tutor. A large majority will interrupt their daily work tasks (and those of their colleagues in the next cubicle or office) to cope with the changes in an informal on-the-job learning method. One way or another, the nation's organizations will pay an additional cost for each new piece and version of technology that enters the workplace.

This is the foundation of the computer-training and computer-learning industry and field. Hundreds of thousands of jobs and thousands of businesses, products, and services exist to support the technology-learning needs of our society. These same forces of change are also direct challenges to those jobs, businesses, products, and services.

The past two decades have been the Wonder Bread years for the computer-training industry. The growth of mainframe end-user computing followed by the introduction of the personal computer spawned our industry by creating an immediate need for training and support services. Many of the first players in the computer-training field got there by accident. If, for instance, you had one more week of experience with Visicalc, the first spreadsheet, you could open the doors of a new training center. If you were able to explain how to send a PROFS E-mail message, you were designated the in-house guru and trainer. Software publishers launched the first Authorized Training Centers as a way of assuring organizations that actual people were available to teach them to use these new and daunting technologies.

We have come a long way in the past two decades. As technology evolves into an everyday reality in our offices, homes, and even briefcases, computer training becomes a more mature and diverse field.

Good-bye, Mom and Pop

The days of the corner "mom-and-pop computer learning center" are almost numbered. In order to operate a full-service training classroom, one needs high-end computers with loads of memory, a high-speed network, and instructors knowledgeable about various configurations and combinations of technology. The capital required to maintain these classrooms and to market effectively to major corporations is changing the landscape of the computer-training industry. Each week I hear of at least two training companies that have merged, been acquired, or joined a national franchise operation. *Expect to see larger players entering the training-and-support business. Watch for the Baby Bells to develop help-desk and support-outsourcing businesses in the next 18 months.*

Outsourcing Rampant

The forces of reengineering and downsizing are driving a large percentage of computer training off the corporate organizational chart. Large-scale and segment-specific outsourcing of computer training is now in vogue. The number of full-time trainers employed by major corporations has shrunk. It is not uncommon to see a computer-training department of only three or four people servicing 10,000 users; primarily, they're involved in the contracting and scheduling of training.

Much of this outsourcing actually occurs right on the property of major organizations. *Corporate classrooms are more likely to have an external trainer at the overhead projector, and some classrooms are even being leased to external training centers for total management.*

May I See Your Certification, Please?

The days of self-certification are over. Software publishers, following the strong lead of Novell, have climbed aboard the certification bandwagon. Every major software publisher has created, or is about to launch, a testing and certification program aimed at the technical population of its user community.

Certification of support staff, trainers, developers, programmers, and even end-users is a goal of the software industry formulated to protect the image of its product. If you have a problem with your database or network and can't get good support from your MIS department, you might end up blaming the product. Certification programs aim to develop an envelope of competency and support around each major system and application suite. *Expect to see more tests and greater emphasis on career-track testing (e.g., Client-server Certified Programmer).*

Planned Expenditures

This point is based more on hope and need than on a perceived trend. One of my major frustrations is the lack of reality budgeting for computer training. Most companies do not link the acquisition of technology with the undeniable need for increased computer training and support. Immediate needs trigger most training requests. But a *planned* approach to technology-skill investment is infinitely preferable.

Organizations must face the reality that the full cost of each new technology includes the cost of formal and informal computer learning and support. *Planning for learning that is added to the technology migration process will allow for longer-term deals with training vendors and also will encourage more strategic decisions about investing in employee skills.*

I Want It *Now* and I Want It *Here*!

A good percentage of computer training comes at the wrong time. It is either scheduled for two months after an employee starts or is on the calendar for six weeks before the employee really needs the application.

Another large percentage of computer training takes place at the wrong location. Workers away from the home office receive less training than their colleagues back at headquarters. Night-shift workers are rarely on the rolls for computer classes. And mobile and commissioned sales staff are the most frequent no-shows in computer-training programs.

"I want my workers to be able to sit at their desks and learn what they need to do their jobs today," said a manager of 35 banking professionals. "Tomorrow, let them learn what they need tomorrow. I can't afford to have my people going to training every time a new package hits the network." She wants her people to learn the new technology but only when they need the information and with as few trips to the classroom as possible. Here are some emerging trends that meet this demand.

Just-in-time training. Upgrades will be taught in shorter classes, perhaps only a one-hour live session with a take-away CBT learning disk. One training vendor now has a one-day Microsoft Suite class, where employees self-teach four or five products in six hours. The trainer provides the motivation, context, and overview; the learners do most of the work on their own, back at their desktops.

Integrating computer training and job training. Most companies still have separate offerings for computer training and job functions. Bank officers go to one training department to learn how to approve loans and then go to the technology-education center to learn how to use Excel or Lotus 1-2-3. Now these two learning tasks are beginning to meld in corporate America. Progressive training departments are combining curricula from the human-resources and technical-training departments to provide single offerings that will teach someone how, say, to issue a loan and use the spreadsheet as a work tool. Courseware developers are responding to this trend by designing new technology that allows customers to edit, resequence, and integrate computer courses with internal content.

The wandering trainer. Organizations are starting to place trainers in the workplace rather than in front of the classroom. By spending their day working at the desktop with users, they can often deliver the critical element of training needed to keep those users productive. One company dispatched its trainers to provide "sneaker-based training," with each trainer spending two days a week in the workplace. In addition to holding impromptu classes, they also were able to tweak configurations of workers' computers and write a couple of simple but crucial macros to simplify a task. When these wandering trainers returned to the classroom, they often dramatically changed the focus of their classes to match workplace reality.

Scheduled help-desk-based training. Some applications can be taught by phone through a scheduled training event. When I hooked up our organization to the Internet, I was given a time to call the help desk, along with a set of reading materials. The technician broke from his stream of assistance calls to spend 90 minutes walking me through a complex set of new programs. It was an efficient and cost-effective way to get me up and running. Blend that with computer-based training or a demo, and it becomes a viable alternative to classroom training for certain users and applications.

Just the disk, ma'am. The thirst is growing for great computer-based training. The growth of CD-ROM technology, the exposure to children's software, and the increased bundling of CBT with applications have preconditioned the marketplace for this category of product. Watch for an explosion of new CBT and learning products in 1995. The open question will be their effectiveness and full acceptance by users. The simple porting of a curriculum from classroom training to disk will not be acceptable. Developers will have to heed the requests of users for the following features in computer-based training.

■ Freedom of sequence, segment, and style. Users want to be able to skip the stuff they know or don't want to know and to learn without having to answer a test question on every screen. They don't want to take the worst parts of a classroom and transfer them to the desktop. They want to make CBT into personal learning, with choice and freedom.

■ Real-work examples. Users want to work with examples from their own workplace, not from the Acme Company. Developers must allow for easy local customization.

■ Linkage to classroom learning. Because users will often use CBT before, during, and after attending a class, organizations want to purchase a training process that integrates desktop learning with classroom offerings. The use of in-class CBT for information transfer and remedial assistance allows larger, more cost-effective courses.

Prediction: *Watch for new players in the business CBT industry. Educational software and entertainment groups have been eyeing the business market as a natural extension for their artists, authors, and marketers.*

Over the Net

Distance learning is here! The amazing spread of the Internet is yielding a new medium for delivering learning services. I recently offered a pilot course called "Training Skills for Teaching New Technology" via the Internet. I asked for a few interested folks to help us experiment with delivering content modules to their desktops via Internet-delivered E-mail. A few dozen responses would have been terrific; instead, more than 4,000 people applied! The economics are intriguing, since it costs us only a few cents a student to distribute the content modules. Several dozen technology organizations are monitoring this course to adapt the approach to their own continuing-education offerings. *As additional tools for network learning are developed and disseminated, watch for the rise of in-house and externally offered on-line courses.*

In Your Face

Desktop video teleconferencing is about to hit in a big way. The cost of live, two-way desktop video will drop to less than $1,000 a desktop by the start of 1996. ISDN capacity is booming in most organizations and even in the home. Currently, it is possible for a live instructor at one site to conduct a class for learners at many different sites, with full instructor access to each desktop. Organizations like Picture-Tel, AT&T, and Intel are leading the way with the enabling technology. The computer-training industry will need to adapt quickly to this new channel of information. *Imagine a pay-per-view computer-training course, delivered to your desktop via the cable, that allows live communication with instructors during the discussion section. It's coming!*

Scattered Computer-Training Buying

We have watched a shift in the point-of-purchase of training materials and services — from a central office to the business units of organizations. Many corporations enable their business units to buy training from any source, including the internal training department. More people, in more scattered locations, are becoming involved in computer-training decisions and purchases.

Chargeback Confusion

Companies are also struggling to develop models for assessing and recovering the costs of training and support. Thinking of these charges as a form of taxation yields some interesting alternatives. Why, for example, charge for learning but give support for free? Does it make sense to provide an incentive for those business units that depend less on help-desk services?

Employee, Pay Thy Way

Several corporations are exploring the concept of sharing the cost of learning investment with the employee. One beverage company requires that all workers have WordPerfect skills the day they start their employment. They can attend free classes in the learning center, but they must pass the competency test before reporting to work. This restriction shifts the salary costs of learning to the employee.

Other groups are considering employee contributions to CNE certification as a way of emphasizing its impact on workers' future earnings and career potential.

Taxes at Work in Learning Labs

The focus on retraining is generating proposals for tax-dollar support for computer training. Witness the proposed legislation before Congress and in local governments to use community-college training services to attract and support business growth.

Bundled Models for Training Services

Training vendors continue to develop models for pricing classes and services. Watch for all-you-can-learn pricing plans as well as national contracts to provide complete training services at a per-desktop annual cost. *The economics of the computer-training business will evolve as the field matures and as learning is recognized as a perpetual portion of the technology-expense budget.*

Summary

Computer training is not a field for the weak-hearted or for individuals or businesses that put a premium on stability. In many ways, computer training is a change-adaptation mechanism. We have our jobs, our training centers, and our learning products because technology changes and people adapt accordingly. To survive in the computer-training field — as a corporate learning specialist, a freelance trainer, or the manager of an applications training center — you must try to stay abreast of every change, experiment with every new technology, and adapt, quickly and critically, new models for providing learning to our workforce. Fasten your seat belts; we're in for an exciting ride!

1

About the Book

The senior managers of a large financial-services organization have convened a meeting to assess the "state of computers" in their business. After an hour of discussion about hardware and software, one brave soul raises the issue of the value of all this technology. "Do our employees really know how to use these new applications? Is our company making a single dollar additional profit after this enormous investment in technology?" The conversation quickly shifts to the need to build the computer skills of the workforce. The computer-training manager is invited to the next meeting.

All the computers in the world don't mean a thing unless people know how to use them. The challenge of this management team, and the challenge of every organization throughout the world, is to help employees master the computer hardware and software that sit on their desks. Every worker in every organization will struggle to learn (or resist learning) new technology. *The Computer Training Handbook* is dedicated to facilitating the computer-skills learning process.

While we use the phrase *computer training* throughout the book, you will see the word *learning* just as often. Learning is the process a user goes through in attempting to master technology. Computer training defines the efforts of organizations to manage or assist learning. In the six years since the publication of the first edition of this book, the need for computer learning has grown enormously, and the profession of computer training has experienced a similar expansion and maturation. Learners make their way through the complex world of technology by attending classes, taking computer-based tutorials, reading books, calling help desks, bothering their peers in the next cubicle, and even asking their young children for help.

This book is a guide to all those variations on the computer-training theme. It can be a handbook for the working trainer, the new trainer, and the computer user who has been asked to train people. It can also be a textbook for students learning about computer training. You can read it from cover to cover or dip into it selectively, like an encyclopedia. It can provide a thorough introduction to the field or an answer to an isolated question. Topics range from the organizational context of computer training to training design, and the tone ranges from the philosophical to the practical. Along with substantial chapters on the fundamental principles of computer training, training design, and adult learning are almost two dozen shorter chapters on specific techniques and technologies.

Computer training is a relatively new field. The first programming courses were delivered only 35 years ago, and people didn't begin to look methodically at computer training until the mid-1970s. Despite its youth, the field shares its foundation with several more mature pursuits, and this book brings together research and practical experience from the fields of adult education, educational psychology, curriculum development, and management theory — not to mention the experience of practitioners in all industries. We have tried to strip the jargon from the theoretical material and translate such material into practical do's and don'ts.

Above all, this book is a guide to decision making. Educational theorist David Berliner has described effective teaching as a series of decisions, and computer training is no different. Who should learn? What should they learn? When? How? How should the instructor respond to learners' questions? And how should the instructor respond when learners don't ask questions?

When decisions about computer training are left to chance, people usually manage to learn. But they don't always learn what is most useful to them, and the learning process can be painful. The only way to have some control over how people learn to use computers is to make some conscious decisions about it, whether you're a manager, a trainer, or another user trying to teach the system to a colleague. This book advocates conscious decisions about computer training, and it should help you make them.

The guidelines in this book apply to almost any situation in which people need to learn to use computers in order to do their jobs. Computer training happens when an instructor stands in front of a class of 20 people or when one person sits in front of a screen-based tutorial. Computer training happens when one person calls a colleague for quick help with a spreadsheet package or when another person leafs through a manual looking for an answer. Computer training occurs every time a call is made to a help or support desk. A retail clerk learning to operate a point-of-sale terminal is receiving computer training; so is an editor learning to use a word-processing package.

Most of our comments are equally applicable to systems that are off-the-shelf or homegrown, simple or complex. You will be able to apply what you read here whether you are teaching users to follow menus, use command language, or fill in fields. And with the distinction between mainframe and PC applications becoming ever blurrier, this material will apply to every imaginable configuration, from stand-alone PCs to vast networks of micro-mainframe links to client-server-driven wide-area networks. It could even be applied to our computerlike phone systems that sit on our desks, many of their dozens of buttons forever untouched. The hardware requirements differ in these situations, as do the job requirements and the level of control users have over their computers. But the principles of effective training are the same.

Who Is the Book For?

This book is for anyone involved with helping people use computers in their jobs. Computer trainers are not the only people with this responsibility, nor are education coordinators, data trainers, DP training specialists, or others with similar titles and job descriptions. The staffs of help desks and computer-support centers spend much of their time training, both formally and informally, and so do users who have gradually or suddenly become the resident computer experts in their departments — lawyers who are particularly good at using LEXIS, NEXIS, or any of the other legal-research databases, nurses who are adept at accessing patient records on the medical-information system, or managers who have mastered a particular spreadsheet package.

Others with training-related responsibilities are programmers and application developers who follow their programs out into the organization to teach people to use them, hardware experts who are constantly asked for help with configuring networks, and other technical experts.

More and more educators and trainers with other subject-matter expertise are adding computers to their repertoires. Corporate training departments are sometimes asked to help bear the massive training burden of organization-wide systems implementation. And as the computer terminal becomes a common piece of office equipment, training for a growing number of jobs will include elements of computer training, blurring the distinction between the trainer and the computer trainer.

Computer training requires three skills: computer skills, training skills, and business skills. Depending on their backgrounds, people with training responsibilities may need reinforcement in any one (or two) of those areas. This book will help fill in the missing pieces.

Techies

> "Every day I come to work and find that our network has changed. New users have been added, new hardware is waiting to be installed, and new code has been shipped by one of our technology vendors. My whole job is staying abreast of technology, but I can barely keep up. No wonder the users get frustrated. More and more, I find myself coaching them rather than wiring network boards."

These are the words of a 12-year veteran of network management who recently attended a train-the-trainer course. His boss realized he needed more than just superior technical knowledge; he needed to know how to transmit that knowledge to coworkers.

Knowing how to use technology doesn't automatically mean knowing how to teach it, nor does knowing how it works. But that's not to say a technical expert can't also be an expert trainer, or learn to be one. This book should be read by "techies" from the perspective of understanding how technical information is absorbed and processed by their users. You could regard this as sort of a minicourse on a new machine — we'll call it the USER 9000 — that has been shipped to your organization. Study how the input and output process of the USER 9000 works. Experiment with a different format of instructions to find out new and elegant ways of explaining technical information. And reflect on your own style as a teacher or support person. Can you keep your hands off the learner's keyboard? Do you use humor as part of your process for helping users cope with bad technology? Have you ever asked for feedback from users on how you provide learning assistance?

Trainers

> Top management at a large financial house asked one of the
> company's most popular sales trainers to help introduce a new
> on-line system to a group of office managers. Word had spread
> about his charismatic, energetic style, and management wanted
> to capitalize on his skill. Still learning the system himself, he was
> reluctant, but he couldn't say no to the VP. His insecurity turned
> his usually humorous interactive session into an irritating
> lecture, and his reputation didn't fare much better.

Just as technical expertise doesn't guarantee training expertise, the
ability to teach marketing or welding or high-school biology or college philosophy doesn't guarantee the ability to teach word processing. And when computer trainers come with the training half of the
package but not the technical half, they often struggle with the same
apprehensions about the technology that they are trying to help learners overcome. Even those who are comfortable with the technology
may need to learn instructional approaches that are more appropriate to the demands of computer training. Along with presenting such
approaches, this book offers trainers insights into their own learning, helping them increase their confidence as computer users.

The role of practice and exercises changes dramatically when shifting
from human-resources-type training to computer-learning situations.
The presence of a colorful, noisy machine in front of each learner can
be a trainer's nightmare. Even the most experienced trainers need to
step back and reengineer their style when entering the world of computer training.

Help-Desk Staff

> "Help desk. How may we help you?" That question often brings forth a request for training, even if the caller doesn't recognize it as such. When a user calls for assistance with the placement of headers or footers on a word-processed document, she is asking for a personal trainer. That is, she wants the help desk to walk her through the process and teach her how to do it. Now!

The MASIE Center has found that more than 37 percent of help-desk calls are really requests for "just-in-time" personal training. In order to recognize the nature of support requests and to provide cost-effective assistance, help-desk professionals must understand the learning process.

Expert Users, or "Wizards"

Those who end up with formal or informal training responsibility because of their visibility as expert users of particular applications have some advantages. They understand how the system is used in the work setting, and learners may find them more approachable than less familiar trainers or technical staff. But they don't always have the license or authority they need to give assignments or check learners' work. Again, knowing how to use a piece of software isn't necessarily the same as knowing how to teach it. Expert users may do what they do unconsciously, and they may not be able to answer learners' questions accurately.

Managers

Managers are crucial to their employees' success or failure in learning to use computers. A manager who expects a user to come back from a three-hour spreadsheet course and immediately teach the others in the group how to use the application probably will be disappointed. And the user may seem to have failed, despite successful completion of the course. The benefits of training also may be lost if managers don't allow sufficient practice time.

Poorly managed training is a hidden cost, manifested in diminished effectiveness and the failure to integrate new systems. Familiarity with the principles of effective training can help prevent this cost, and this book will help managers understand the training process and the measurable effects of their training-related decisions.

MIS Departments

With the growth of client-server technology, the training and supporting role of MIS departments is expanding. Increasingly, MIS departments, in a consulting capacity with operational units, are being asked to craft business solutions. Part of this process involves delivering training and support services.

Application developers are developing on-line help systems and other performance-support modules to lower the cost of training and supporting users. In addition, in order to stay competitive, every MIS professional in the world is going through a retooling process to gain skills related to new and emerging technologies, ranging from client-server to multimedia to global Internet access.

MIS professionals sometimes are directly involved in training; in some companies, MIS trains people from other departments as well as its own staff. But even those who don't have training responsibilities should be interested in developing and delivering effective computer training. The best hardware and software in the world is useless unless people can and do use it. MIS increasingly recognizes training as part of the delivery system of new software; as such, training is at least partially an MIS responsibility.

Learners

This is not a book to teach you how to use a computer. After the first edition came out, we received a call from a housewife in Seattle who had just bought a copy. She had spent eight years as an elementary-school teacher and was intrigued by the prospect of reentering the workforce and using her skills. She said she really enjoyed reading the book but still didn't know how to use a computer. We referred her to a local training center in Washington state, where she eventually took a few courses in word processing. And guess what? Two months later, she was working as a computer trainer!

This book is aimed at helping people understand the learning and training process as it relates to computer technology. It would be wonderful if every organization offered a class on "how to learn" for its workforce; the result would be much more assertive, self-aware learners. Feel free to share relevant segments of the book with your learners to help them understand their own learning process.

2

About Computer Training

What percentage of the workforce requires computer training each year? One hundred percent! Every time a piece of technology changes, an upgrade to an application is shipped, a new employee is hired, a reorganization is announced, or a new procedure is implemented, computer learning is required.

Work in a modern organization cannot be changed without a change in the technology environment. And that change drives the need for computer training. In other words, 100 percent of the workforce will have its computing environment altered somewhat in the next calendar year, and, as a result, will need to learn new skills and procedures.

In all of the situations described above, some degree of learning is inevitable. What is *not* inevitable is learning that allows people to make optimum use of the computer in their jobs, with minimal loss of productive time and minimal frustration. That requires some forethought on the part of management. It requires a conscious attempt to answer the question, "How are people going to learn to use computers?" When that question is taken seriously, the answer usually has something to do with training.

About 20 to 30 percent of the time, people learn to use computers in situations that are readily recognizable as training — that is, in formally organized classes offered by in-house training departments and information centers; via hardware, software, or training vendors; or through colleges, universities, and their continuing-education divisions. But the vast majority of people learn to use computers on the job, informally and individually. Most of this learning occurs without managerial involvement or input. Sometimes learners are left on their own with self-study materials such as computer-based tutorials, videotapes, audiotapes, and special manuals serving as instructors. Often, the colleague in the next cubicle or office is the only source of guidance and support. And frequently, these learners have only the vendor's documentation for reference.

Not all managers recognize the importance of providing employees with some structured experience for learning about computers. Some seem to assume that people will learn by osmosis, simply by having hardware and documentation on their desks. Others hope the systems themselves will do the training, invoking the myth of user-friendliness. "You don't need training," they say. "The instructions are right there on the screen."

Unfortunately, few people learn well by osmosis, and "user-friendliness" is not quite as functional a concept as the popularity of the term suggests. It is typically understood to mean "easy to use," but what does *that* mean without a clear sense of the user's skills and needs? The qualities that make a program appropriate or easy to use change as a user gains knowledge. A feature that tells new users what to do may also limit what they *can* do. A driver making his or her first trip to a new destination welcomes explicit directions; several trips later, those directions are superfluous. Similarly, a software feature that is helpful on Day 1 may be unnecessary on Day 2 and annoying by Day 7.

Managers often ignore the importance of training in the name of saving money. In organizations where there is a "tax" on formal training, managers will choose not to train an employee in order to avoid direct billing to departmental budgets. But not training at all or training insufficiently has its own costs. In the extreme, people don't use their computers, so the organization's investment in hardware and software begins to go to waste. Or people use the systems but use them inefficiently and with excessive dependence on their peers or assistance from a formal support function like the information center. Every time a user relies on a formal support function, the organization pays at least $25 in overhead and salaried time. Every time a user goes to a colleague for support, it costs between $25 and $200.

Insufficient training can also lead to the need for retraining, and sometimes it leads to the unnecessary replacement of software or systems. Granted, some system modifications are warranted. No matter how many new training approaches are tried, the amount of time spent trying to master a particularly complex set of screens may far exceed the resources needed to simplify the screens. But just as often, lack of use or inefficient use is a training, not a system, problem.

> A hospital went through three different patient-information systems in seven years. Each time, the staff indicated that the system in place was inadequate. But eventually, it became clear that none of the staff had ever been convinced of the benefits of the system or shown how to use it quickly. The problem was finally solved — not with another system replacement but with a massive effort at training the staff on the system's use and its benefits.

What Is Good Training?

Once managers are convinced of the importance of training, how can they make sure the training provided is sufficient? The primary goal of computer training is to create computer users — not to teach people *about* computers but to teach them *how to use* computers in their jobs. To accomplish that goal, training must be performance-oriented and job-specific. And it must not be expected to stand on its own. Training is only one of three separate tools that organizations can use to create competent computer users. The other two — documentation and support — are every bit as important. Organizations must acknowledge that users will have more to learn *after* they've been trained, and they must make appropriate resources available to them.

> **Can you imagine an airline deciding to buy the new Boeing 777 plane and not making a major budget commitment to training? Would an airline tell its pilots to take some free time and play with the new aircraft? In that industry, every decision to purchase equipment is matched with the decision to invest in reskilling staff. When will we have that same luxury in the computer field?**

Who Provides Computer Training?

Because computer training is a relatively new need, it is rarely administered from a clearly defined spot on the organizational chart. Before the era of personal computers, most people who used computers were either technical experts or staff using a specific application. These individuals generally required some training, but there were relatively few of them, and the necessary training was provided within the narrow channels of their field. The widespread need for training in computer use has arisen during the last decade — as the advent and proliferation of PCs and micro-mainframe connections have made computers available to virtually everyone and as more and more organizations have begun to automate their routine operations.

The first organizations with formal computer-training functions were the first to go "on-line" — airlines, insurance companies, and banks.

They had to train enormous numbers of employees to input and retrieve data in high-transaction environments. Usually the MIS function undertook this task, with analysts and programmers serving as trainers. Since then, computer training has become an increasingly widespread activity, as likely to originate at the local departmental level as in the MIS department. It may also be provided by a separate function altogether or by some subset of the MIS function.

In any organization, the actual training may be provided by full-time employees who work for a computer-training unit. Or, trainers may be employees who are "borrowed" from other units to teach a specific class. Finally, trainers may be hired from outside the organization; such outsourcing of training requirements can mean using a freelance trainer to teach an advanced technical class or contracting the entire training function to a third party.

People who provide computer training are no longer just technical experts. Data-processing professionals have been joined by those with experience in teaching and training and by others who are experienced users of the systems that need to be taught. In fact, they have been joined by people without any training or computer background at all, whose titles and job descriptions are as varied as their résumés. They are called computer trainers, data trainers, DP training specialists, and software instructors. They are solution consultants and analysts, help-desk supervisors, support specialists, managers, and supervisors. They are expert users in every imaginable line department. And they are less-than-expert users who nonetheless are asked to help when a colleague has to learn the system.

The job of computer training is as subject to variation as its place in the organization. One thing is certain, though: Whatever the organizational structure for computer training, it's not permanent. As technology continues to evolve, so will the ways computer training is used in organizations — and the way its use is supported. As long as computer technology continues to evolve, so will the field of computer training.

Another thing is just as certain: *How* an organization approaches computer training suggests *how well* its users will succeed. Too often, hardware and software decisions get all the attention, while users are left to fend for themselves. But the ultimate gains from hardware and software decisions hinge directly on training decisions. If people lack the skills to use it, the best spreadsheet available will never accomplish its intended purpose. Managers who expect to evaluate the results of their hardware and software decisions must understand the role of training in the use of their purchases. Otherwise, they may misunderstand the reasons for system problems, make poor decisions in the future, and never realize the optimum returns on their investments in technology.

The following anecdote about an organization guided by the mistaken perception that computer expertise resides in the system rather than in the users illustrates the importance of a conscious commitment to training.

A major retailer installed a system to disseminate sales and marketing data, but its various division managers didn't want to bother with the logistics of scheduling and didn't want employees leaving their desks and phones to attend computer training. Instead, they distributed the vendor's manual, along with an abbreviated guide to using the system and the phone number of the help desk. As a result, the help-desk staff grew quickly from one to eleven and has stayed that large. Instead of facilitating learning, the management of this organization made a permanent commitment to facilitating use. That is, instead of making a one-time investment in training each user and then providing minimal support, management is paying through the nose for daily support.

3

A First Look at Adult Learning

"What's the big deal? You go to class or you read the manual, and you figure it out! I learned how to use a computer without any fuss or bother, so why are we holding these people's hands?"

"Are adults different from children when it comes to learning?"

"I just can't understand the users' attitudes. You'd think these people were being asked to work a nuclear reactor. Why are they so resistant to change?"

For many adults, walking into a classroom can be like going back in time. All it takes are the rows of desks and the chalkboard, and suddenly we're 14 again. But, of course, we're not children, and although trainers may use some of the same techniques that high-school teachers use, they use them to accomplish very different goals with very different audiences. Most often, the business of training is *performance* rather than *knowledge,* and adult learners have job responsibilities to which they expect to apply what they learn. Adults are also used to having a much greater degree of overall responsibility in their lives than children in school classrooms are.

For much of this century, researchers and practitioners have studied the phenomenon of adults as learners and developed teaching and training approaches suited to the needs of those learners. Their findings reveal a few major characteristics that pertain to most adult learners and that trainers must consider when working with them.

■ Adult learners are self-directed rather than dependent. Habits formed in predominantly teacher-directed elementary, secondary, and even post-secondary education may cause learners to look to trainers for direction and motivation. But because adults are used to relative independence in other arenas, training that encourages dependence is not likely to succeed. This means that objective setting and the evaluation of learner performance should be mutual processes, not the sole responsibility of the trainer.

■ Adult learners bring a lifetime of experience to the learning situation. Instead of considering learners empty vessels to be filled, trainers should recognize and value their experience and use it as a resource. Because adults are motivated to learn by their life situations, it is hard to motivate them to learn things they don't consider relevant and immediately useful.

■ Adult learners dislike memorization; they particularly dislike being *told* to memorize. Although they prefer to learn gradually, through familiarization and repeated use, many adult learners feel compelled to memorize if they sense that information won't be available after the instructor has spoken. Handouts reduce memorization anxiety by putting course content into a lasting form.

More than 30 years ago, European adult educators coined the term *andragogy* to refer to the art and science of helping adults learn, as distinct from *pedagogy,* the art and science of teaching children. Adult-education proponent Malcolm Knowles introduced the term to this country, and the concept of an alternative to the traditional teaching model spread — along with the idea that each model has appropriate uses, in different situations, for both adults and children.

Andragogy versus Pedagogy		
Assumptions	**Pedagogy**	**Andragogy**
View of trainee	Dependent	Self-directed
Experience	Of little value	Rich experience
Time view	Someday	Needed now
Orientation to learning	Subject-centered	Problem-centered
Acceptance need	Peer/trainer	Need satisfaction

This model would explain an adult learner demanding the following from his or her learning experience.

Self-directed. "Let's just focus on the features of the application that I'll probably use when I go back to my workstation. I don't really need to know about headers and footers. Can we skip ahead and look at tables, since my boss is always giving me a ton of data to include in reports?"

Rich experience. "I want to try that now! Hold off for a minute while I see if that feature actually works on my machine."

Needed now. "Can you walk me through formatting again? I've got to get this report out by 4:30, and you did a great job of explaining it to me last month."

Problem-centered. "Can we have a few examples from a real-world business to give us a better understanding? Do you have any case studies of organizations that have actually linked Groupware with HR databases?"

Need satisfaction. "I really liked this course! It was super to be able to actually do some work with the presentation program and build slides for a talk I delivered the next day. The feedback from the instructor was great!"

The insights from this andragogy/pedagogy model brought new approaches to the training and human-resources fields. Trainers began to focus on building motivation for learning in students. The assumption was that once a learner wanted to know something, he or she would find a pathway toward that knowledge. Trainers began to use the term *facilitator* to describe a shift away from the front-of-the-classroom model to that of a coach.

Ten years ago, I had to explain adult-learning theory to a wide range of technical professionals embarking on computer-training assignments. A discussion of andragogy versus pedagogy didn't seem appropriate, so I designed something I call the Masie Model of Indexing, which I describe in the following chapter.

4

The Masie Model of Indexing

"Hey, it really works! I didn't believe it would when I saw you demonstrate it."

"Isn't this spreadsheet just like the football-pool program we have on the mainframe? You change one box and the whole sheet changes."

"I know we covered that in class this morning, but I think I must have dumped everything from that section. Could you explain it one more time?"

Nothing is more interesting than watching people learn. Over the past 20 years, I have taught more than 30,000 adults in a variety of settings. Yet every time I walk into a classroom, I am amazed at how interesting we are as learners.

The Masie Model of Indexing came from my desire to explain, simply and humorously, adult-learning behavior to folks without any teaching background. I strongly believe that if you want to change people's behavior, they have to understand what they could do better or differently. In other words, if we want nonteachers to be better trainers, they must understand how learners respond to them.

To illustrate the Masie Model, I'll introduce you to Lisa and Elizabeth, both of whom just received new computers and need to learn how to use them.

Lisa. Today is Lisa's 11th birthday. Her parents purchased a personal computer for the occasion. Lisa has had only minimal exposure to computers in school. She needs to learn how to use her new PC.

Elizabeth. Elizabeth is 41 years old and works in a real-estate office. Her manager has just purchased a real-estate software package. She is getting a desktop computer to track all of her real-estate sales. She needs to learn how to use her new PC.

How will these two people differ as learners? If you were responsible for teaching each of them, on a one-to-one basis, how would you proceed?

Participants in my seminars frequently give these responses:

- Lisa wants to have fun, so give her games.
- Lisa will bore easily, so try to keep her attention.
- Elizabeth must know how the teaching will affect her.
- Elizabeth wants to learn how to do actual tasks in her job.

Research on how children learn technology emphasizes the need to keep students *stimulated*. Lisa will respond to programs that have color, action, sound, movement, and interactivity. She will learn as long as she is engaged, but her concentration would falter if the teacher described the function of each key on her keyboard.

Another relevant fact about children as learners: They rarely own any data. Because Lisa doesn't have any data, she's not afraid of losing any.

That's why children, when stuck, are quick to reboot, or restart, the computer system.

Adults respond to *functionality*. Elizabeth wants to know that this program will actually help her complete certain work tasks related to the sale of a house. She will focus on her job and how it relates to her current system, and she may be concerned about how this program could change her job or her status in the organization. She will also worry about the loss of critical data. Just try to get her to turn off the computer before she knows *exactly* where copies of all her customer files are! Adults focus on data and function.

Different File Formats for Different Folks

Another difference between Lisa and Elizabeth is that they have different formats for filing information in their brains. Apparently, children and teenagers have a unique ability to create "temporary sequential files." For example, on the first day of the school year, Lisa might create a "file" in her brain with the word MATH at the top. Over the next nine months, her teacher would download content from this curriculum that would go into Lisa's MATH "file," with little reference to other files. Since the teacher probably wouldn't relate the math content to the social studies lessons, this file would be self-contained.

Throughout the school year, Lisa would ask herself (or occasionally ask the teacher directly) the all-important question: "Will it be on the test?" Depending on the answer, she would place a significance flag next to each item marked "probable test question." Young learners know from experience that only a small percentage of content from each class ever appears on the exam. Therefore, the sorting criteria for Lisa is testing probability.

At the end of the semester, Lisa will take the test after studying the flagged items. Eventually, she will erase most of the MATH "file." (If you doubt this, define the following terms: *log, arc, cosine, tangent,* and *quadratic equation.*)

One researcher found that youngsters will score better on exams when the test items are presented in the exact order of the original learned material. In other words, Lisa will do better if she takes a test that follows the sequence of the file — hence, my conclusion that young learners have "temporary sequential files."

Adults, on the other hand, performed differently in that same research study. The order of the test items did not affect their performance, which suggests to me that adults have "indexed files."

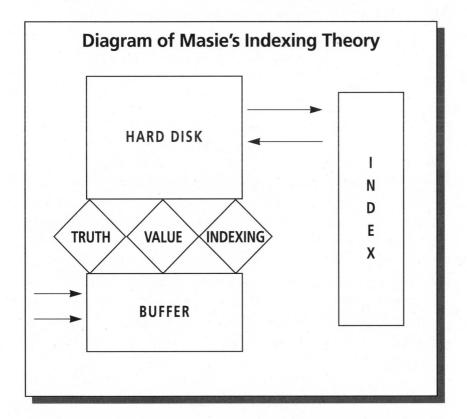

Imagine that we could take a group of learners from computer-training classes to a virtual x-ray machine. The schematic diagram above illustrates what we might see when we looked at their brains.

Item	Purpose
HARD DISK	The long-term accessible storage area for information. This is the target for all learning and training activity.
BUFFER	The short-term holding area for information just received by the learner. Information stays in the buffer while the learner considers its future.
T - TRUTH TEST	Is this information true?
V - VALUE TEST	Is this information of potential value?
I - INDEXING TEST	Can I relate this information to the current contents of the hard disk?
INDEX	The table of contents for all information stored on the hard disk.

Hard disk. This is where the learner stores all information. The hard disk contains tens of thousands of useful and random pieces of information. Lisa has the ability to write directly to her hard disk. The problem that Elizabeth faces is that most hard disks get write protected in one's early twenties.

Buffer. Since Elizabeth's hard disk is write protected, we are forced to deliver all training to the door of her buffer. Think of the buffer as the temporary storage area where all new information lands while it is being processed. In fact, these words are going into your buffer as you read them.

Some learners have major buffer problems. There are some who have "morning-only buffers." Try teaching these people before 10 a.m. Others shut their buffers down after 3 p.m. Still others have "auto-wipe" buffers, which seem to erase all information as soon as it is shared.

There are also different sizes of buffers. Elizabeth might have a buffer that can handle 30 items; in other words, she can keep 30 items under consideration while she decides if any are worth moving to her hard disk. But what if she were in a class with an instructor delivering 40 items? She might participate in the "first-in, first-out" cleaning process. This would yield questions like, "Would you tell us how to sign on again?"

Or Elizabeth might have one of those "garage-door" buffers, where she drops her pen and takes a buffer break while she processes the information she has already received.

Every learner applies three tests to each new piece of information — truth, value, and indexing.

1. Truth Test

Should I believe this information? Learners want to know if they can trust the information being presented. Many learners do not really trust the procedures and processes their instructors teach them. The reasons are many.

- Salespeople have exaggerated the product, claiming it was easy to use or quick to install.
- Instructors have lied in the past.
- They know their equipment differs from that used in class.
- They think the instructor has a special edition of the software with a password issued by God. "Of course, it will work on *their* machines, but wait until I try it back at the office."

Our experience has shown that adult learners do not learn — or test the truth — just by watching an instructor or fellow worker push keys. Not until they press their *own* keys with their own fingers and get the desired result is the Truth Test passed. All around the world, learners validate this by exclaiming, "Hey, it really works!" Do you think they'd say that if they really believed *your* demonstration?

If the Truth Test is not passed, the information tends to go in one end of the buffer and out the other. If it is passed, then learners are merely one-third of the way home to learning.

2. Value Test

Will I ever use this information? Learners can see something as true, but they still want to know if it is of value to them. They want to focus on the features and functionality they are most likely to use. Elizabeth might see that the real-estate-management software allows her to track new prospects, but if she has a good file-card system, why bother with software? Why learn about lease writing if she hasn't handled apartment rentals in her 12 years at this agency? No wonder she examines each nugget of information about the computer system from the perspective of its impact on *her*.

The problem with the Value Test is the "maturity" of the user: New users tend to make bad choices about what might be important in a program. That's because most computer systems are able to change the way we work. While we are learning the system, we are thinking of our current mode of work and applying the Value Test to old habits. For example, when I purchased a laser printer for my office, the employees couldn't see why they would ever want to use more than three fonts. Two months later, they were begging me to buy *more* fonts. Experience changes the needs of learners and their perception of value. This is one reason why follow-up training can have such an impact on learners.

It's easy to see why instruction that is generic and nonspecific is often ineffective. Users listening to an instructor who isn't talking about *their* work realities may have difficulty seeing the value of new material. For example, it is easier for a lawyer to see the value in software that features samples of legal briefs than one focusing on generalized word processing.

If information cannot pass the Value Test (or its cousin, the Truth Test), it will never see the hard disk. But there is one more test, which relates to new and existing material.

3. Indexing Test

How does this information relate to what I know? The Indexing Test addresses a great fear of learners — that they are running out of mental hard-disk space. They fear that if you did a disk check, it would indicate they have only a few hundred bytes free. This forces them to become very selective about how they use their remaining hard-disk space.

> **Actually, there is no evidence that adults lose the ability to learn new material as they get older. Not until we reach our 80s does biology really affect the ability to grasp new information. However, one's self-perception about that ability has a great impact. When a 55-year-old claims to be too old to learn, it's a case of self-fulfilling prophecy.**

In order to preserve their disk space, adults seem to make certain rules that govern their approach to assimilating new information.

- Relate all new material to everything learned since birth.
- Do not create any new file folders.
- Link all new information to an existing folder.

This process is called *indexing*. Essentially, adult learners take each feature or function that is being taught and run a quick scan of their hard disk, looking for something familiar. That is quite easy for a user migrating from Lotus 1-2-3 to Microsoft Excel or from dBASE to Approach. It may, however, require a stretch to find a relationship for the concept of Visual Macro Scripting. Users sometimes relate information to the strangest pieces of data, and it often results in stories about distant relatives who are using weird pieces of software— all in the name of finding a relationship. Once I can relate new information to old information, I create an index entry. Indexing is a process of appending new to old and keeping a notation in a table of contents. The index becomes a quick path to information that is stored in a very personal fashion.

Users whose information passes the Truth, Value, and Indexing tests will learn new computer skills. I've been teaching this model for the past 10 years because of my beliefs about the ways people learn. Here are a few of my core assumptions about learning.

■ The most important phase of the training process is *not* the delivery of information. People, text, or machines can do that.

■ The most important phases of the training process *are* the Truth, Value, and Indexing tests. This is where human beings play critical roles as coaches, trainers, and providers of peer support. Great instruction occurs when the learner has an easy way to test for truth, to test for value, and to index the new to the old.

■ When learning failures occur, it is usually because of a difficulty with the Truth, Value, or Indexing tests. Rarely does a learner not hear the information. The problem lies in the processing.

■ Learners can learn how to learn. The more they become aware of their own learning process, the more they can help. If, for example, I know I will need to see value, I will talk to my manager before going to a class to determine which projects will require this software.

Take a few moments to discuss these ideas with a colleague or friend. We have found that the Masie Model of Indexing can help turn on a lightbulb in both new and experienced trainers as they ponder their own approach to instruction. Consider some of the following "aha"s that learners have shared after adopting this model.

"I now teach in smaller chunks, allowing for the three tests on an ongoing basis. We used to do lecture in the morning and a lab in the afternoon. Now we blend the practice throughout to facilitate the Truth and Value testing."

"We group our learners in pairs as soon as they come into class. After receiving each major concept piece of our programming seminar, the pairs take five minutes to discuss the new content. This encourages better questioning and a more in-depth mastery of the concepts. We now use 'indexing' as a prime method of instruction."

"As we built a CBT system for a client, we asked each learner to select one of 15 job titles in the organization. All examples they saw and worked on reflected the type of information processed by their job choice. This value-based feature got a thumbs-up from our client and their learners."

The best instructors are not always the best talkers. They are the people that just seem to know what learners need, what learners do, and how learners think.

5

Learner Resistance

"I don't have time to go to training!"

"Don't tell me they're going to change our system again! This is the fifth time in 10 years the patient system has been changed. I'm not going to learn a new system."

"But I don't type!"

"I'm a COBOL programmer. How can I learn a GUI interface after 20 years of doing line code?"

All these learners are exhibiting a healthy response called resistance. It is healthy because they're not convinced that learning this new content in the way suggested is in their best interests. A society or an organization where people express their concerns is basically healthy. We can use their statements to help us form a more effective strategy for computer learning.

The term *computer-resistant* has worked its way into our everyday vocabulary and usually brings to mind a stubborn traditionalist, often a self-proclaimed computerphobe who considers the computer an early arrival from the Space Age and refuses to acknowledge its existence. But most computer-resistant people have more specific reasons for not wanting to learn how to use computers, and even experienced computer users may resist further training. If, for example, a secretary has been using state-of-the-art word-processing software and then switches jobs, she's not going to be particularly enthusiastic when she finds Version 1.0 of the ABC Writing Program on her new desk.

Resistance also exists in highly technical quarters. For example, the move to retool, or retrain, mainframe technical workers has met with major resistance. Tens of thousands of programmers who followed a very traditional career path are now being told to alter their work process and programming style — immediately. From a career and employment perspective, it's a valid suggestion, but it generally is strongly resisted.

Recognizing and overcoming learner resistance are prerequisites for an instructor's success. Instructors may be tempted to take resistance personally, to try to ignore it, or to deny its validity. But if they accept it, they can find out exactly what the learner is resisting and why. Only then can they intervene, and only after resistance is overcome can training accomplish its goals.

It helps to think of the various forms of resistance to computer training as falling into four categories.

Resistance to Learning

The word "I" is a fairly reliable clue to resistance to learning. When you hear "I'm too slow," "I don't learn that way," "I can't type," and the like, you pretty much know what you're up against.

People often resist learning because they don't think they'll succeed. Their reasons for predicting failure vary: "I'm too old" and "I'm not mathematical" are a couple of classics. "I'm too busy" is another common protest; sometimes that's exactly what the potential user means, but frequently it's an excuse to avoid anticipated failure.

People who make these protests are not necessarily resisting the idea of using the computer. In fact, they would probably like to use it. It's the idea of *learning* that they're resisting, and they are likely to feel this way regardless of the particular system being taught.

> The CEO of a company has come to depend on daily sales reports. Recently, MIS has implemented a new client-server system to allow him to request personalized reports. Week after week, he has canceled his appointments with the trainer to learn to operate the new system. Given his dependence on the reports, the problem apparently stems from his resistance to learning the new system.

A mismatch between user learning style and instructor training style can also result in resistance. A learner who prefers hands-on, trial-and-error experimentation isn't likely to be delighted with a lecture. Unfortunately, a negative attitude toward the learning situation may become a negative attitude toward learning the system at all.

> An employee responds enthusiastically to the announcement that she'll be given a PC and taught how to use it, but when she finds out that her training will take the form of a video and a self-study workbook, or that she'll be one of many in a large class, her enthusiasm fades. In fact, she becomes reluctant to learn. When asked about this, she explains that she had been expecting one-on-one instruction and doesn't feel confident she can learn without an instructor's undivided attention. Her apprehension is caused not by the computer but by the learning method.

People who are very resistant to learning might not show up for training at all. If they do, they're likely to be extremely reluctant participants. Rather than trying to talk these learners off the moaning couch, the trainer should provide an opportunity for immediate success — ideally, at the keyboard. The conviction that "I won't be able to do it" usually doesn't stand up long in the face of accomplishment.

Instead of launching a conventional introduction to Windows and personal computers, try this alternative. Before learners arrive, turn their computers on, boot them up with the word-processing software, and compose a brief letter for each screen, including — and *misspelling* — the learner's name. The desire to correct the spelling of their names will sway even the most reluctant learners. Before you know it, people who have vowed never to set finger to keyboard will be racing the cursor around the screen.

Positive role models can also help overcome resistance to learning, as can efforts to show people that learning is inevitable. Hanging the walls of a training room or training center with photographs of alumni is one good way to provide these motivators.

> One company introduced its new E-mail system with a videotape of the company president learning to use the system. At the end of the video, he turned around and said, "It was tough to learn this system, but I managed! I have your mailbox ID, and I'll be sending you messages regularly."

Resistance to Using

Some learners have no qualms about the learning process itself, but they simply don't want to use the new system. Maybe they're intimidated by it. Or they see it as a possible threat to their jobs. Or they're already accustomed to even more sophisticated systems. When these individuals protest, they often mention the system itself: "This system is too slow and too cumbersome," or "It's not my job," or "The other system was faster, and it had color and a mouse!"

The best way to overcome this kind of resistance is to sell the benefits of using the new system, hardware, or software. But benefit selling can backfire if it emphasizes benefits primarily to management. Remember, for example, that a faster system is not necessarily positive if it threatens to reduce the workload and, therefore, the hours of paid employment. That's why it's important to let learners know how the system will benefit *them* directly.

Examples of Benefit-Selling Words

Management Phrases	*Worker Phrases*
Faster	Less boring
Cheaper	More marketable skills
Productivity	Elimination of errors
More company control	More user choice

Benefit-selling vocabulary that is meaningful to learners may differ markedly from what is meaningful to management. Many organizations think they are selling the benefits of a system to a worker, only to find they are extolling management benefits.

Resistance Due to Inadequate Information

This form of resistance is often signaled by the word *they*, as in "They never told us about this" or "They're always pulling this kind of thing." Other signs of this form of resistance are comments like these: "I don't know what this is all about" and "I don't know what I'm doing here (in class)."

When people haven't heard anything about the implementation of a new computer system until they are sent to training, their reactions can range from bewilderment to resentment, and they take these feelings to training. The obvious solution to this kind of resistance is to notify learners in a timely fashion about future training programs. But that's not always within a trainer's control. If people show up for training without really knowing why they're there, they should be referred back to their managers for more information. And if that information isn't available, training should be postponed.

Resistance to Change

The introduction of a computer system represents a change in the learner's job. Some people dread change and will do anything to avoid it. Trying to deal with this kind of resistance in the training environment itself is nearly impossible and can take a trainer's attention away from teaching.

That's why trainers should respond to learners who are resistant to change by referring them to their managers, supervisors, union stewards, or others in positions of authority. Another solution is to involve these change resisters immediately in some activity, inviting them to ignore or transcend their resistance. If you manage to get their attention and provide a fairly immediate opportunity for accomplishment, this approach can work.

Resistance Overview

Every time a group assembles for computer training, it's a good bet that some forms of each of these resistance styles will be present. A trainer who anticipates learner resistance can provide preventive measures within the course to cope with its many forms.

Contracting for Learning

The trainer can go a long way toward overcoming learner resistance, but the learners themselves must also do some of the work. By introducing a learning contract, trainers can help ensure that investment in the learning process is mutual. The concept of contract learning is based on the premise that adult learners are self-directed, rather than dependent on their instructors, that they are motivated by their own needs, and that responsibility for setting goals and evaluating learning is mutual.

A Sample Learning Contract

Employee: Sara James

Unit: Sales

Software: ACT Contact Manager

Application: Sales Contact and Prospecting

Method of Learning: Sara will participate in a three-part learning segment. The first phase will be a self-study tutorial titled "High-Powered Contact Management." The second phase will be a small-group clinic to be provided by the training department. The final stage will involve spending an hour with Doug Jones, an experienced user of ACT; the focus of this discussion will be to help Sara format her own screens for contact management.

Responsibilities: Sara will devote at least six hours to the self-study section. Sara's manager will release her for the clinic and allow at least four additional hours of practice. The training department will provide examples of contact reports relevant to Sara's work.

Skills/Objectives: As a result of this learning contract, Sara will be able to develop a personal database of all contacts and use ACT for all daily outbound and inbound sales calls. She will be able to provide her manager with monthly analyses of sales efforts and focus her energy on the top 20 percent of the market potential grid.

Background: This is Sara's second package on a PC. She has mastered a spreadsheet and database. In addition, Sara has tried ACT several times and has worked with a PIM located on her Wizard palmtop computer.

(Sara, her supervisor, and a member of the training staff would sign this contract.)

6

Procedural and Navigational Users

Some people rip open the shrink-wrap on new software boxes and are installing within seconds. They would never think of looking at the manual unless all else failed.

"How can I surf on the Information Superhighway when I am a very structured person? I want to know exactly what to do and exactly what I will see on the screen when I take an action. Are there any nonsurfing pathways to the Internet?"

Why do some people seem so much more comfortable experimenting at the keyboard than others? How can we keep them from exploring?

Using a computer can be a finite, well-defined activity or an open-ended, unstructured one. The difference depends on both the nature of the system or software package and the user and the requirements of the user's job. The two basic styles of computer use can be described as *procedural* and *navigational*; these terms represent extremes, of course, with a predictable continuum of intermediate styles in between.

Procedural users perceive the operation of a system or software package as a finite series of specific linear procedures. They perform tasks by making particular keystrokes. This is not to suggest that procedural users are limited in their capability; they may, in fact, be very accomplished in the finite realm they have mastered. They are, however, dependent on material they have memorized or on procedures-based documentation, such as cheat sheets.

Navigational users approach systems with a broader understanding of core procedures and functions they can apply to multiple situations. They are more comfortable experimenting with the system and tend to try unfamiliar keystroke combinations more readily. Instead of job-specific aids, the navigational user relies on more thorough documentation.

Each style of use has benefits and drawbacks. Procedural users tend to require little support as long as the systems they work on and the procedures they perform remain stable. And because they don't experiment, they tend to stay out of trouble. But when they need to perform unfamiliar tasks, they are reluctant to press keys in search of a solution, so they're less likely to find solutions on their own.

Navigational users tend to use in-depth documentation or on-line help to solve their problems. But because they spend more time experimenting, they devote less of their time at the keyboard to the primary task. They also risk getting into trouble in their experimentation — not only within their own tasks, but by wandering into realms of the system where they shouldn't be.

The 1990s have seen desktops become increasingly visual and graphical. Windows, Unix, OS/2, and other graphical interfaces have shifted the balance of power toward the navigational approach. By definition, a mouse is going to lead a person to navigate and travel across the screen. While there still is a need for procedural users, they probably should develop core navigational-level skills to operate successfully in the current computer environment.

Personal inclination and personality play a role in determining whether users are procedural or navigational. For example, people who are inclined to experiment will become navigational users, given any choice. But people also work in the styles they've used with other computer systems, or they adopt the styles they see around them or in which they are trained.

It may be to an organization's or department's benefit to decide what kinds of users it wants and to train them accordingly. These don't have to be permanent or absolute decisions; they can be job-specific or even time-specific. (Some users may be procedural for the first few months on a system and then be encouraged to become more navigational.)

Procedural use is particularly appropriate for routine, repetitive tasks like retail checkout or data entry; navigational use is particularly appropriate for people who work in field offices without readily available support or on systems that change frequently.

Whoever makes decisions about user style should ensure that the chosen styles and the established support systems are suitable for their respective users. Otherwise, employees may not use their computers appropriately. Remember, though, that no matter how carefully an organization tries to determine users' styles, people ultimately use computers the way that makes them most comfortable. And that often means working procedurally with one application and navigationally with the rest, or vice versa.

When computers were installed at a large retail chain, it was decided that the retail clerks would be procedural users and the managers would be navigational. However, it turned out that most of the clerks were high-school students who already had navigational exposure to computers, and the managers had already been trained procedurally in most other aspects of their jobs. The clerks immediately started fooling around at their keyboards, even bringing in their own disks to use when work was slow. When asked for help, the managers could only refer to their manuals. Eventually, the clerks were given navigational leeway, and the most proficient clerk was assigned support responsibility.

Decisions about style of use should be communicated explicitly through training and even through management policy statements. Trainers can shape users by acting as role models and by using certain types of documentation and training techniques in class. How much they encourage users to learn by discovery also influences user styles.

Training of procedural users usually involves lots of memorization and emphasizes specific actions, presenting them in terms of keystrokes. Trainers of navigational users suggest that users find things out for themselves, even if this makes users uncomfortable at first. Navigational users are also shaped by so-called reference-based training, which teaches people how to use reference material.

Help-desk professionals appreciate the distinction between procedural and navigational users because it helps them determine what kind of support to provide. For instance, some people who call help desks want a very point-A-to-point-B kind of assistance. Others want a person along for the ride as they attempt to figure out a solution. By testing the waters for style early in the call, the help-desk professional can provide the most useful kind of assistance.

7

Learners' Thinking Styles (and Other Learning Differences)

> *"There are 10 people in my class every Monday. Three seem to take endless notes. Two are always ahead of me. One asks the strangest questions. Are these differences genetic or learned?"*
>
> *"Mary was doing end-of-the-month sales summaries in two hours. Joe still can't get a file up on the screen, and we've been at this for three days. Why the difference? What can I do?"*
>
> *"Why are some people always asking 'Why?'"*

A training professional (or novice) can make three disastrous errors when it comes to perceiving learners.

■ Assuming that all learners are like you and that they approach learning the way you do

■ Assuming that learners know how they learn
■ Assuming that you can easily determine how learners learn

The truth is that learners are diverse, learning styles are moving targets, and learners are difficult to read. Every learner presents the trainer with different challenges. A software package that one person finds easy to use may seem complicated to another; a function that one user finds practical, another may consider absurdly inconvenient.

It's not uncommon for trainers and computer support staff to chalk these differences up to personality and shrug them off — especially when they can't figure out how to overcome them. However, these diverse reactions to learning about computers are actually caused by identifiable differences in the way people think and learn, differences confirmed by a growing body of research on the workings of the human mind. Trainers and designers of training who understand learning differences are able to reach a wider audience and provide useful remediation and support when users encounter difficulties.

Further research will encourage the development of new approaches to training. But we already have more insight into how we can create successful computer users than we did 10 years ago. This chapter will concentrate on a theory of individual differences that was fundamental in developing the Sagamore Design Model, which will be introduced later.

The Thinking-Styles Theory

The thinking-styles theory is an outgrowth and synthesis of work done by dozens of researchers and educators. Special credit is due Jim Bellanca, from the Illinois Renewal Institute, and Neuro Linguistic Programming practitioners for their contributions. Readers who have taken style inventories such as Myers-Briggs or Performax will recognize elements of those models, which we have integrated into our thinking-styles theory.

Various researchers have discovered that people think in four fundamentally different ways, but most are capable of using all four kinds of thinking and do so, at different times, in different situations, for different tasks. Most people, however, tend to prefer one style or use one style most naturally and most often. This "default" style is usually the one we rely on in stressful situations. And because learning new skills is often stressful for adults, default thinking styles are likely to dominate in computer-training situations.

The thinking style that dominates at a given time plays a major role in the way an individual learns and uses new knowledge and skills. If people are expected to learn to use computers successfully, information must be made available to them in a way that suits their thinking styles. That means that computer trainers — as well as those who design interactive learning programs, write documentation, and provide support — must recognize and understand the characteristics of each style. They must also be aware of their own styles and know how to adapt to those of learners and users.

As you read these descriptions of the four thinking styles and try to recognize your own, remember that most people use all four styles at one time or another. Each describes a stereotype, and few people consistently exhibit any one style to the exclusion of the others.

Reflective Thinking

Reflective thinkers look at things subjectively, relating new information to their own experience and constantly considering how they feel about what they are learning or doing. Reflective thinkers become actively — and usually, verbally — involved in this process of integrating new information. But when they're confused, they often shut off their computers to give themselves time to think.

The most common question from a reflective learner is "Why?" But it's a personalized "why," not an abstract one: "Why do we use a totally different language on the computer?" "Why do I have to enter my name if Windows already has that information in an .INI file?"

Reflective thinkers also tend to be highly sensitive to organizational politics and are more likely than other learners to talk about them overtly, asking questions like: "Does this feature mean we're not going to do color printing with external vendors?"

Implications for Training

Reflective thinkers tend to:
■ compulsively relate new information to previous experience;
■ monitor the classroom process, quickly providing feedback when the instructional style shifts;
■ participate actively in large- and small-group discussions;
■ have as many comments as questions;
■ initiate after-class discussions with the instructor;
■ introduce political and organizational concerns into discussions;
■ dislike passive instructional methods like videotape and low-participation lecture;
■ prefer a lecturer who can tell a good story; and
■ join user groups. (See the "User Groups" minichapter, pp. 208-210.)

Implications for Support

The typical support call from a reflective thinker is a long, involved story about the job in progress when the problem arose, the disastrous results of the problem, the calls to friends and relatives for advice, and so on. Support providers can help most effectively by trying to explain why the problem arose and telling a story about the same problem happening to someone else.

Implications for Documentation

Reflective thinkers are not likely to use generic documentation and may, in fact, have extremely negative reactions to it. They want to see examples that relate specifically to their organizations and jobs rather than those of the Acme Corporation variety.

Implications for Technology-Delivered Instruction

Initially, reflective thinkers will react negatively to computer-based training because their style favors a learning model that involves human intervention. Developers could build in a virtual set of colleagues for them to meet and interact with on the screen. They could create case studies that allow for personalization. And they could encourage the sense of wandering that characterizes reflective thinkers.

Conceptual Thinking

Conceptual thinkers want the whole picture. They want to understand what's going on behind the screen and are not satisfied by screen-level information. They need to visualize the workings of the software or system in a structured, organized way, and if such a structure isn't provided, they'll create one in their minds. They ask lots of "What is it?" questions in an attempt to fit what they are learning into these models.

If an instructor says, "This system has eleven major features, but I'm only going to explain the four that you'll be using," the conceptual thinkers in the group are sure to ask about the remaining seven features. They don't stop asking questions until they're confident that they've acquired all relevant information.

Implications for Training

Conceptual thinkers tend to:
- be more tolerant of lecture than other learners, as long as it's sequential, logically organized, and interesting;
- ask questions that force an instructor to cover a topic in more detail than is really of value to users;
- take prolific and meticulously organized notes; and
- ask the instructor to repeat information — not necessarily because they're confused but to fill in gaps in their notes.

Implications for Support

When conceptual thinkers call for support, they provide more detailed information about the problem than the support staff can possibly use. Unlike the personal stories of reflective thinkers, though, this is technical information; perhaps even including the serial number on the back of the computer. Support will be most helpful if it is presented in terms of the whole system, referring to a system map, if one is available, or to the manual.

Implications for Documentation

Documentation should include visual "maps" of systems or software to keep conceptual thinkers from having to construct their own models or to ensure that their conceptualizations are accurate.

Implications for Technology-Delivered Instruction

Conceptual thinkers desire two options when learning by means of a technology-delivered approach. First, they want a total overview of the information, in the form of a content map or outline. Second, they want to go through the process step-by-step, and they welcome additional layers of detail being made available throughout the course.

Regular checks for understanding will help conceptual thinkers, as long as they don't feel patronized.

Practical Thinking

On the old TV show *Dragnet,* there was an actor named Jack Webb who was always asking for "just the facts, ma'am." Practical thinkers are the Jack Webbs of computer training, and "Just the facts, ma'am" is their credo. Practical thinkers diligently edit out any superfluous information and are constantly on the lookout for shortcuts, macros, and other ways to simplify their computer work .

When an instructor says, "This system has eleven major features, but I'm only going to explain the four that you'll be using," practical thinkers ask, "Are you sure we need to know all four?"

Practical thinkers don't want to leave the training setting until they're sure they know how to apply their new computer skills to their jobs. To make sure, they ask questions like: "How would I use that feature?" "What does that do for me?" "Can you give me the quick version of that?" They want to put their fingers on the keyboard and work through the procedures rather than listen to an extended lecture.

Practical thinking is sometimes undervalued, largely because the testing systems used in most schools tend to associate intelligence and capability with conceptual thinking. It's worth noting, however, that practical thinkers are often the most successful learners in computer training, with greater transfer of new skills to daily use than most other learners.

Implications for Training

Practical thinkers tend to:
■ keep trainers honest, holding them accountable for the ability to transfer learning back to the job;

■ prefer guided practice to any other training activity, especially theoretical lecture; and

■ take sparse, tightly edited notes.

Implications for Support

When practical thinkers call for support, they usually express some anxiety about "fixing the problem." They will be most responsive to help expressed in terms of a nuts-and-bolts solution.

Implications for Documentation

Practical thinkers are partial to streamlined documentation. They are great fans of cheat sheets and may create their own miniature versions by sticking adhesive notes onto their terminals. (See the "Cheat Sheets" minichapter, pp. 168-170.)

Implications for Technology-Delivered Instruction

Practical thinkers want to jump straight to the hands-on sections of a computer-based training course. They want choice and should be allowed to sequence their learning to receive procedures first, followed by optional conceptual segments.

Creative Thinking

Creative thinkers love to play, thrive on change, and hate boredom. They learn about the limits of systems and software by testing them. If an instructor says, "The only key that activates the printer is F3," creative thinkers will press all the other keys just to make sure there isn't another way to do it.

When a creative thinker's hand goes up, the question is likely to begin, "What if . . . ?" Creative thinkers concoct their own shortcuts and often try to take applications far beyond their intended use. For example, a creative thinker might realize you could use a spreadsheet as a word processor and then create a search-and-replace macro instead of using the search-and-replace command already programmed into the word processor.

Implications for Training

Creative thinkers tend to:
- prefer unguided practice to any other instructional activity;
- avoid boredom in ways that may be threatening to trainers — by, say, introducing unrelated topics or launching into their own unguided practice;
- thrive on plenty of validated practice time;
- have difficulty learning within an established structure;
- require some one-to-one time with the instructor; and
- appreciate opportunities to design their own learning experiences through individual learning contracts.

Implications for Support

By the time creative thinkers call for help, they've often gotten themselves into serious trouble, but they mask their desperation by asking for "suggestions." They are most receptive to support that takes the form of elegant, out-of-the-ordinary solutions to their problems.

Implications for Documentation

Creative thinkers are likely to develop their own job aids and alter the documentation provided to suit their needs; they may even develop some of their own documentation.

Implications for Technology-Delivered Instruction

The creative thinker may be an unhappy camper if given only one choice of media for training. Our experience has shown that a tightly controlled CBT package won't work with this style of learner, who wants total freedom of movement and approach, and loves to "surf" a bundle of resources. Consider giving creative thinkers a CD-ROM with all available documentation and loads of examples. A visit to an on-line forum focused on an application will also be greatly appreciated.

Trainers Have Thinking and Teaching Styles, Too

Trainers are people, too, with our own styles and preferences. As teachers, we find some learners easier to work with than others. And like everyone else, we incorporate aspects of all four thinking styles into our work. The best trainers move frequently among all four, but most trainers tend to have dominant styles. Here are some stereotypes of the way the four thinking styles manifest themselves — in the extreme — in training.

Reflective. Trainers who are reflective thinkers are personal in their delivery and very social, even empathetic, in the classroom. They care a lot about every learner's success — and that every learner not only uses the software but likes it, too.

Conceptual. Conceptual-thinking trainers want learners to understand how the software or system works, to have a model of its connections and relationships. They usually want to cover the entire system and are not very helpful to learners who want edited-down versions. Once learners have demonstrated competence on certain procedures and are advancing to new ones, conceptual trainers may simply say, "This new procedure is a lot like Procedure X," and thus lose learners who don't think conceptually. When trainers allow their conceptual thinking to prevail, their learners may understand the content but not be able to apply it.

Practical. Trainers who think practically are concerned that learners can *use* the course content. They often oversimplify the material so that users can master a series of keystrokes without understanding the concepts behind them. Practical trainers are also likely to prepare cheat sheets for learners. If practical training is taken to an extreme, learners may become extremely dependent, procedural users.

Creative. Creative trainers, eager to show learners the entire breadth of the system or software, are likely to vary their training designs frequently, leading to discrepancies between their lesson plans and what actually is taught. This can be highly frustrating for learners. At their worst, creative trainers create games and simulations that become more compelling than the information they are supposed to teach.

Bridging Trainers and Learners

Trainers can and should learn to incorporate all four thinking styles into their teaching. But assuming that dominant thinking styles are distributed fairly evenly throughout any population, the style a trainer uses at any given time is ideal for only 25 percent of the group. That means the remaining 75 percent is probably somewhat confused or frustrated.

How can we make sure that training isn't lost completely on any learners? Do we try to reach people in the styles they revert to? Or do we expect them to alter *their* styles in order to accommodate *ours*? Elementary-school teachers attempt to expose their students to multiple styles of thinking and try to develop less-used thinking skills. But adults are usually locked into their dominant thinking styles, and trying to change them is beyond the means or scope of training. In other words, trainers — along with designers of training materials, documentation specialists, and support providers — are obliged to stretch beyond their own default styles and attempt to match their learners' styles.

It would be easier to meet learners' needs if we could categorize those learners by thinking style. Unfortunately, we can't, since most learners shift from style to style at different times and for different kinds of information. In one-to-one training, trainers can watch learners carefully enough to determine their dominant thinking styles and even their patterns of shifting between styles. Clues can be found in the kinds of questions learners ask, the ways they function at the keyboard and in groups, and the aspects of the system that seem to interest them most. Learners' use of documentation and cheat sheets and their approaches to note taking are also revealing. In a large group, though, it's almost impossible for a trainer to note these clues for every learner. The only solution is to provide a variety of materials and to shift training approaches frequently.

Later we will discuss the Sagamore Design Model for structuring lessons in a computer-training course. The model, a simple, six-step approach to delivering instruction, is based, in part, on the diverse nature of learners' thinking styles. Here's a preview from the model, showing how each stage of a lesson can stimulate the learning of each thinking style.

Sagamore Design Model — Thinking Styles

Stage of the Model	Thinking Style Stimulated
Set	
Context	Conceptual
Motivation	Reflective
Objective	Practical
Information Transfer	
Organization	Conceptual
Diversity of Style	Creative
Check for Confusion	All
Guided Practice	Practical
Unguided Practice	Creative
Check for Understanding	All

Since each stage in the Sagamore Design Model meets the learning needs of one or more thinking styles, following it is a good way to ensure that every style gets some attention every hour, even without knowing exactly which styles are represented by the learners.

These brief periods of activity may do little more than tickle each learning style, but that can make the difference between keeping a learner's attention and losing it. If you're a practical thinker, you'll probably be more willing to sit through 15 minutes of lecture if you know that guided practice is next. And even if you don't quite grasp the procedures when the instructor first explains them, you'll have a better chance during practice. Without such opportunities to use their preferred thinking styles, learners feel locked out of the training. Their confidence goes down and their resistance goes up.

Learners' questions and confusion give instructors another opportunity to accommodate different thinking styles. If information has been delivered in one style, it's a good idea to choose another one for clarification or remediation.

Once trainers begin to recognize the signs of different thinking styles, they can adapt their delivery accordingly. In fact, they may realize that they already have been making these observations and adaptations intuitively but have lacked labels for the different styles. For example, a trainer who returns to the office and says, "That group today sure wanted the 'quick and dirty'" is actually noting the predominance of practical thinking in a training session.

Trainers who are secure in their command of the material they're presenting are usually more willing to depart from their own preferred styles. Newer instructors tend to be less flexible, as do those approaching burnout.

Thinking Styles, Documentation, and Support

Recognizing diverse thinking styles is as important for providers of documentation and support as it is for trainers. Along with the basic manual, an ideal packet of documentation contains something for everyone — sales literature to give reflective thinkers an idea how the product would benefit them, a systems map for the conceptual thinker, a cheat sheet for the practical thinker, and a prediction of future developments to keep creative thinkers interested.

On the telephone or in person, the effectiveness of support depends heavily upon the support provider's ability to match users' thinking styles. If users can't follow the thinking behind the help they receive, they may get solutions to their immediate problems but probably won't remember how to solve the same problems again.

Other Learning Differences

Thinking styles are not the only differences among individual learners. Those for whom English is a second language may have difficulty understanding oral and even written explanations. At least 27 million adults in this country are functionally illiterate, and many more have poor reading skills. While many of these people have managed to function in their jobs so far, the ability to read is becoming more important as crucial information is presented on computer screens. Obviously, text-based training materials are of little use to learners with serious reading problems.

Any computer-training session is also likely to include some careless spellers, some people with poor hand-eye coordination, and others with severe "math anxiety" who panic when they see numbers. Poor spellers can take advantage of spell-checking programs — but not for entering commands on-line. People with shaky hand-eye coordination may lack confidence using a mouse.

Regardless of how their minds work, learners also come to training with individual expectations — about the training and about their own capacity to learn. Whether these expectations are based on rumor, past experience, or anything else, learners may become resistant if the training experience doesn't engage them. And more resistance means less learning. It's important for trainers to know what learners expect so they can help them deal with any discrepancies.

Finally, learners' roles in their organizations influence the way they behave — and learn — in a training setting. The need to maintain an image of power and status can prevent a learner from asking questions and, therefore, from really learning, as can the need to maintain secrecy about one's organizational role or even the sense that one's work is underpaid or undervalued.

Summary

This litany of individual differences might suggest that trainers must be experts in educational psychology, learning disabilities, adult literacy, and organizational psychology in order to do a good job. Obviously, that's unrealistic, but those who provide training, documentation, and support should be aware of the differences among individuals and be prepared to address them. All learners and users are composites of their personalities, their educational experiences, and their basic approaches to handling responsibilities. It is the trainer's mission to provide the most effective support to every individual by acknowledging his or her unique approach to learning about computers.

8

Needs Assessment

"How do I know what to teach?"

"Sometimes I don't know why certain people are in my class. Why do managers send staff who don't really seem to need this application?"

"Is there a way to make sure people learn what they need to know?"

Training can seem like a guessing game. The trainer walks into a classroom and starts to guess. Who will come to class? Why are they coming? What do they know? Which applications have they used? How do they learn? What is their attitude about learning? What styles of learning do they represent? Can they type?

Sometimes we know the folks coming to class, and the answers to these questions are already in our personal knowledge bank. Other times, the sponsor of the class has told us some of the characteristics of these learners. But often we don't know the learners at all when they walk through the classroom door. And whatever we don't know will prompt a lot of educated — or uneducated — guesses.

At first glance, planning the training for a particular system or software package might seem simple. Why not just show them how it works? Because that's not enough. (And even if it were, *that* is not as simple as it sounds.) Remember, effective computer training does much more than teach people about the computer; it teaches them to *use* the computer to *do their jobs*. But learners have different jobs and different uses for the computer in those jobs, as well as different attitudes about the computer and about training. And they learn best in different ways.

Training will accomplish its goals only if it acknowledges these differences and is responsive to the learners' job-related needs. Planning for training should also include a thorough look at the nature of the hardware and software to be taught. And finally, the trainer's own knowledge, attitudes, and presentation style will affect the way training is conducted, so this information should be included in planning as well.

The process of collecting all this information is called *needs assessment,* and it is as important to effective training as a thorough medical examination is to an accurate diagnosis and effective treatment.

> **Suppose you call the doctor's office complaining of nasal congestion and a persistent headache. When you arrive for your appointment, the doctor checks his schedule and says, "Oh, you're here with a cold." Then he writes you a prescription and sends you away. Because he hasn't asked you any questions, the doctor hasn't determined whether your ailment really is a cold, an allergy, or some other kind of infection. Nor has he checked to see if you might be allergic to the medication he has prescribed. Because of his negligence, you might not get better and you might get worse. Your trust in the doctor is likely to diminish, and you may end up spending a lot more money than you'd planned.**

Our experience indicates that trainers often gather *some* information in advance. But under pressure to get their courses ready, they also make a lot of informed guesses, waiting to get the real story when their students arrive. Sometimes they fail to find out anything at all about the learners and their requirements for using the computer on the job.

Suppose you limit your information gathering to guesswork, or you neglect it altogether. Your training is likely to lack appropriate, job-related examples and cover too much, too little, or the wrong material. You might spend too much time on unimportant material and not enough on essentials. You probably won't communicate as well as possible with your audience, and your inability to make appropriate material accessible to learners will necessitate more questions, answers, practice, and explanation. Your learners will probably need post-training support, if not more training, and either one of these will increase the original training expenditure.

Besides helping you design an appropriate and efficient program, needs assessment will also help you determine whether you are really competent to teach the course and give you the option to bail out if you discover you aren't. If you do proceed with the training, your knowledge of your audience will enable you to handle a wide range of contingencies, and this preparation will boost your self-confidence.

The Assessment-Conscious Trainer

The trainer who is committed to a needs-assessment-based approach to training is on a quest for information about the learner, which you will gather through formal and informal questioning and observing. This will be a blend of overt and covert intelligence gathering. You will never have the time or ability to get all the needs-assessment information you desire, but your curiosity will enable you to absorb more data about the learners and, consequently, make more deliberate decisions about the training process.

We have developed a series of needs-assessment questions, methods for gathering information, and suggestions for using it, all of which should prove useful as you prepare to train. But the most important message in this chapter has more to do with a certain state of mind than with specific questions or survey formats. How much information you gather and how you gather it are less important than how receptive you are to information about the learners, their jobs, and the relevant systems, and how aware you are that such information can positively affect your training.

The following lists of possible needs-assessment questions are not intended as model questionnaires, since they could produce more information than most trainers would have time — or in some cases, license — to find out. Their purpose is to encourage your curiosity and suggest the range of information that can be useful in planning and delivering training.

Assessing the Learner

Following is a "wish list" of data that would be beneficial to know about each and every learner. Some of this information is not easy to collect and may even be ethically difficult to obtain, but a trainer would appreciate knowing it before walking into a classroom.

Needs-Assessment Data About Learners

Name of learner
   Job title
   Job function
   Number of years on the job
   Number of years in the company

Gender

Ethnic or cultural background

Computer experience
   Typing experience and speed
   Attitude toward computers
   Does learner own a computer?

Attitude toward classroom learning
   Types of favorite and least favorite teachers from school years
   Reader or nonreader
   Learning disabilities
   Note-taking habits
   Frustration tolerance
   Eyesight and reading-glasses adjustment

Current level of stress on the job

Voluntary or involuntary participation in class

Previous exposure to corporate training department

Educational background

Manager's attitude toward use of computers

Experience with using documentation or on-line help

To find out *everything* about the learners that might inform your training would be too time-consuming, not to mention intrusive. But even if you don't collect all this information, and even if you don't consciously use all that you do collect, each fact you have will help you in some way — even if subconsciously. If you can visualize the group while you're sitting in your office doing your planning, you'll find it easier to create learning activities and anticipate questions and problems. And the more background you have on learners, the more comfortably you'll handle the range of situations that arise during training.

Some information, such as age and sex, will be available to you through observation rather than formal data gathering. And although you probably wouldn't design a course differently based on the age or gender of participants, you're likely to approach each class and each participant a little differently if you are sensitive to these details. In a class with fifteen women and two men, for example — or two women and fifteen men — you'll have an idea of the source of any discomfort among the minority. And knowing the approximate ages or, at least, generations of the learners will help you select metaphors and explanations that make it easier for participants to index new information. Large age gaps among participants may also create some discomfort that deserves your attention.

Assessing the System or Software

Later chapters will help you decide which features of a system or software package to include in your training. But first, you should ask some general questions to help anticipate learners' reactions to the material.

■ How intuitive is this software?
■ Is the software conducive to navigational use?
■ Once the program has begun, is each "next step" obvious?
■ Is the software menu- or command-driven?
■ Is the software similar in format or usage to other popular packages? Are there any counterintuitive features of the software?
■ Is the software language filled with jargon or technical terms?
■ Have the developers renamed common terms with their own language?
■ How much of the package is keyboard- versus mouse-driven?
■ What are the learning and support features of this package?
■ Does the program contain learner-assistance tools such as tutorials, on-line help, or performance wizards?
■ How confusing are the error messages?
■ Are there logging and tracking components?
■ What is the character of the documentation?

■ Are the support and learning features obvious or hidden?

■ What degree of personalization is allowed/required?

■ How vulnerable are other packages to the changes this program makes?

■ How difficult is it to install and remove this package?

■ Are there alternate-language features of this software?

■ Does the software require special audio or video capacities?

■ How "buggy" is the software?

■ When are the next major and minor software releases scheduled for this package?

■ What is the reputation "on the street" and in the computer magazines concerning this package?

■ What systems or applications within the corporation is this package replacing?

■ What is the general feeling toward adopting this package?

■ How involved have the users been in selecting this package?

■ How good and extensive is the help-desk service for this application?

■ How long does it take a new or an experienced learner to master this software?

Assessing the Work Context

The following set of questions yields information about how the software, hardware, or system will be used in the workplace. It also covers managerial expectations, which have as great an impact on learners' jobs as their basic responsibilities.

■ What core work tasks will this package be used to accomplish?

■ Will this package be used in conjunction with other packages?

■ Will it import or export data to or from other programs?

■ How frequently will it be used? How many days or hours a week?

■ Are other people in the office using it, or will the learner be the only user?

■ Will everyone use the same version?

■ Are there people in the office area to provide support? How will this support be implemented?

■ If this system is already in use, what are the local customs for its use? (Do people complete optional information screens? How are fields filled in and files named?)

■ Which aspects of the program will be used frequently, which will be used occasionally, and which will never be used?

■ What are some examples of the job tasks for which the software will be used?

■ With what hardware is the software used? How fast is it?

■ How are the keyboards configured in the learner's office?

■ What kinds of job aids are developed and used in the learner's office?

■ How soon does the learner need to be up and running?

■ Will the learner have to support and teach others?

■ Have learners been briefed on the new technology and sold on its benefits?

■ How does management want you to handle resistance?

■ Does the learner's manager use and/or understand this technology?

Assessing Your Own Needs

It is critical that trainers also assess their own needs. You bring a host of experiences, backgrounds, styles, preferences, and prejudices to the learning process. You also bring a default style to the process of assisting others in learning new technology. In other words, you have a comfortable and familiar way of explaining and teaching. This may work in most circumstances but not in the one you are about to encounter. Trainer, know thyself!

■ What is your attitude toward this software?

■ Do you like or dislike the software?

■ Would you use this software at home?

■ How do feel about teaching this class?

■ Are you energized or bored with this content?

■ Are you teaching at your favorite or least favorite time of day?

- Have you had a chance to use this software?
- What are your skill and comfort levels with this technology?
- When you were a learner, what was most confusing about this package?
- What did your trainer do that was helpful or confusing?
- As you begin teaching this class, what is your stress level?
- How bound will you be to your notes and documentation?
- How comfortable are you handling advanced users of this package?
- Have you ever taught these types of workers before?
- What happened the last time you taught these learners?
- How much time have you had to prepare for this class?
- Have you been provided with adequate courseware for this class?
- Will the equipment in class be checked prior to the day of training?
- Are there adequate course materials for this class?
- Do you plan to wear clothes and shoes that are appropriate for the class?

Collecting the Data

You can collect these data in a variety of formal and informal ways, each of which has advantages and disadvantages.

Surveys

A printed survey, mailed to participants before training, can gather a lot of information, but its validity may be questionable because you don't know whether participants have — and have given you — a complete picture of their training requirements. You may also be disappointed by the number of completed surveys you receive, since a 40-percent response rate is considered high for mailed surveys. (One way to increase the return rate is to personalize the forms with the participants' names.)

Interviews

Participants may be willing to tell you more in person or over the telephone than in writing. In-person interviews provide another benefit: nonverbal communication that helps you gauge attitudes. But interviews can be time-consuming; you should allow from 10 minutes to an hour per participant.

The Grapevine

Your own colleagues can be a useful, if less formal, source of assessment data. People who have previously conducted training in a department where you are about to train will be able to brief you about the audience, management expectations, and other contextual factors. But don't expect this information to be totally objective, especially if it focuses on personality-related issues.

Your organization's human-resources-development department or function may also be a good resource for job descriptions and, on occasion, profiles of participants' learning styles.

Last-Minute Assessment

If you're not able to use any of the preceding techniques before beginning training, you can still gather a lot of information on the spot. Open your class with an informal poll of the participants. Or arrive at the training room early enough to chat informally with the participants as they come in. Don't avoid on-the-spot information gathering just because you've mailed out surveys or spent hours on the telephone cross-examining your participants. There is always more to find out.

Validating the Data

Once you've collected this information, make sure it's accurate. While people aren't likely to tell flagrant lies in response to your questions, they may have conscious or unconscious reasons for omitting certain information or even providing misinformation. They may not feel comfortable describing complicated organizational situations to you, or they simply may not know the answers to some of your questions.

People's attitudes and awareness may also change, and they may tell you different things at different times, so it's important to keep your data current. A needs assessment is useless if you wait too long to apply the information.

To validate needs-assessment data, present a summary of your findings to the learners themselves or to others who know about them — managers, supervisors, or other trainers. To some extent, needs-assessment information also validates itself during training. If your teaching examples are effective and you feel well prepared for the class, you can be almost sure you received valid information. Obviously, the ultimate test of an accurate needs assessment is successful training.

Using the Data

Uses for the validated data vary. In some cases, they will be the basis for critical decisions. For example, you may have to ask some learners to find alternative training if their job needs don't coincide with those of others in the class or if their skill levels are considerably lower than others'. You may decide to lengthen or shorten the course, or invite a guest speaker to address issues important to the learners but not part of your repertoire.

If you are designing the training yourself, this data will enhance your design process. If you are using a packaged set of course materials, needs-assessment data will help you fine-tune the already completed design. In either case, you won't be able to use all the data for specific, advance decisions. If, for example, you are teaching a particular software package to people who will use it in a variety of ways, you won't be able to address all their needs directly. But what you can't build explicitly into the training design will be tucked away in reserve. Your awareness of the users' range of applications will prepare you to answer their questions and provide an appropriate variety of examples. As we mentioned earlier in this chapter, just having the data helps prepare you for training by allowing you to visualize the class. And that congruence between your expectations and what actually happens will raise your confidence considerably.

Coffeepot and Restroom Needs Assessment

The most significant needs-assessment data are often found not on printed forms or via a telephone survey, but around the classroom coffeepot and in the restrooms. It's true! The coffeepot is the place where truth starts to flow. Get to the coffeepot before class starts, and you'll encounter great nuggets of data. The trick is to *listen* rather than *lecture.* The other place to gather data is in the restrooms. One trainer heard some very critical and important feedback coming from the next stall during a restroom break. Had she not overheard this conversation, she wouldn't have known how resistant some of her learners were.

Summary

Conducting a needs assessment is the best way for trainers to avoid guessing their way through a class. The more you know about the learners, the software, and the business context, the less you'll need to guess.

9

Objectives, Targets, and Goals

"We spent more than $75,000 on training classes for all our divisions' staff. I sent each employee to classes on word processing, electronic mail, and our corporate-information database. Most people said the courses were good, but there are hundreds of phone calls to the help desk, and the majority of our group feels they really haven't learned much. What happened? "

This manager thought she was contracting for learning. Instead, she contracted for training. As her tale of woe continued, we found that she bought 18 hours of training on applications and not a minute on how to do everyday work in the office. This happened because:

1. She bought training that had fuzzy objectives.
2. The learners attended training that had fuzzy objectives.
3. The learners mastered fuzzy skills.

The issue of objectives is one of my hot buttons. I see more wasted training dollars, more frustrated managers, learners, and trainers, and more misunderstanding created by poor or fuzzy objectives. In fact, when we began to revise this book, the section on objectives was the first one that was significantly rewritten. The computer-training profession *must* take a more aggressive and accountable approach to developing objectives that affect learning realities.

In many books on training, this chapter would be predictable. First, the authors would say you can't reach a goal if you don't know where you're headed. Then they would take you through (as I did in the first edition) a model for writing a good objective. The theory is that if training designers write clear objectives, the trainers follow those objectives, and the class will be held accountable for them. As a result, everyone will stay on course.

While this may be true in theory, life is much more complex. So this second edition takes a different approach to objectives. My goal is to provide two things: a rationale for developing (rather than writing) objectives and ammunition for defending those objectives from an inevitable assault.

Learning involves making a series of strategic decisions. Learners, their managers, the trainer, and others will make a series of decisions that shape and alter the learning experience. The trainer, for instance, will decide to shorten the class to three hours or extend it an extra day. Learners will decide to take the intermediate course rather than the introductory seminar. Learners' managers opt for one seminar rather than another because of the list of topics on the agenda. Each of these decisions is strategic and predictive of success or failure in the learning experience.

The primary decisions to be made in a computer-skills learning experience involve the content, level, outcomes, and format of objectives.

Content

A number of questions concerning course content should be asked. What content will be covered in the course? Will the course address one specific spreadsheet or the general features of all spreadsheets? Will the course cover the basics of a package, or will it include advanced macro capacities? The designer and/or teacher of a course has to articulate the content of the class. In general, the computer-training industry does not do an adequate job in this arena. When The MASIE Center recently gathered training agendas and course booklets from a wide range of internal and third-party seminars, we found that most included only 50 to 100 words on the content to be covered. A typical description read like this:

> **Intro to Word Processing**
> This course for beginners will cover the basics of creating, editing, and printing simple documents. In addition, it will address such productivity features as spell-checking, grammar assistance, and style sheets. Four hours at the Brown Learning Center.

Managers selecting this course for their employees have no guarantee what their training dollars will buy. Will learners receive an overview? Will they actually perform each of the tasks? Will they walk away being able to accomplish a work task? Answers to these questions are not readily apparent in this terse course description.

I suggest that content be specified in two formats in the computer-training field. The first lists the actual features or functionalities that the instructor will address. The second lists a series of work tasks that encompass these features and functionalities. The first listing would contain such phrases as "defining a cell," "moving pictures from slide to slide," and "using the spell-checker." The work task list would give the learner such phrases as "developing a departmental budget using a spreadsheet" or "creating a complex memo, including graphics and columns of figures."

A good tool for developing the content components of objectives can be found in Chapter 10, which focuses on VCP. VCP stands for vocabulary, concepts, and procedures listings, and it provides a simple way to do a complete inventory of a software package and choose those elements to address in a course.

The content component of objectives becomes the first part of a contract with the learner. The training provider states exactly which software functions and features will be addressed. A manager can decide which employees should attend the class by comparing its content with the needs of learners who will use this computer technology.

Level

The level of sophistication, or difficulty, of the class is often stated in a fuzzy fashion. No wonder learners frequently complain that they didn't know the level of a training class prior to attending! A clear statement about class level answers the following questions.

- What experience or knowledge is expected of the learner as a prerequisite?
- What experience is *not* expected of the learner?
- What will be the experience of the other learners?
- What will be assumed as learner experience and, therefore, be built into the class design?
- What will be the "rate" of training, predicated on an assumed level of learner sophistication?

An inadequate statement of level objectives would be: "This course is aimed at users with experience in Lotus 1-2-3." Such a vague statement doesn't help employees make a personal decision about their qualifications to attend, and it doesn't communicate what to expect if they do come to class. Some internal and external training departments use fuzzy objectives purposely to attract a large number of learners to a specific class, an approach that can deceive both the trainer and the learners.

I suggest a statement of level that is as clear as the one that follows.

Prerequisites: All learners will be expected to be current and competent users of Windows (3.1 or 95) software. They will be able to launch applications, use the file manager, and configure printers and communication ports.

Level of instruction: The trainer will teach with the assumption that all learners are comfortable with computer concepts and are able to absorb new program applications and features quickly, with minimal background provided. Technical, "behind-the-screen" aspects will include memory management, networking models, and program debugging.

Who should not attend: Learners who are beginning to use Windows software and those unable to alter their .INI and .SYS files should not attend this course.

Outcomes

The outcome component of the objective is part of the "money-back guarantee." This is what the learners and their managers are buying. The objective should be framed with a specific, work-related outcome. Here's a good example.

After attending the seminar and completing a postclass assignment of 10 hours, the learner will be able to design, format, and produce a four-page newsletter, including the use of imported .GIF graphics, conversion of .TIFF files, trapping, and all aspects of prepress. This objective will be met when the learner creates a final project that receives the manager's approval of content and the technical approval of the training department.

There is nothing vague about this objective, and it obliges learners, the trainer, and the manager of each learner to assume responsibility for their roles in the instructional process.

Format

Of the many models for writing objectives, one of the best is titled *Developing Instructional Objectives,* an excellent resource in this area by Robert Mager, the objectives guru. Mager takes his readers through an elegant process for writing clear, usable objectives.

Personally, I don't worry too much about the actual language of objectives. I'm more concerned about their *use.* They must indicate exactly what participants will be able to *do* after they've successfully completed the training activity. These should be attainable goals so that the training provides participants with some experiences of success.

Some organizations, especially those with well-established training departments, require that objectives be stated in a very specific format. But regardless of organizational style, written objectives should emphasize the word *do* over the word *know,* and *tasks* over *knowledge.* Training goals may include some knowledge acquisition, but that knowledge is usually a vehicle for accomplishing certain tasks. And objectives should focus on the tasks rather than the knowledge.

Here are three ways of stating the objectives for the same database course.

1. *Ninety percent of the learners will be able to display their knowledge of database procedures by creating a 10-field file including character, numeric, and memo fields.*

2. *Users will be able to create files including character, numeric, and memo fields.*

3. *As new product lines are released, users will be able to alter the order-entry program to include new-product information.*

Any one of these formats allows learners to deduce why they're learning what they're learning and what they'll be able to do with it back on the job. Such clearly defined objectives make it easy for the trainer to know what constitutes success, and the objectives can be used as the core of the learning contract established between learner and trainer. When objectives are openly shared with managers, it's easier to ensure that training helps learners acquire the skills those managers want them to have.

The ultimate test of objectives is the ability of the learner, the trainer, and the learner's manager to know if the objectives were met. Too often, the instructor perceives that the objectives (of training) have been met, while the learner doesn't have a clue if the objectives (of learning and doing) have been met or not. The training profession needs to demystify objectives and adopt a more customer-friendly language of service.

10

Vocabulary, Concepts, and Procedures

"Our instructors were always complaining that they couldn't cover all the material during class. After we started to do a vocabulary, concepts, and procedures inventory, the complaints diminished dramatically. Now, there's a much tighter fit between content and time. The VCP gives us a clear sense of what is in and what is out of the course. Today, we use the VCP to structure the development of our computer-based tutorials."
—Mark Wilson, Blue Cross/Blue Shield

The VCP inventory was a "shower idea" — it came to me one day as I was in the shower thinking about a client's problem. The client wanted to categorize the content of a new software package; in other words, he wanted a process to organize the thinking about each new software application that came into the organization. As I showered, I thought about what we computer trainers do, and I realized we spend our time teaching three types of content.

- ■ **V** = vocabulary (new terms and what they mean)
- ■ **C** = concepts (how things actually work)
- ■ **P** = procedures (which keys to press)

Why not do an inventory, or analysis, of each software package from these three perspectives? The result would provide a basis for selecting or not selecting the content of a course. I tried it out in my next train-the-computer-trainer course, and it was an instant hit. Ten years later, thousands of organizations have validated the simplicity and applicability of this shower-inspired tool.

Let's start at the beginning of the design process. When you've completed the needs assessment, you have a better understanding of how learners will use the system or software you'll be teaching. But you still have to determine exactly *what* to teach so they can accomplish the required tasks.

All trainers have to do some preliminary thinking about the content of a course, but the nature of the subject matter makes this process particularly complicated for computer trainers. Any piece of software presents a vast universe of teachable items. If you look closely at Excel, for example, and count every item, aspect, field, and subfield it represents, you'll come up with more than 1,700 items. A full-fledged word-processing package includes about 1,500 teachable items, and the number in a complex statistical package can reach the thousands.

Deciding What to Teach

Even if you *wanted* to teach every detail of a given software package or system, you could never fit them all into the time allocated for training. Besides, few learners want to learn all that much, and they don't need to unless their job requirements are quite extraordinary. On a day-to-day basis, the average desktop-application user needs only 30 to 50 of the pieces of information you could teach; a skilled user might require 100.

Furthermore, most computer applications are considerably more open-ended than almost any other training topic, from stress management to basic selling skills to crane operation. When you teach people how to use a computer — even for a specific set of procedures — you are teaching them to operate a technology through which they can wander in ways and directions that might differ from those you have chosen. Even if you teach a very finite set of procedures, you can't prevent learners from encountering other aspects of the system, by accident or by intentional exploration.

So how do you decide which items to teach — especially considering that different users need different groups of items? It's tempting to avoid the decision-making process altogether and launch into a so-called comprehensive overview of the material, promising learners that you'll cover everything. But if you take this approach, your coverage of the material will inevitably be cursory. Learners will have to judge for themselves which items are important, with little basis for their judgments, and they may never get sufficient explanations of the material they really need to use.

Just as dangerous is the "get-'em-started" approach, in which trainers begin with the initial procedures, such as logging on, and continue sequentially until time runs out. This approach is based on the faulty assumption that learners will be able to figure out the rest of the material for themselves.

If you want to make sure users learn what they need to know, you must make explicit decisions about course content. And in order to select and eliminate teaching items from the total universe, you must have that universe at hand.

The VCP inventory is a technique for cataloging the vocabulary, concepts, and procedures — that is, the teachable items — of any hardware, software, or system.

Conducting a VCP Inventory

The resources you will need to conduct a VCP inventory are the software itself, the on-line and print documentation, and any available job aids. Once you have collected these resources, you simply scour them for all teachable items, which you record in three lists.

Vocabulary

The vocabulary list includes all words and phrases that have special meanings either in the world of computers or relating to the product being taught. The word *screen*, for example, has two different meanings in "computerese," and both of these differ from its non-computer-related meaning. A screen can be a single page of displayed information, and it can also be the surface of a monitor where information is displayed. (And it can be, among other things, a sheet of wire mesh that keeps bugs from flying through an open window.) Other words, such as *file* and *record*, are also used differently from one product to another.

When you're compiling the vocabulary part of the VCP, ask yourself how each term you encounter is used, and add it to your list if there is even a remote chance that learners might not be familiar with its computer-context use. Note that the definition is just for your reference; the list includes only the terms themselves.

Each vocabulary item you write down may be a clue to others. If you put *cursor* on the list, for example, users will eventually have to learn that the cursor is the blinking indicator on the screen that shows where new input will appear when you press the keys. Along with *cursor*, then, your list should include *screen*, *input*, and *keys*.

Don't worry about the length of the vocabulary list. Some software packages have as many as 100 items that might require definition or redefinition by the trainer. It's better to include items you might decide not to teach than to risk omitting something important.

Concepts

Concepts are the principles behind the operation of the system or software. They help learners understand how and why various aspects of the product work the way they do. If, for example, you explain how to move information from one computer to another, learners will have to understand the concept of the telephone line as a link.

Users don't need conceptual knowledge in order to operate computers, but a basic understanding of how the system works can boost a user's self-confidence. And it is essential for navigational use.

Because concepts are hard to identify, the concept list can be the most difficult part of the VCP to construct. Concepts are neither listed in the index at the back of the manual nor provided on the help menu. They don't flash on the screen when they are implemented. But you can sometimes identify concepts by thinking through the words in the vocabulary list and asking yourself whether each is tangible or abstract. The abstract ones probably belong in the concept list. You can also try applying this half-in-jest rule of thumb: If it takes more than two sentences to explain, it's probably a concept. Of course, a generalization like that isn't absolute, but concepts usually require fairly elaborate explanations.

Procedures

Procedures are specific actions a user performs on a computer. Typical procedures in a telecommunications package, for example, are specifying the baud rate, setting colors on the screen, and starting a call. Some procedures are simple, single-keystroke actions; others require 20 or 30 keystrokes.

To develop the procedures list, go through the software manuals and screens and list every procedure that can be performed with the product. Don't leave anything out, and don't worry about the sequence in which you ultimately will teach these procedures. Just choose categories that make sense to you at the moment. The procedures for a telecommunications package, for example, might fit into these categories:

- Setting up the program
- Preparing to send data
- Dialing and sending data
- On-line commands
- Terminating the call
- Utility functions

Since concepts and procedures are related to each other the same way theory and practice are, you might find some concepts lurking in the procedures list, particularly when you realize that several procedures fit together as manifestations of a broader concept. For example, individual function keys initiate procedures, but function keys also represent a concept — that is, special devices for performing procedures instantly.

You can create the three lists in any order you like. Some trainers do procedures first, moving on to vocabulary and then concepts. Others reverse the order, and still others move among the three lists while reviewing the resource materials. A word-processing tool that allows you to set up three windows makes it particularly easy to jump from one list to another.

When you're finished with your VCP lists, show them to three or four people familiar with the subject matter. They will undoubtedly add items you've missed, helping you ensure that your list is complete.

It should take a full day to prepare a comprehensive VCP list for any software package. Yes, it's time-consuming, but once you've completed a solid VCP, it will require only minor revisions over time and will be useful to people throughout the organization.

After completing this review process, you have one last set of decisions to make before beginning to select the teaching items from the VCP that will be the basis for your training design. Ask yourself whether you're teaching only the product you've completed the VCP for — a software package, for example. Or will you also teach learners to use some hardware? Do they need to learn even a minimal amount about a secondary piece of software, like DOS or a mainframe operating system? If the answer to any of these questions is yes, you'll need to do a VCP inventory for each of those additional products.

If the participants in your training session will perform a particular job task for the first time, along with learning to use the computer, you should also develop a VCP for that task. Finally, you may want to do a VCP for the business itself. New hires are often unfamiliar with the nature of the business they have just joined, and that lack of knowledge can prevent them from doing a thorough and effective job.

Developing a business VCP can seem like an overwhelming task. But it's likely to be heavier on vocabulary than on concepts or procedures. And it can be extremely worthwhile for new-employee orientation as well as training in specific tasks. Until you've done a business VCP, you really can't be explicit about what you expect people to know about the organization and its business, about what you're teaching, and — just as important — about what you're choosing not to teach.

Example of a VCP Listing for New Internet Users

Vocabulary	Concepts	Procedures
Gopher	Global networking	Log-in
Telnet	Freeware	Pinging
TCP/IP	Network manners	Telnet
Worldwide web	Internet providers	Join newsgroups
IRL	IP addresses	Subscribe listservers
Mosaic	On-line services	Domain names

A VCP list also has uses beyond the design of training. Distributed to systems, documentation, and support staffs, the VCP provides a common language for talking about the content of training. It also can be used as a skills-assessment technique during new-employee orientation — at, say, a company that develops large, industry-specific systems. New employees at such a company usually receive both technical and industry-related training; by checking off areas of familiarity on an industry-related VCP, they can avoid unnecessary training. A VCP list also lets you compare your company's or client's training needs with the content of externally purchased courseware or live seminars.

The VCP Analysis

If you plan to use the VCP to design training, your next step is selecting the items to include in a course. When developing training on request for users with certain job descriptions or computer-related task requirements, you can construct course objectives based on the results of your needs assessment. These objectives will guide your VCP selection or analysis. On the other hand, when designing training for multiple users from different jobs or for unknown users, you will have to choose the vocabulary, concepts, and procedures that seem most relevant based on the nature and structure of the software.

Either way, there are some broad guidelines for making your selection. Although they are not universally applicable, you should find them dependable in most situations.

Vocabulary

In choosing words and phrases from the vocabulary list, remember that learners can master only a limited number of new ones in a given time period. Try to limit your vocabulary choices to about six to eight words per hour of training; ten words per hour is certainly the maximum you should expect students to learn. If you need to teach more words than that, decide which are most important for your learners and distribute a glossary covering the rest.

Concepts

You should also limit the number of concepts presented to no more than three per hour. Choose those that really will help people understand what they are learning. If you're giving learners an introduction to the Internet, for example, it's essential that they understand the nature of the Net and the global nature of data. There are, of course, other concepts related to the Internet — T1 connections, domain name registration, and firewalls — but these are not as immediately applicable to what the learners will be doing and will only confuse them by competing with the crucial concepts for their limited attention and retention. You obviously will teach more concepts to navigational users and those with more sophisticated user requirements.

Procedures

If you have made an appropriate selection of vocabulary and concepts, you can be more generous with procedures, especially when providing enough documentation to make memorization unnecessary.

Some VCP Applications

Over the past 10 years, we have received lots of feedback from trainers about the ways they have used the VCP inventory. Following are two gems that came across our desk.

The VCP as an Evaluation Tool

One trainer in Kansas used the VCP to elicit evaluation data from her learners. She took a sample of 15 items from the VCP and created a VCP Model of Evaluation Survey using the the following scale.

1. I fully understand and can use this.
2. I basically understand it and will try to use it.
3. I am a bit confused but will figure it out.
4. I am very confused.
5. I don't plan on using it.
6. It wasn't covered in class.

After the learners completed this exercise, they kept a copy of it and gave one to the trainer. It was a perfect way for her to see how confused they were when they left class. She always slipped in a "ringer," an item not covered in the class, to see if they were responding honestly.

The VCP as a Random-Access Agenda

A colleague of mine from London has adapted the VCP to provide his learners with ongoing choice and needs assessments in an advanced programming class. He hands out a VCP of the entire course contents the first morning of class. Each day, the learners vote on which items they would like covered and how much emphasis should be placed on each one. This technique allows my friend to skip information the learners already know and devise a sequence that makes sense to them.

As you develop new ways of using the VCP, please tell us about them at emasie@masie.com.

11

The Sagamore Design Model

It's 9:02 a.m. and time to start class. The instructor steps to the front of the room, and the group quiets down. After some opening comments and activities, the first lesson is about to begin. Is there a formula for presenting the information in that lesson in a logical, engaging fashion?

Very few books and only a few hundred articles have been written about the art and science of computer training. But there are tens of thousands of books and hundreds of thousands of articles about the art and science of education. We need more active links between what we have learned from the study of learning in schools and the practice of computer training in corporate settings. The Sagamore Design Model is one of those links.

Early in my career, I spent lots of time in teacher-training workshops and institutes, where I became familiar with the work of two educational masters: Madeline Hunter and Jim Bellanca. Hunter's model for looking at effective teaching focused on a series of steps that teachers could follow to teach a lesson. The goal was to develop a language for describing effective teaching actions that administrators and teachers could use to improve learning. Jim Bellanca took Hunter's work one step further, applying a series of practical models for developing lesson plans and teaching classes. His goal was to link Hunter's paradigm with the thinking-styles work.

Jim and I cotaught our first class on training the computer trainer in the early 1980s. We advanced the Hunter/Bellanca model yet another step by translating this structure to the reality of teaching a computer-skills class. I dubbed this the Sagamore Design Model, named after the Sagamore Lodge and Conference Center, located near my home in the Adirondack Mountains of upstate New York.

Thousands of computer trainers have since used the Sagamore Design Model, which is the courseware-development focus of several major publishers in the U.S. and Europe. The model is an instructional format that can facilitate the design and delivery of both classroom- and non-classroom-based training. It is also a philosophy of learning. Every time I assume a teaching or coaching role, I naturally use the Sagamore Design Model, which articulates six activities that generally occur, in varying sequences, when adults learn to use computers.

1. The Set: Preparing the learner for learning
2. Information Transfer: Transferring new information to the learner
3. Check for Confusion: Checking to see if you have confused the learner
4. Guided Practice: Structured, hands-on practice of new information
5. Unguided Practice: Lablike practice of new information
6. Check for Understanding: Checking for mastery of new information

Research shows that teachers who consistently incorporate these activities have a higher success rate than those who don't. And Hunter has found that learners require these activities as elements of their learning and will attempt to accomplish each one, with or without the teacher's cooperation. The Sagamore Design Model places the learner and the trainer on the same side of the learning fence.

By applying this model to their training, organizations can accelerate and ensure the occurrence of its components in a logical, productive pattern. The model doesn't have to be applied literally and sequentially. Its six steps need not occur in the same order or even during class. Also, like most models, it represents an ideal that is almost impossible to replicate perfectly, given the constraints of technology, time, and money. But all aspects of the model should be included at one point or another during any learning experience.

The Sagamore Design Model can serve as a guideline or even a template for developing training — whether an instructor creates a formal, written lesson plan or improvises a plan as the class goes on. But it has other uses, too — as a standard for adapting purchased courseware, evaluating instructor performance, and evaluating the usefulness of various technologies for the delivery of training. (Many of the minichapters in the Techniques and Technologies section of this book mention the correspondences between specific training tools and the stages of the model.)

The Set

The set, which always occurs at the beginning of each course segment, is designed to take into account the characteristics of adult learners; its function is to create a sense of anticipation within learners, to make them want to learn. It does this by stating the course objectives, establishing a context for the course material, and motivating the learners. These three goals can be accomplished in any order, and the whole set shouldn't take more than five minutes.

Objectives

Stating the course objectives in practical, accomplishment-oriented terms prepares people for what they are about to learn. This is particularly important for practical thinkers who will commit their attention to a class only if they know what they'll gain from it. Objectives should be written on a flipchart or handouts so learners can refer to them for refocusing if they become distracted.

Context

When you set the context, you let learners know how the upcoming material relates to material they may already know and material you have taught earlier in the course. Adults tend to grasp and remember new information more effectively when they can relate it to already familiar information; by setting the context, you help them do this. This is particularly important in computer training, which, more than other types of training, involves tasks that replace existing manual procedures. Learners can best grasp new procedures by seeing how they relate to familiar ones.

Motivation

As adults take responsibility for their learning, they tend to make judgments about whether course content is of value. This part of the set encourages positive judgments — by means of stories that sell the benefits of the system or software being taught, by asking the learners questions that help them deduce that value, or by demonstrating what learners will be able to do when they've completed the course.

The more actively learners are involved in each part of the set — with raised hands, their own stories, or even just smiles, laughter, and nods — the more effective it will be. Make sure to stop and clarify if you see any confused looks. The set is the launching pad into the rest of the training, and if you lose learners here, you may have lost them for the duration.

Information Transfer

During this stage of the process, the course content is delivered to learners. The delivery vehicle may be an instructor, a set of printed materials, videotape or audiotape, a computer, or any combination of these.

Whether you are designing the training yourself or delivering someone else's design, information transfer requires many decisions — from determining the overall content and delivery medium to more detailed matters concerning instructional style and how much time to spend on each chunk of information. (Chunks are logical, "digestible" segments of the overall course content.) A good rule of thumb sets a 20-minute limit on the time spent using the same instructional style and medium to discuss a given topic.

Check for Confusion

Learners may ask questions throughout the information transfer, and you should be ready and willing to answer them at any time. It's also important to stop and actively solicit questions after each chunk of information transfer, because some learners are timid about asking and others may be so confused they don't know what to ask. This solicitation may mean asking individual learners to paraphrase what you've talked about, to explain which areas they're most or least confident about, or to describe how they might apply this information to a particular task.

If hands don't go up immediately, don't assume that no one has questions. Just wait a minute (actually, about 10 seconds) and give learners time to register the fact that you've finished lecturing, to scan the information they've just received, to identify the area of greatest confusion if there's more than one, and to formulate a question. Then they usually conduct a "stupidity check," asking themselves how their questions are going to be perceived by other learners, the instructor, or even themselves. Finally, they scan the room to find out whether anyone else is about to ask a question — giving them confidence to ask theirs or causing them to wait. This process takes eight to ten seconds — much more than the two or three seconds most instructors tend to wait.

Ask learners to try answering their colleagues' questions instead of answering them all yourself. This helps them test their understanding of the material, reinforces their new knowledge, and boosts their confidence if they're correct.

Guided Practice

Soon after each chunk of information transfer, give learners an opportunity to put their fingers on the keyboard and apply the information you have just delivered. The instructions for guided practice should be very directive, requiring learners to carry out specific procedures. Otherwise, it will be difficult for the instructor or the learners to determine whether or not they have absorbed the material. Most guided-practice exercises have a right answer. They shouldn't contain any trick elements, and if they allow too much creative leeway, learners will have questions about the exercise itself rather than the procedure.

In classroom training, guided-practice exercises can take the form of cooperative learning. They shouldn't require more than 10 minutes each, and learners should know how much time they are expected to spend on each exercise. Written instructions give learners something to refer to if they forget the oral instructions. The trainer should circulate throughout the room during guided practice, checking to see if learners are having difficulties and being available for questions. Since guided practice is the learners' first opportunity to apply new information, they may come up with questions that hadn't occurred to them earlier; in fact, one purpose of guided practice is to elicit these additional questions.

Unguided Practice

Unguided practice allows learners to apply their newly learned skills and procedures to actual work or, at least, to realistic, job-related tasks. Learners can select from a variety of problems or bring actual work to class. It's not necessary for all participants to do the same exercise; in fact, if they have different jobs, they'll benefit from doing different exercises. When class participants have similar jobs, they can complete their unguided practice in cooperative learning groups.

Unguided-practice exercises don't require a single correct solution or even a particular approach; they may even include some ambiguity about which procedures to use. Because it departs from the specific procedures learners have been taught, unguided practice tests their understanding of the concepts underlying these procedures. And by providing a sense of accomplishment, unguided practice helps lock new skills into learners' memories.

Unguided-practice exercises can take anywhere from 20 minutes to two hours. They should include some real challenges, so instructors may have to do some figurative hand-holding — more for some students than for others — especially during longer projects. Unguided practice can be assigned as homework, but don't expect high success rates.

Check for Understanding

Before delivering a new chunk of information, make sure learners understand the last chunk. You can check for understanding implicitly by means of guided and unguided practice, or you can regard it as a separate activity. Just asking learners if they understand is not enough; they should be required to perform some procedures that demonstrate their understanding. Since this may be the last time learners are in a situation where they feel comfortable asking questions about the material, it's important for them to have that opportunity. This activity also lets trainers do some quality control, checking to catch any bad habits learners may be forming.

Thinking Styles and the Sagamore Design Model

Besides accomplishing an essential part of the learning process, each step in the Sagamore Design Model satisfies the needs of learners with particular learning styles. By following the model, the trainer makes sure every style gets some attention every hour, regardless of which styles are represented in the class.

Design Tips

There is no magical formula for sequencing course content. Two trainers can be equally effective teaching identical content in entirely different sequences. The same holds true for the different parts of the VCP list. Some people like to teach concepts first, then procedures; others like to start with procedures, then fill in the conceptual explanations, interspersing vocabulary throughout.

Your assessment of learners, your own style, and the nature of the software will all help you determine the appropriate sequence. If you know your audience has an interest or a background in a particular procedure, start with that. And if everyone definitely needs to learn a certain procedure, teach that early in the class so people who don't need more in-depth coverage can leave early.

While there's always latitude concerning the specifics of training delivery, make sure you follow these basic guidelines.

■ To help prevent boredom, don't stack all the vocabulary at the front of your design.

■ Some instructors have a tendency to continually review old material. A certain amount of review may be important, but it's just as
important to keep moving forward.

■ Let people know when you're teaching a procedure. Because practical thinkers may edit out the nonprocedural content, you want
to be sure you have their attention.

■ Don't be afraid to experiment. Your confidence and ability to create
effective sequences will improve with time and practice.

Techniques and Technologies Introduction

Readers of the first edition of this handbook have provided us with continuing feedback on its various components. The next 23 chapters cover the most frequently mentioned topics, which became known affectionately as the "minichapters" during the writing of this edition. Most are indeed shorter and have a specific focus, whereas the other chapters tend to be more conceptual.

Useful to both new and experienced trainers, the minichapters were designed for quick, easy reference. Each concentrates on a particular approach, technique, tool, or technology commonly used in designing or delivering computer training. Although their formats vary slightly, we have, when applicable, briefly defined the topic, described its major uses, and discussed its implications from both instructional and managerial points of view.

The minichapters are divided into two sections, Techniques and Technologies, with specific topics presented within each section.

Techniques

Chapter
Number   *Title*

12   Classroom Environment
13   Classroom Management
14   Cooperative Learning
15   In-Class Reading
16   Lecture
17   On-the-Job Learning and Training
18   Rebooting Learners
19   Self-Study
20   Simulation

Technologies

Chapter
Number   *Title*

21   Audio Learning
22   On-line and Internet-Based Learning
23   Cheat Sheets
24   Computer-Based Training
25   Flipcharts, Blackboards, and Whiteboards
26   Handouts
27   Interactive Video
28   Large-Screen Projection
29   Classroom Networking and Mirroring
30   Overhead Projectors
31   Slides
32   Video Teleconferencing
33   User Groups
34   Video Learning
35   Performance-Support Systems

12

Classroom Environment

The classroom's seating arrangements, lighting, temperature, and noise level are as critical to training effectiveness as the course design and instructor. Total control over the physical environment may not be possible, but as a trainer, you can take certain steps to make a classroom more conducive to learning.

Seating Arrangements

Unless the seats and equipment are permanently installed, you must decide how to set up the classroom. The most common seating arrangement — straight rows of desks and chairs — is often least effective. Learners strain to see you over each other's heads and terminals, and the whirring of PC fans can render clear communication impossible. Going from terminal to terminal to check learners' progress and offer remedial help is likely to be both inconvenient and disruptive.

On the other hand, staying at the front of the room limits instructors' contact with learners and often results in choral teaching, where learners are directed through specific keystrokes and learn only to imitate. Finally, if the rows are close together, it's difficult to rearrange the seats to form cooperative learning groups.

As an alternative to straight-row seating, try arranging desks or tables in a U-shape, with learners facing in. Or, terminals can be positioned around the periphery of the room, facing the walls, and another set of chairs or tables arranged in rows or a U-shape in the middle. Terminals facing the walls work especially well for guided and unguided practice, and the midroom seating can be used for instructor demonstrations, thus eliminating the problem of competing focuses.

Seating Plans

You may also want to base seating assignments on information about the learners. Naturally, seating should reflect a sensitivity to physical handicaps. To produce varied exposure to other learners, participants from the same departments and organizations should be seated apart.

Another option is to change seating assignments daily or after breaks. This increases participants' opportunities to learn from each other and may influence their participation patterns. Moving talkative learners to the front of the room will help you monitor them, while moving quiet participants up encourages their participation.

Lighting

Whatever the instructional setting, consistent lighting is preferable to shadowy lighting. Also, brightness levels have been found to affect learners' moods and involvement, and a room that's too bright is no better than one that's too dark.

Lighting also influences the type of projection technology used. In a room with directional lighting, overhead projectors produce a fairly crisp image with the lights on. Diffuse lighting, however, causes an overhead projection to wash out. Large-screen projections of computer displays require diminished lighting for a crisp image, unless rear projection is used. Slide presentations require a darkened room.

The individual workstations in some well-appointed training classrooms are outfitted with adjustable lighting. This is a costly but worthwhile addition.

Temperature

Room temperature also has a definite effect on learners. As with lighting, the key is to avoid extremes whenever possible. When subtle temperature control is not an option — which it rarely is — choose a slightly cool room over a warmer-than-average one.

Ventilation

Few training rooms have sufficient natural ventilation. A well-placed fan or two can help prevent stuffiness.

Noise

With their fans humming in unison, a roomful of PCs can be noisy. To maximize your vocal projection, avoid standing next to a PC and make an effort to circulate throughout the room while lecturing.

Distractions

Unfortunately, not all training occurs in specially designed class-rooms. In fact, noisy offices and shop floors are more often the site of on-the-job training. Trainers in these situations should take measures to forestall learners' distraction — by putting up screens around workstations, flying labeled helium balloons, or posting "Training in Progress" signs. Best efforts aside, you should prepare for lower attention levels in such settings than in a classroom.

13

Classroom Management

(AKA: climate-setting)

The thermostat, the light switch, and the seating plan aren't the trainer's only environmental controls. You also create the emotional climate of the classroom, subtly influencing learners' feelings about training and their expectations of success.

No matter which instructional approach you take — or whether the instruction is informal, one-to-one training at a learner's desk or an actual class — the following classroom-management guidelines can enhance the chances of training success.

Greetings

You can make participants feel welcome by meeting them at the door, shaking hands with them, and introducing yourself. A friendly greeting also helps dissolve any last-minute anxiety or resistance to learning.

Next, indicate where participants should sit and what they should do until the class begins — read a handout, fill out a questionnaire, experiment with a keyboard, go through a brief introductory computer-based tutorial, or perform another suggested activity. This directive is likely to meet with participants' approval if the reasons for the requested actions are clear.

House Rules

The first 10 minutes of training have a powerful effect on how learners perceive the entire training experience. By starting right in, you establish control. Critical as it is, however, instructor control must not be at the expense of participants' trust. After all, adults are used to a certain degree of control in their lives, and they'll resist a learning process that challenges that control. They're far more likely to feel comfortable and confident if they see the instructor's control as contributing to their learning success.

Establishing "house rules" is another way of achieving balance of control by letting learners know what to expect during training. How free are they to interrupt with questions, for example? An instructor who encourages interruptions makes it easier for learners to ask the real-time questions that can make the difference between confusion and learning.

Another house rule covers note taking. Without guidelines, some learners may spend the session trying to write everything down, getting much of it wrong, and retaining little. Ideally, note taking is limited to vocabulary and concepts, since 100-percent accuracy in notes on procedures is rare.

Learners should also know what they're expected to do if they finish practice or other independent activities ahead of the rest of the group.

Introductions

Trainers can conduct classroom introductions in a variety of ways. Once again, the traditional approach — in which participants introduce themselves one by one — is not the most effective. That method can be lengthy as well as costly, considering organizations are paying at least $35/hour (or more) per person for training. In addition, people don't listen very carefully to others' introductions when they're absorbed in preparing their own. As an alternative, instructors can distribute class rosters that provide job information and are alphabetized by participants' first names. Another introduction exercise involves beginning the session with an informal verbal poll on participants' organizations and jobs.

Jargon

Many words and phrases familiar to instructors are gibberish to learners' ears. To facilitate understanding, trainers and training materials should introduce and explain each new phenomenon, *then* name it. Encourage learners to interrupt whenever they hear terminology they don't understand.

Breaks

Particularly when learners are sitting at CRTs, frequent, short breaks are helpful. Limiting uninterrupted instruction to 50 or 60 minutes is a good rule of thumb. It's also important to control the length of breaks by restarting promptly at the announced time and to explain assignments before breaks; that way, learners who return to the classroom early can get started.

On-the-Spot Decisions

Instructors can't make all their classroom-management decisions in advance. Every training session includes unexpected questions, conflicts, and other surprises. One participant may produce an illegal copy of a disk. Another may start and sustain an argument about terminology. Another may introduce the topic of salaries. Appropriate responses to such situations aren't listed in any course guide, but every instructor needs a personal plan or pattern for developing them. Ideally, such responses are based on the instructor's previous discussions with colleagues and managers or on a corporate policy for inappropriate classroom behaviors. The conduciveness of the classroom environment to learning depends as much on these spontaneous decisions as on those included in the lesson plan.

14

Cooperative Learning

(AKA: working in groups, sharing a terminal, breakout groups, buzz groups, rebooting activities, small-group discussions)

Cooperative learning is any activity in which two or more learners work together, sharing their knowledge, experience, and problem-solving skills. Much more than learners working together in assigned groups or doubling up at computer terminals because of a hardware shortage, it is an instructional technique that requires intention and structure to be effective. Cooperative learning may not decrease overall learning time, but it does reduce lecture time and the instructor's role in remedial activities.

In their 25 years of studying cooperative learning, University of Minnesota professors and researchers David and Roger Johnson have compared the effects of three learning structures: cooperative groups; large groups, whose learners work in parallel but independently on assignments; and individual assignments, in which information transfer and practice take place in a self-paced medium, such as a workbook. In almost all of their 300-plus research projects, the Johnsons have found that cooperative learning yields the highest level of group

performance. Furthermore, individual performance levels in cooperative activities are as high as those in other situations, and frequently higher. Cooperative learning especially appeals to the reflective,
practical, and creative types of thinkers, who prefer activity to lecture.

All types of organizations across a wide range of industries use cooperative learning. This approach is particularly well adapted to training in field offices and other settings where limited space and
equipment make it necessary for learners to share terminals.

The introduction of cooperative learning often elicits some protest; for-
tunately, the most commonly expressed concerns are ones easily set
to rest. For instance, some people worry that the emphasis on group
performance may impede individual learners' progress. This is not a
factor in corporate training, however, since no one is held back from
achieving job competence. Most organizations, after all, prefer a broad
base of trained system users to a few individuals who've mastered a
spectrum of seldom-used features.

Many learners, and their managers, who oppose the sharing of terminals during training mistakenly believe that the amount of individual computer access determines training value. This assumption
is especially true in organizations that bill training expenses to specific departments, making managers particularly value-conscious.
However, the observer's role in cooperative learning is not a passive
one, and participants can learn as much from coaching and discussion as from actually pressing keys. (Facilities permitting, you can
provide the best of both worlds by assigning learners individual
practice at their own terminals and time working together at shared
terminals.) Management can diffuse unenthusiastic reactions to cooperative learning by assuring learners of its positive instructional
applications and ability to help them upgrade their skills.

Cooperative-learning activities provide various opportunities for
learners, rather than the instructor, to deliver course content. Each
group member might learn a specific topic — through CBT, lecture,
reading, or any other medium — then teach it to the others. Or,

after covering the fundamentals, you can distribute a handout explaining the next segment of material and ask the members of each group to go over it together.

To check for confusion at the end of each lecture segment, groups can spend a few minutes discussing your major points and drawing up a list of questions for you or for each other. Distributing handouts with a series of questions for learners to answer is another technique that brings confusion to the surface for clarification.

For guided practice, group members can work on exercises together or independently but with help from each other. For unguided practice, each group can simulate a job-related situation involving the application they are learning. In a class on an accounting package, for example, one participant might be the bookkeeper, another the controller, and another an irate customer presenting a problem for the others to solve using their new skills.

Cooperative learning offers the same cost advantages as instructor-led training, and more. Doubling up participants at terminals is an obvious way to cut equipment costs, and by taking advantage of peer support, you can increase the number of people in a class without decreasing the availability of assistance.

Advantages

Peer support. Assistance is more readily available to participants in cooperative learning than to individual learners. Confusion and counterproductive habits generally are spotted sooner in a group than by an instructor making the rounds. Also, because learners' grasp of new information is similar, they can often explain and clarify in ways that make the most sense to each other. For this reason, many learners are more comfortable asking peers than instructors for help. The emphasis on peer assistance in cooperative learning introduces participants to a way of acquiring understanding and support that continues beyond training. Finally, helping their peers gives learners a chance to affirm their understanding while boosting their self-confidence.

High involvement. Because cooperative learning encourages active participation, areas of learner confusion are readily apparent to both learners and the instructor .

Emphasis on competence. The outcome of cooperative learning may not be superior individual achievement by training's end. However, nearly 100 percent of learners attain a defined set of skills through this instructional mode.

Relevance. Cooperative learning pushes participants to think practically. With learners' active involvement in the material comes an almost automatic application of the concepts to their job tasks.

Popularity. Most people end up liking cooperative learning—even some who initially resist it. The Johnsons' research shows that cooperative learning not only receives consistently high ratings for learner satisfaction but also reduces disciplinary problems. Of the 25,000 to 30,000 people they have trained, only about 35 have remained opposed to cooperative learning. While some say they resent paying a lot of money to sit in groups of their peers rather than learn from an expert, very few ask for their money back.

Flexibility. A classroom set up with 12 workstations will allow you to teach 24 people, two per terminal, cooperatively.

Efficiency. Cooperative learning can save instructor time because simple, "How do I push Enter?"-type questions can be handled at the group level.

Disadvantages

Expectations. Learners who equate training with learning from an expert may be disappointed, even angry, when asked to work in groups. Shared terminals can heighten those reactions, since many people believe maximum "hands-on" time is a prerequisite for learning. Early on, you should explain the benefits of cooperative learning and try to dispel the myth that hands-on time is best.

Influences of personality. Any antagonism that participants bring to the training setting can negatively influence a group, as can extremely dominant, passive, or passive-aggressive personalities. However, careful group selection can prevent these problems.

Tips

The success of cooperative learning depends on a number of factors, including the following.

Group size. The ideal number of learners in a group varies according to activity. Two is most comfortable for working at a terminal, while groups of three discourage the dominant-subordinate relationships that can evolve with pairs. David and Roger Johnson recommend a maximum of seven people in a group, but in computer training, a group that large is appropriate only for an activity such as discussion that doesn't involve actual procedures at the terminal.

Group composition. In the corporate setting, instructor-selected groups provide more balance and freedom from distraction than self-selected groups of friends. After getting to know participants better, you can compose groups that are less likely to experience interpersonal conflict.

Choosing students of various abilities for a group is the best way to ensure full-group performance. It allows the most competent learners to assist those having problems, thereby reducing pressure on less competent learners. Grouping by similarities should be based on common job situations or application needs rather than comparable skill levels. Occasionally, instructors allow advanced learners to move ahead in a group; however, assembling a group of slow learners is a virtual setup for training and learning failure.

Uses of competition. It's important to avoid competition *within* groups, but cooperative learning thrives on subtle, well-managed competition *between* groups. In fact, a certain amount of competition among groups occurs naturally. If it doesn't upstage the learning process itself, intergroup rivalry can enhance motivation by reinforcing a group's sense of collective responsibility. When teaching in a graded setting, instructors might announce that each member of a group will receive the grade that's the average of the group's performance. Although grades aren't typically an issue in the corporate setting, a climate of friendly competition can nonetheless foster a sense of group accountability. In training a class of programmers, for example, you might give all groups a list of error-filled code, with the goal being to identify and correct more errors than the other groups.

When groups report on their work following a cooperative learning session, stay in the collective accountability mode by calling on members at random. Or, try asking learners who need extra practice instead of letting the reporting responsibility fall to the group's "secretary."

Time allocation. Every cooperative learning activity needs a set time limit. Establishing this limit can be challenging, because it's hard to predict exactly how much time groups will need, and no two will work at the same rate. If you provide more exercises than participants will be able to complete, everyone will complete something, but no one will run out of work. Any remaining exercises can be taken home for extra practice.

At the beginning of a course, no cooperative learning session should exceed 10 minutes. This time limit allows monitoring of learners' attention spans and decreases the risk of alienating learners opposed to the method. By the end of a three-day seminar, however, you may have learners working cooperatively for 40 minutes at a stretch.

Other Tips

■ Cooperative learning by no means absolves the instructor of responsibility. Rather, it shifts your responsibility to a sophisticated managerial task — shaping and monitoring group activities. The skill with which you perform this task will determine the success of your cooperative-learning sessions. Providing explicit written instructions for all group activities will save learners time and help ensure training success.

■ If you monitor group activities too closely, participants won't rely on each other. Too much distance, however, can cause them to feel abandoned and deprived of your expertise. In the beginning, get involved when you observe a particularly dominant participant taking over a group, or when a group is sidetracked by a major disagreement. As time goes on and group activities are more extended, monitoring can decrease.

■ If you control the classroom setup, try arranging terminals so that they face the walls and positioning chairs in a U-shape in the middle of the room. This pattern allows class members to sit together for lectures, then break into groups around terminals for cooperative learning. It also enables you to assist one group without disturbing the others.

Future Trends

One of the current trends in management technique and philosophy focuses on the role of group and team operation. Quality-management and work teams fit naturally into the cooperative-learning model. Teams that manage daily work processes should also team up for learning. Watch for additional team-based learning models in the workplace.

Developments in both hardware and software are making computer-based instructional technology available to learner groups as well as individuals. One such application is a computer-based tutorial that shifts control back and forth between two learners.

Internet and Groupware models of knowledge dissemination are creating new opportunities for technology-based cooperative learning. The ability of learners in separate locations to work as a cooperative team is a truly exciting innovation and is sure to produce new models for learning.

15 TECHNIQUES

 **In-Class Reading**

Reading is the core of computer learning. Learners read computer screens, the instructor's whiteboard notes, handouts, courseware, and software manuals. Likewise, reading is the core of on-the-job learning. Many people don't recognize reading as learning, however. Try this simple experiment: Lean back in your chair for an hour at work and read a computer magazine. Chances are at least one colleague will remark, "Must be nice to have time to read!" We often undervalue the role of reading as an integral part of learning.

Vendor manuals, third-party manuals, magazine articles, and customized materials can be used to deliver information in an instructor-led class. Many instructors are reluctant to include reading in their repertoire of classroom activities, however, because they anticipate learners' negative reactions. Indeed, much precourse material sent to participants goes unread, as do handouts distributed during multiday sessions or at the end of a course. Some learners have an aversion to reading in general, but even those who like to read may protest when valuable class time is spent on activities that can be done outside class. If they are brief, well structured and matched with learners' sophistication levels and the course content, reading assignments can be a useful component of classroom training.

When you have large quantities of information to deliver, alternating between lecture and reading assignments can provide welcome variety. You might have learners follow their reading with cooperative-learning activities. This allows them to note important or confusing points, answer prepared questions, or discuss the material's content with other group members before your check for confusion. Accompanying reading with group activity helps justify its use for resistant participants.

It's a good idea to have extra reading assignments on hand for learners who finish assigned activities early. Written materials can also be supplied to learners who miss class, need remediation, or are interested in supplementary, nonrequired information. Naturally, individual learners have unique reading preferences. Anecdotal reading material appeals most to reflective thinkers, while conceptual learners prefer more structured material. Whereas practical learners are most interested in reading that focuses on procedures, creative learners appreciate lists of hints, tips, and shortcuts .

Advantages

Self-pacing. Unlike listening to a lecture, reading allows learners to set the pace. They are free to concentrate on difficult passages for as long as necessary, skim familiar information, go back to refresh their memories, or stop to rest. This flexibility is especially helpful for learning complex concepts or phases of procedures.

Active involvement. Reading doesn't have to be passive. By underlining crucial passages and recording personal notes, learners are better able to grasp and retain new information.

Comprehension. Learners with first languages other than English may comprehend more by reading than listening. One-on-one follow-up discussions are still recommended.

Disadvantages

Aversion. Even when reading assignments are carefully selected and structured, there will still be learners who hate to read, think of themselves as poor readers, or read painfully slowly.

Perceived value. As mentioned earlier, some learners do not think of reading as a worthwhile class activity. They may complain about having to come to class to do something they could do on their own. Consider this another opportunity to share the rationale for your instructional choices with your learners.

Tips

■ Three to five pages is a dependable maximum length for most classroom reading, especially at the beginning of a class or course.

■ Use reading assignments to provide breaks after long group activities or as transitional activities between lectures and keyboard practice. In classrooms where learners double up on computers, half can work on reading assignments while the others are at the keyboard. After lunch and at other times when low energy levels may cause learners to drift off, intersperse reading selections with talk-oriented activities.

■ Once learners have participated in a cooperative activity, you'll have a better sense of how fast they work. This will help you decide how much time to allow for reading assignments.

■ Try to allow sufficient time for learners to finish reading assignments, but don't hold the majority back waiting for a few slow readers. They'll have a chance to grasp the information when you summarize it and respond to other learners' questions. They can also return to the written material after class.

■ Distribute handouts when you're ready to use them. If you hand them out earlier, some learners may insist on reading them immediately, regardless of what's happening in class.

■ Producing materials that are well written, visually appealing, and easy to follow will help counter potential learner resistance.

16 TECHNIQUES

Lecture

(AKA: demonstration, short explanation, theory session, backgrounder, overview)

Lecture — the verbal transfer of information from instructor to learners, interspersed with varying degrees of learner participation — is the most widely used form of training instruction in the United States. This is partly out of cultural habit, since the lecture method is so familiar from our years of traditional schooling. To go back even further, lecture is a first cousin of storytelling, one of the most ancient, captivating forms of information delivery. Lecture that borrows a sense of drama and pacing from the age-old art of storytelling can be quite enjoyable for learners.

As a training technique, however, lecture is overused! Too many trainers feel that their job focuses on the presenting of well-structured, polished presentations. In fact, many train-the-trainer programs are little more than public-speaking seminars. While the role of lecture or demonstration is critical to the success of the learning event, we need to remember that it is only a portion of the instructional task. That is why The MASIE Center urges trainers to reduce the instructional time spent lecturing and increase time spent on the interactive, processing-focused aspects of learning.

The nature of adults as learners puts special demands on a lecturer's approach. By shortening the duration of uninterrupted lecture, inviting learner participation in a variety of ways, and using a U-shaped seating arrangement (or some other variation from the straight-row pattern), you're more likely to engage adult learners.

Another reason for the popularity of lecture is that many instructors see it as the best way to maintain control over class time and content — as a sort of guarantee that learners will absorb large quantities of information. Unfortunately, these assumptions are unfounded. More accurately, lecture is a safe way to protect your lesson plan and your ego from learners' questions — especially those not easily answered.

To be really effective, lecture requires a high level of instructor self-confidence. No matter how good an entertainer you are, lecture audiences are most interested in your knowledge of the material. In choosing lecture to teach a software package you don't know very well, you risk misrepresenting the product and damaging your training reputation.

As for the "guaranteed absorption" assumption, just because learners listen to large quantities of information doesn't mean they learn. If you think of the human mind as a computer, with the long-term memory simulating a hard disk and the short-term memory acting as a buffer, lecture is basically a buffer-filling technique. It delivers information to learners' short-term memories but may not help them understand it in a way they can remember. Without the opportunity to relate new information to something they already know, learners are unlikely to achieve long-term retention. They may not even retain what they've heard through the end of the lecture. Instructors can come closer to guaranteeing learner absorption of information by familiarizing themselves with situations in which the participants will be using computers and referring to these scenarios often.

Like any training method directed to large numbers of learners, lecture is subject to the "multiplier effect." This effect can have negative as well as positive consequences. If the trainer misunderstands a particular function, everyone taking the course will misunderstand that function. If the trainer decides learners don't need to know a certain function, no one will learn it. On a more positive note, lecture provides an efficient platform for conveying corporate standards and general operating procedures needed by large numbers of people.

Lecture is a cost-effective method of information transfer when delivered by an effective lecturer, supported by minimal technology, accompanied by a variety of participatory activities, and received by learners who are motivated and mentally engaged. It lets you train 40 people at a time, or 80, or 200. If the system or application changes, modifying the lecture material is not an expensive proposition. And thanks to a variety of participation options, lectures can be customized to specific learners' job needs at no extra cost.

If lecture is not accompanied by practice, you save money on equipment and system time. But like many such savings, this one has a downside. Educational researcher David Berliner found that when learners are not actively engaged, their need for remediation increases — and both support time and further training time cost money.

Lecture can be the sole method of instruction or one of several; it can be used for one-to-one instruction as well as for groups. Specific uses of lecture involving different degrees of participation are described in detail later in this chapter.

As a rule, the more learner participation a lecture incorporates, the more effective it is. An instructor who does not encourage learner participation should try using audiovisual aids to engage learners as much as possible.

Listening to a lecture is the default learning style for conceptual thinkers, who typically make up 25 percent or more of a training audience. These individuals are capable of doing their own indexing, while other types of thinkers may need personal assistance and other kinds of activities to retain new information.

Pure lecture can be used for the set and information transfer, and, with minimal participation, the check for confusion. For guided and unguided practice, and the check for understanding, lecture should be supplemented with an interactive activity.

Advantages

Familiarity. It's both the good news and the bad that learners are comfortable with lecture. When they walk into a room and see a podium and an overhead projector, they know what to expect. In the role of lecturer, you won't have to deal with overt resistance or complaint, but you may not elicit much enthusiasm, either. (See Disadvantages.)

Predictability. Allocation of class time is relatively easy and dependable.

Uniformity. If you're introducing 150 users to electronic mail, the help desk will have a clear sense of what they've learned. Lecture provides a forum for explaining corporate standards to everyone who will be working on a system.

Flexibility. Once a lecture-based lesson or course has been developed, any instructor can use the script. It's also much easier to change a lecture script than a videotape, audiotape, or CBT course to accommodate even slight changes in subject matter.

Ease of supervision. A training manager can evaluate the instructor's work just by walking into the classroom.

Low social risk. Some instructors feel more comfortable dealing impersonally with learners, especially if the audience is composed of their superiors.

Role modeling. Like any learners, new computer users learn by observation, and instructors serve as models. Learners can watch where the instructor rests the manual, what he or she does while the system is processing, and so forth.

Authority. A good lecturer will become a trustworthy expert to whom learners can go with their questions and learning-related problems.

Disadvantages

Familiarity. Predictability has its flip side. Learners may be so accustomed to lectures that they go on "automatic pilot" when they see a podium and an overhead projector. They may have unconscious or even conscious blocks against learning from a lecture.

Learner passivity. When active participation isn't required, it's difficult for the instructor to monitor learners' understanding or detect their confusion levels. Even visible signs, like eye contact and head-shaking, are not always accurate indicators of receptivity and comprehension — as I once discovered upon thanking a responsive participant for his eye contact. It turned out that the man spoke hardly a word of English and had understood nothing. If you already know the learners, you'll be better able to read their facial expressions and body language, but few trainers are that lucky.

Risk of layered confusion. Without feedback, an instructor can't be sure of learners' understanding. This is a particular concern when teaching concepts that build sequentially. If learners misunderstand the first concept in the series and the unaware instructor proceeds to the next, there's little chance of learners grasping any of them. If you're teaching someone to use a spreadsheet program and the user creates a mental image of a file as a screen without your knowing it, the user will be completely confused when you start talking about copying files.

Inefficiency. Lecture might seem like a fast, efficient way to deliver information, but that doesn't make it a fast, efficient way to learn. If information comes at learners too fast, they don't have time to "index" it to discover whether they need clarification. And of those who realize their state of confusion, only five to ten percent are likely to raise their hands and ask for clarification. Even if the instructor has invited interruptions, people don't like to make their confusion public. If they ask questions at all, they usually wait a while. Unfortunately, an instructor needs about twice as much time to answer questions on topics no longer under discussion. Asked belatedly, the questions themselves may need more explaining, and the instructor must reestablish the context to answer them effectively.

Lack of job relevance. Unless the instructor has information about learners' jobs to build into the lecture, learners aren't encouraged to relate new material to their jobs. Even when the lecture includes job-related material, the instructor has no way of knowing whether learners are making the necessary connections to their own jobs.

Risk of dependence. Lecture can create dependent, procedural users if it doesn't include opportunities for experimentation. Dependence on the instructor is often established via lectures, and users may have difficulty adjusting to others' styles of explanation.

Tips

■ If learners ask you to repeat lecture points, don't take their requests literally. Simply repeating the original comment slowly and loudly—a common teaching mistake—won't solve comprehension problems and will likely frustrate the learner. On the other hand, offering an entirely new explanation of the point in question may create new confusion. The best way to help learners understand confusing material is to offer a slightly modified version of the original explanation or concept.

■ Avoid introducing exceptions and complex procedures before learners understand the basics.

Variations on the Lecture Theme

Short explanation. Whenever learners ask questions, even during nonlecture activities, instructors tend to switch into lecture mode for their answers. This gear-switching tendency can present quite a trap. By launching into a full-fledged lecture during an individual or a cooperative practice session, you bring learners to a full stop. If their attention is divided, neither the short explanation nor the practice activity will be effective. Instructors need to make sure they understand the nature of learners' confusion. Beware, especially, of providing more information than the learner needs. If you launch into a review of an entire topic when a learner is missing only one detail, you'll waste time, frustrate the learner, and possibly miss the crucial detail again.

Overview. A number of trainers use lecture to create a structure at the beginning of a lesson or course. Sometimes this takes the form of a rapid, benefit-selling demonstration. Other times, it is a quick pass through the screens of an application for the purposes of exposure and vocabulary building. The need for such an overview depends on the audience, and you should make sure it's necessary before doing it. An overview that does a good job of establishing a general understanding of the topic can cut down on the need for later hand-holding. Don't make the mistake of assuming that students are learning simply by exposure, however. If you overload them, it won't do any good to say later on, "Remember when you saw this screen earlier?"

Demonstration. Demonstration, in which the instructor performs the procedure being explained, is particularly useful when you break the procedure into manageable chunks, with a check for confusion at the end of each one. During demos, be sure to tell learners whether you're expecting them to learn from the demos or whether you're just showing them the system's bells and whistles. Even if you're not intending to teach, your audience's natural curiosity may push your demo over the line into a training event, and you should be prepared to do their questions justice.

Theory session. Lecture is often used to explain the concepts behind procedures, and if you're teaching a system that includes anything more than menu-driven commands, you'll need to include some theory in your course. But calling a lecture segment a theory session will alienate learners who don't think of themselves as — or who aren't — conceptual thinkers. You can avoid these "allergic reactions" by interspersing bits of theory throughout a lesson rather than dealing with the theoretical components in extended, isolated segments. It's a good idea to begin thinking about integrating theory with vocabulary and procedures at the VCP stage.

Lecture with Participation

Of the teachers you remember most vividly, the entertainers probably come to mind first. Charisma and pizzazz come in handy when lecture is the primary mode of instruction. Now think a little harder, recalling the teachers from whom you learned the most; the jokes and anecdotes probably fade. Often, the teachers we learn the most from are those who require us to actively confront our own ideas.

New trainers often worry about not being good speakers, much less good actors. But entertainment value is much less critical to good teaching than providing learners with opportunities to stretch beyond their previous experience. By allowing learners to externalize what's been going on in their heads, participation gives them — and their instructors — an indication of how well they're learning it.

While most instructors teach best when comfortable with the method they are using, participants' comfort with the instructional style is just as important. Effective instructors monitor learners' reactions constantly and adjust their techniques when necessary. If, for example, you notice that learners have stopped taking notes or asking questions during a lecture, you should solicit their participation to reestablish a higher attention level.

Opening a lecture to learner participation may feel risky to instructors who lack confidence in their knowledge of the material. But each of the following variations on the lecture method allows a different degree of control, offering trainers at any experience level the opportunity to choose a comfortable style.

Random-access lecture. If you want to tailor a class to learners' interests while retaining a maximum amount of control, try this lecture type. Prepare discrete lecture modules on certain topics, then select and sequence them according to learner interest once you've covered the fundamentals. For example, if you're teaching an accounting system and you've covered the basic reporting concepts, why not let learners select the specific reports they want to see demonstrated?

There are several ways to manage the selection process. You can ask learners to brainstorm the types of reports an accounting system might produce, then deliver the corresponding lecture modules. (You'll need to edit out reports learners have no need to know and arrange sequence-dependent topics accordingly.) Or, you can distribute a portfolio of handouts on all report types and ask learners to rank them according to their interests.

Solicited participation. Soliciting participation from individual learners is the easiest way to get participation without risking the awful silences that can fill the classroom when participation is voluntary.

You need to ask for participation with a great deal of finesse, or learners will get the impression that you're testing them and will be reluctant to risk wrong answers. Following educator William Purkey's use of the word "invitational" to describe the instructor's role, try setting a tone that makes people feel they have been invited to participate. If you explain and justify your approach to participation early on, learners will understand what's expected of them and why. But even with these explanations, you'll encounter learners who are reluctant to participate. Respect that reluctance; you'll only alienate these learners if you continue calling on them.

You can invite participation as often as every few minutes. If you're demonstrating how to fill in the fields on a screen, ask someone to provide the appropriate information. Or, ask a question that requires learners to apply material you have just covered. If you're doing a demo, ask learners to direct your actions.

The way you respond to incorrect answers is as important as the way you elicit those answers in the first place. Suppose someone gives an answer that's wrong but makes sense in light of a previous action. By simply saying, "That's wrong," you're likely to offend the learner. Instead, say something like, "I can see why you gave that answer. It would have been right on the previous screen, but that's not what we do this time." It's usually a good idea to provide the right answer immediately instead of asking someone else for it, which might make the original respondent feel inferior. If you do call on another person, don't let the eager hand-wavers monopolize your attention.

A seating chart or tent cards can help you call on learners by name, and you should encourage learners to get acquainted and refer to each other by name. Change the seating plan during breaks, at lunch, or between days of training. This will force people to circulate beyond their limited groups of colleagues and friends.

Many training consultants suggest that you state your question before calling on someone, requiring everyone to listen to the question. However, if you call on someone *before* stating the question, that learner can listen particularly carefully and feel better prepared to answer. You risk a lower level of overall class attention this way, but you decrease the chances of embarrassing individual learners.

Voluntary participation. Instead of calling on specific people to answer specific questions, encourage learners to raise their hands or interrupt with comments, questions, and suggestions. Don't expect this kind of participation to happen automatically— you'll need to use solicited participation or random-access lecture first to get learners into the habit of participating.

The Socratic method. With both voluntary and solicited participation, the bulk of the information still comes from the lecturer. The Socratic technique, named for the ancient Greek philosopher credited with its origin, uses questions that elicit most of the information from the learners themselves.

When teaching a computerized accounting system to a group of learners familiar with manual accounting procedures, you might begin by asking them to make lists of the reports, information screens, and other features they would include in automating their company's accounting process. Basically, you are asking them to design a hypothetical system. When they finish, show them the system you're teaching and ask them to compare the two in order to better understand the one they're learning.

You can also intersperse the Socratic method throughout a conventional lecture. This technique is particularly effective for verbal and conceptual learners. Instructors who use it should be well respected by learners and have a high level of confidence in their knowledge and ability to apply the technique.

Cooperative-learning-oriented lecture. If you are using cooperative-learning activities (see also the minichapter titled "Cooperative Learning"), try introducing a few basic features via lecture, then have learners deduce subsequent ones in their cooperative groups. Be careful not to present too much material in the lecture segment, or you won't leave anything for learners to do. Including too little, on the other hand, prevents them from continuing on their own. Because checks for confusion occur during the cooperative work, which is less closely supervised, distribute printed materials to help prevent layered confusion.

17

On-the-Job Learning and Training

(AKA: OJL, OJT)

Less than 20 percent of future computer learning will take place in computer-training classes. Most employees will learn how to use computers at their desks, with the help of peers. The challenge of providing effective on-the-job learning can be met by managing that process and supplying the tools and assistance learners need to master the new technology.

The acronym OJT (for on-the-job training) has been used by industry insiders for dozens of years. It originally referred to training provided by supervisors or appointed peers during the course of an actual job. For years, banks have used OJL (on-the-job learning) as the final stage of teller training. The majority of training done in defense plants during World War II was conducted via OJL. OJL cuts a wider path than OJT. It refers to all learning-based activities, overt and covert, in the workplace.

I organized the first on-the-job learning conference in 1993. The participants described their organizations' efforts to begin managing the OJL process and to raise OJL's status within their training departments.

OJL is a versatile, multifaceted training technique. It can be used to provide new skills or to support users in the application of existing skills. It can handle all stages of the Sagamore Design Model. Formal and planned or informal and spontaneous, OJL works with an audience of one learner or several.

Users or managers can request on-the-job learning, which is a useful supplement to other forms of training. OJL can fill in the gaps for new hires waiting to attend classes, employees who have missed scheduled classes, and users seeking remedial training or support. Another appropriate use of OJL is to upgrade skills originally learned in a class.

If you asked corporate training directors or information-center personnel how employees in their organizations learn computer skills, they'd likely point to a catalog of class offerings, all but ignoring the role of OJL. On the other hand, asking department managers the same question reveals that fewer than half of their computer users have taken training classes. And this pattern of users being trained on the job is just a glimpse of the shape of things to come.

There are several reasons for the discrepancy between perceptions of effective training and how learning actually happens. Because OJL is rarely monitored, records of its use are scarce. Training directors tend to downplay the use of OJL because of its threat to their budgets — there's no reason to increase departmental budgets for instructors and materials if employees are learning computer skills from their colleagues at their desks.

When large numbers of people need identical training, a class can be most economical. In most other instances, OJL can be a real money-saver. Despite its "soft costs," OJL isn't free. Rather than showing up in the training budget, the expense of this method is absorbed by the supervisory function, other users' productivity losses, and computer support.

The use of on-the-job learning is increasing steadily, and management can no longer afford to ignore it. If organizations hope to get the most out of their technological investments, avoid the spread of bad computing habits, and perpetuate organizational computing policies, managers and supervisors must actively monitor, evaluate, and manage OJL.

Management must take definite steps toward validating OJL. Some companies have added OJL management to supervisors' job descriptions. Others, in an effort to monitor on-the-job acquisition of computer skills, require new users to become registered by passing a qualification test.

The legitimization of OJL may seem like a threat to established training functions, but even computer trainers should recognize its importance. Say you work in a training department that is perceived as the organization's service unit and considered responsible for all end-user computer training. That responsibility may not be explicitly stated in your department's mission, but if you have any responsibility for end-user training, top management isn't likely to let you off the hook when end-user computing performance is unsatisfactory. User support staffs rarely bother to find out where users have acquired their skills — or their confusion. In the long run, the training function is likely to be held accountable for end-users' computing performance, whether these users have attended classes or not.

Advantages

Cost. OJL can provide a high-effectiveness, lower-cost approach to delivering workforce skills.

Spontaneity. OJL can be delivered within minutes after a training need is perceived. This is especially true for informal training, but even more formal OJL doesn't require as much planning as a full-fledged class. This makes it particularly inviting for users who "don't have time for training" and those who need experience with a system or an application before enrolling in a class. The benefit of on-the-job learning in such circumstances is strongly felt in high-paced, reactive environments like brokerage firms, banks, and retail stores.

Low visibility. Because OJL is more subtle than other forms of training, it's generally met with less resistance by senior executives, expert users, and others reluctant to admit they need training. It has become a common method of training temporary employees, staff assigned to special projects, and others who may not warrant a major training investment. (See Disadvantages.)

Peer training. Helping their coworkers gives peer trainers an opportunity to hone and expand their skills. Experienced users doing OJL inevitably return to the manual and learn new features and functions, especially if the system has been revised. This sets an example for the learners, who see the importance of keeping up to date. Finally, helping less proficient users is a good way to build self-confidence and a sense of competence.

Job-related. Because OJL learners work with real systems and applications rather than hypothetical exercises, they have little difficulty transferring their new skills to the job.

Disadvantages

Low visibility. Unmonitored, OJL can perpetuate inconsistent or incorrect information, bad user habits, and negligence of corporate policies. This lack of structure leaves organizations vulnerable to "wizard" users who may create shortcuts that ignore rules regarding system use. Before calendar and clock cards, for example, unsupervised OJL allowed millions of impatient users to bypass date and time prompts, leaving management without important records of file creation and updating.

Lack of tools. Without appropriate training materials and job aids, on-the-job learning can become on-the-job watching. But the users who deliver OJL may not have the time or skill to create such materials. If you know of supervisors who are training their employees, or employees who are training each other, consider supporting their efforts with practice files, checklists, manuals specially edited for training purposes, and other relevant instructional aids.

Inconsistencies. There is a downside to OJL's use as a stopgap technique for providing training before employees can get to a class. Unless on-the-job trainers know what's going to be taught in the class, they may leave out crucial concepts or introduce irrelevant ones. Or, they may teach shortcut versions of procedures that users should understand in full. You can help learners who will attend one of your classes (rather than one offered by an outside vendor) by providing on-the-job trainers with materials consistent with your own.

Impact on customers. Productivity is expected to drop as employees master new skills. This transition period can be particularly stressful, however, when the job in question involves customer transactions. An honest, to-the-point explanation can minimize this stress for both users and customers. Just as a grocery store should label a checkout line being used for training, so might a customer service representative tell a telephone customer, "By the way, I'm a new employee, and my supervisor is on-line in case any problems arise."

Lack of training expertise. Effective instruction requires good communication skills as well as subject-matter expertise. Frequently, those who deliver on-the-job training are expert users but not skilled communicators or instructors. Worst case, they may be new trainees charged with training others before getting sufficient practice themselves.

Subjectivity. Experienced users typically have strong attitudes, positive or negative, about the software or system, and they may pass these on to new users.

Support dependency. Because on-the-job learning focuses on procedures and even shortcuts, minimal conceptual background is gained. Users tend to be procedural, and their confusion level tends to be high. Often dependent on support, they lack training in how to learn from the support they get. The net result is prolonged handholding by the support center. However, a diligently monitored system of OJL could help defray high support costs by providing an on-the-job support network. The support function would keep records on competent users' areas of expertise and refer other users and their questions accordingly.

Future Trends

Here are some of the trends The MASIE Center has observed in the on-the-job learning segment of the computer-training field.

Sneaker-based training. Trainers and help-desk staff are being released from their traditional roles for several hours a week to provide a walk-around, at-the-terminal-based form of instruction. This "sneaker-based training" combines structured demos, practice sessions, question-and-answer segments, and hands-on tweaking of the user's configuration or system.

Temps as trainers. Growing numbers of temporary-employment agencies are placing their temps as OJL resources. An organization's major migration to a new operating system would be an ideal opportunity to hire a group of of OJL folks to work with individual business units on swift conversions.

OJL "transcripts." Workers will want to document and prove their learning as they master skills outside the classroom. Certification trends are extending to learners who have taken an OJL approach.

OJL training. OJL coaching skills are not the same as traditional training skills. For that reason, several vendors and universities are offering OJL training seminars, aimed at developing coaching and remediation skills in key personnel.

18

Rebooting Learners

(AKA: refresher, active review, competency checks)

Sometimes learners are just "down," especially in the morning or after lunch. *Rebooting*, a term borrowed from the vocabulary of computer use, has been adapted by trainers to describe a set of techniques for restarting the learning process in low-energy learners.

A computer isn't ready to compute the moment you turn it on; nor will it always be ready to perform a particular task when you are. Likewise, learners aren't automatically ready to pick up where they left off when they return to training after lunch or at the start of a new day. Just as computers need to be warmed up and booted — to have the needed operating system and programs installed in memory — learners go through a warm-up process that I'll describe here in computer-related terms.

Imagine that the learner's brain is structured like the inside of a computer. There's a hard disk for long-term memory and a buffer for receiving information, storing it temporarily, and making it available for the short term. When trainers explain new concepts and demonstrate new procedures, their words and actions go into the learner's buffer, or short-term memory. As learners begin to understand how the material relates to other, more familiar information, the data goes into long-term memory — the human equivalent of the hard disk.

Each new skill acquired or concept learned has its own location, or "file," in memory. This site usually relates to the location of the previously mastered knowledge that helped the learner grasp the new material.

In light of this metaphor, imagine that learners have "dumped their buffers" upon returning to training after lunch or an overnight break. The course material is no longer fresh in their minds. Some has been forgotten altogether, some has been stored in long-term memory, and some has been moved to different "files" as learners arrive at new understandings. The learners' buffers, then, are full of other issues and information — the phone calls they've just made to their offices, news items they heard on the car radio, their lunchtime conversations, the fires they should be putting out back at the office. As they find their seats, stow their briefcases, greet their colleagues, and receive new handouts, learners prepare to replenish their buffers. They begin searching their long-term memories in an attempt to access the information learned in the previous session.

Unfortunately, the most common start-up techniques don't take this "learner limbo" into account. Many instructors immediately present new material, neglecting the fact that learners are still settling in and trying to recall material from the previous session that may be required to understand the new material. Other instructors restart by asking if there are any questions on the old material. Learners often do come up with questions between sessions but are not usually focused enough at the beginning of class to ask them.

Some instructors resume class by reviewing the previous session's material in new terms. This is a dangerous technique, one apt to confuse learners and possibly undo the previous session's learning. A quick review of the old material using the same format and terms isn't much better, because it puts learners in the passive listening mode. The alternative, rebooting, actively involves learners in refreshing their memories and preparing to learn new material.

Rebooting activities focus on material from the previous session that is particularly confusing or that relates to the new lesson. In the simplest rebooting activity, learners work in teams of two or more, checking the instructor's list of items to see if they understand them, helping each other when necessary, and writing up their questions. After about five minutes, the instructor calls on people for definitions, poses questions that delve more deeply into the material, solicits learners' questions, and encourages other participants' responses.

Rebooting can also take the form of computer-based exercises that drill learners on procedures from the previous session. These activities may require learners to detect errors in a computer operation the instructor is performing. An instructor might ask learners to list the previous session's procedures in the order of their probable use on the job, or in order of their difficulty to understand. Finally, learners can reboot by creating job aids for tasks involving the previous session's material.

Advantages

Enforced interaction. By giving learners an immediate opportunity for active, verbal participation, rebooting almost guarantees that their attention is engaged when the instruction recommences.

Peer teaching. By teaching each other, learners have the chance to test their own understanding. Discovering that one can explain something to someone else is also a great confidence booster.

Observation opportunity. Rebooting gives the instructor a few minutes to move around the room, observing the class and getting a sense of how well each learner has grasped the material.

Efficiency. Rebooting clusters remedial time at the beginning of the class rather than letting it take up time throughout. Because learners have a specific opportunity to refocus on the previous session's content, it's less likely that time will be needed for that process during the rest of the class. And once learners' attention is engaged, it's likely to hold for the new material as well.

Reassurance. When rebooting is a regular feature of an instructor's classes, learners can count on it as a "safety net" when they get confused.

Tips

■ If your rebooting content includes a series of procedures, try presenting them in a different sequence than how they were taught. This ensures that learners' ability to remember and use the information isn't limited to a particular order.

■ Rebooting shouldn't take much more than six to ten minutes — three to five minutes for the group discussion and three to five minutes for the whole-class discussion. Longer sessions may be a sign that the material wasn't well taught in the first place or that you are trying to accomplish too much in rebooting.

■ Rebooting techniques can also be used during class as structured checks when learners seem confused, or for teaching complex topics.

Reboot List for Client-Server Concepts Seminar

■ Requester
■ Client Modules
■ SQL Search
■ Network Models of Data Sharing
■ Groupware
■ Code Libraries

■ Retooling of Programming Skills
■ Data Validation

Author's note: Sometimes, trainers themselves need to be rebooted. When teaching multiple-day courses, I notice a difference in my energy level from Day 1 to Day 2. The first day, I'm pumped up with the excitement and nervous energy of teaching a new group and a new class. But by the time Day 2 rolls around, I'm more relaxed, and that can be a problem. As much training energy is needed on Day 2 as on Day 1, and it has to come from the trainer.

I've discovered that rebooting is a surefire way to energize myself as well as the learners. It gives everyone a chance to get back into the learning process and to warm up our brains and even our voices. It also gives me a few moments to move around the class and take care of any individual needs without putting the whole class on hold. I'm such a fan of rebooting that I won't teach a class without it!

19

 **Self-Study**

(AKA: individual learning, independent learning, self-paced learning)

*In 1994, the number-one selling series of books in the computer section of bookstores was the **DOS for Dummies** titles. The millions of users who bought **Windows for Dummies** were among the vast majority that used self-study as a primary or secondary method of learning.*

People often learn to use computers on their own, inside or outside formal organizations, relying on manufacturers' documentation or materials specifically designed for learning — like computer-based training tutorials, workbooks, or videotapes and audiotapes. Outside of formal organizational and academic settings, self-study is probably the most common method of learning to use computers. Most people who buy computers for their homes learn to use them by reading the documentation, using a tutorial disk (if provided), and reading third-party manuals. Users who work in organizations without established structures for training also tend to teach themselves.

Although self-study is often used in place of classroom training, self-study materials can be used to supplement instructor-led training. Likewise, instructors often incorporate self-study in their classes. The use of self-study assumes that users can, on their own, acquire the necessary knowledge and skills to do a job. However, self-study carries no guarantees; materials must be appropriate, and learners must be adequately prepared and motivated to succeed.

The effectiveness of documentation for self-study depends on both the learner's skill level and the nature of the documentation. Novice users are likely to have more success with tutorials designed specifically for learning, and some tutorials are geared toward specific audiences. Random-access procedural manuals allow individuals to design their own learning sequences. Users who have experience and don't need hand-holding can take advantage of this method, obtaining information in ways that match their own thought patterns.

Given the nature of self-study, organizations that choose it as the predominant mode of training — or even one of many — should monitor its use carefully. Don't assume, for example, that just because manuals exist or the company library is stocked with videos, users will read or watch them *and* learn from them. Self-study can be less expensive than instructor-led training, especially if the cost of materials is distributed over many people. But a class is a more dependable way to deliver information to a large group, and its lack of support expenses can make it even more cost-effective.

Whenever possible, at least one alternative training method should be available for learners lacking the motivation to train themselves and those whose learning styles are poorly served by the available materials. Even with such alternatives in place, all self-study learners should have support readily available.

Learners with some experience in navigational computer use are best able to teach themselves. That's why self-study is a more appropriate training choice for organizations that encourage navigational use than for those that encourage and reinforce procedural use.

Advantages

Convenience. Self-study allows users to learn at the time and place of their choice, eliminating the need for travel.

Flexibility. Learners engaged in self-study at their desks are more available to attend to work-related issues than those attending off-site classes. (See also Disadvantages.)

Portability. Learners can read training manuals at home or while commuting, and videotapes and audiotapes also can be taken home. However, these methods are most effective when accompanied or followed by keyboard practice.

Disadvantages

Underinvestment in training. Self-study is not always monitored. Managers too often assume that users provided with relevant training materials will learn the required skills, or that the existence of a manual is a sufficient substitute for training. In fact, selecting self-study as the primary training approach can be a way for management to avoid making any other decisions about training. Unfortunately, users don't always learn what they need to from self-study.

Standardization. Most self-study materials are generic and multi-functional, having been developed for use by as many types of learners as possible. As a result, these materials may not be quite suitable for anyone.

Inadequate materials. To begin with, self-study tools are not always appropriate for learning. Conventional user manuals are a classic example. Even those that are sequential often bear little resemblance to the procedure the users will follow in performing their first on-the-job tasks.

Interruptibility. Learners who stay at their desks for self-study typically have a hard time avoiding work-related interruptions.

Dependence on support. Any use of self-study usually leads to greater learner dependence on support than is observed in instructor-led training. Support demands escalate as the suitability of self-study materials for a given audience decreases. For instance, if users are expected to learn by reading manuals, those who don't like to read will rely especially heavily on support.

Tips

■ When evaluating or designing self-study materials, make sure they provide multiple sets of examples and ample opportunity for testing and practice throughout. To supplement off-the-shelf material, try creating supplementary materials with organization- or job-specific examples.

■ Remember that self-study learners need to be motivated not only to learn, but to learn independently.

■ If new users will be learning from a conventional manual, construct a substitute table of contents or customized learner's guide directing them through the manual in a sequence suited to their specific learning and application needs.

■ Consider asking learners who've recently completed a course of self-study to develop self-study materials for future students. Some learners take great notes. These pages, typed and edited, are an example of the many low-cost approaches to generating self-study materials.

■ Every major developer of classroom-based courseware is currently working on a document assembly that allows trainers to create custom versions of the learner booklets. This courseware should be regarded as a learning tool, not just a peripheral to the training event.

20

Simulation

(AKA: case studies, role-plays, games)

A simulation is a realistic, job-like situation created to serve as a vehicle for any part of the training process. Simulations can be developed to varying degrees of depth. At one end of the spectrum are "what if?" questions that merely require learners to imagine specific work situations. At the other end are full-fledged dramas in which learners are completely immersed — for example, the training floor at an investment banking firm or a simulated checkout line at a grocery store.

Some simulations require learners to apply newly acquired skills to tasks they might encounter on the job. In a word-processing course, for example, after you've taught document creation and basic editing, have learners transfer the names and numbers from a manual card file into a word-processing file — a task their bosses might well assign.

To simulate reality even more closely, ask learners to bring in work they've been doing manually and have them figure out how to do it on an automated system. To show the limits of the system or software, design a simulation around an impossible task, or one likely to produce undesirable results.

Simulations also work well in cooperative-learning groups. A simulation can include multiple roles, or learners can take turns posing hypothetical problems for each other, often within an established structure. (With this approach, you'll find that learners usually set much higher standards for each other than an instructor does.) Intergroup competition can be a motivating force in group-simulation activities.

Simulation can be used for all steps in the Sagamore Design Model but is most frequently and effectively used for unguided practice. Make sure learners have a solid command of the training's basic skills before being exposed to the unexpected twists and turns of simulations. Particularly appealing to reflective thinkers, simulations may be dominated by these learners if groups aren't carefully monitored.

Advantages

Authenticity. Because simulations bear such strong resemblance to job situations, they make new skills and concepts particularly easy for learners to relate (and take back) to their jobs.

High risk/low consequence. Simulations give learners the chance to try out actions that might have costly results in real life. For example, they can find out what happens when the system crashes without actually crashing the system.

High involvement. Participation in simulated activities is compelling, almost irresistible, and can help overcome some forms of learner resistance. For those who resist computer training out of fear, a "what if?" scenario can draw out the fear so it can be dealt with. Others resist learning on the grounds that they won't have time to use the new skills on the job. Simulations take the steam out of these "doubting Thomases" by allowing them to use the new skills in a job situation before they've even left training.

Conduciveness to questions. By thoroughly involving learners in the content, simulation activities stimulate more, and more sophisticated, questions.

Versatility. Because there are usually multiple ways to simulate tasks or procedures, learners can practice their new skills in various ways.

Disadvantages

Bad reputation. In surveys of training participants, role-playing repeatedly turns up as the least popular training technique. This is not surprising, considering that some training settings use role-playing to force participation. A nontheatrical learner forced to get up and act in front of a classroom may become "allergic" to role-playing. Such mandatory participation seems especially objectionable in computer training, where the skills in question have little to do with dramatic presentation.

To make the most of simulations and avoid allergic reactions, eliminate emphasis on theatrics and avoid the term *role-play*. Also, use the lesson introduction to explain your inclusion of simulation activities. This will make learners more comfortable with them. And since many learners are wary of these activities, work to gain management's endorsement of their use in advance.

Open-endedness. Because they are open to so many possibilities, simulations require thorough preparation and as much advance structuring as possible. Provide written instructions and be prepared to spend time answering learners' questions about the simulation assignments.

Interpersonal conflicts. The high degree of learner involvement may allow repressed interpersonal conflicts to surface.

Time. Simulations often take more time than other practice activities. That time may not be available, or learners may wonder why it is not being spent on a lecture, which is often perceived as more valuable.

Humor and Games in Training

Joel Goodman, director of The HUMOR Project, Saratoga Springs, New York, has spent his adult years looking at the constructive uses of humor in the classroom. Bob Pike, president of Creative Training Techniques International, Inc., has dedicated his company to the dissemination of high-energy and humor-filled approaches to learning facilitation. These two pioneers have developed great insight into humor's role in the classroom. Here are some contributions from their findings.

■ The root of HAHA is AHA. Focus on truth . . . it is the funniest.

■ There is a great difference between jokes and humor. Humor is natural among any group of people; jokes are plans for eliciting laughter that live on index cards.

■ Humor should come from learners, not from the podium.

■ Games can work . . . if you believe in them. Don't apologize and link them to work or learning objectives. A great example of this involves using a computerized version of Jeopardy. Put together a low- or high-tech simulation of the Jeopardy game board and have users choose questions. As soon as a learner selects "Paradox for $50" or "Netware for $100," you're off and running! It's a great model for testing knowledge in a fun way.

21 | TECHNOLOGIES

Audio Learning

(AKA: tapes, cassettes)

Listening is a powerful component of the learning process. This fact has made audiotape learning programs extremely popular for a wide range of topics. However, audiotapes are probably the least appreciated and most underused medium for computer training.

Audio training was popular for microcomputer training quite briefly, before training in other media became available. (Scriptsit, one of the first microcomputer word-processing packages, was issued with an audio tutorial.) And until interest was diverted to the development of computer-based training and interactive video, steps were made toward developing audiocomputer linkages. By connecting the player to the computer, a learner could control it with the keyboard, and the computer could activate the player. But with the rise of other technologies and the growth of the computer-training profession, the use of audio for corporate computer training has declined to almost zero.

Audio is widely used in schools, however (IBM's Write to Read program for children is an example). While it should not be used as the only method of training — it's less appropriate for novices than for experienced users — it has a vast number of uses.

Audio is an obvious medium for self-study and a convenient way to deliver training to a geographically dispersed audience. Classroom instructors can use it as well to supplement other methods of information transfer and guided practice. Job-specific tapes allow instructors to customize segments of a course to individual learners, in effect delivering multiple lectures simultaneously. Tapes are useful for learners who have missed class or need remediation and for non-native English speakers who can play them back to reinforce concepts they may have missed. (These learners also may be able to find tapes in their native languages to supplement English-language lectures.)

An information center can distribute audiotapes to new users needing basic skills before attending a class, and tapes are a good way to disseminate standards for on-the-job training to line managers. Experienced learners can use tapes to further explore software on which they have received initial training.

Because audio training is more effective with experienced users than with novices, it is particularly valuable for upgrades. Packaging an audiotape with a manual is a good way to sell current users on the advantages of a new version, and learners' taped accounts of their uses of a system can be helpful for supplementary benefit selling after training.

Clearly, the more geared toward auditory stimuli a learner is, the more suitable audio training will be. Conceptual thinkers seem to follow audio training best. A tape including storytelling or specific information they can relate to personally may appeal to reflective thinkers.

Audio can easily introduce a lesson, although it may not be possible to set the context for each situation in which a tape is used. For information transfer, audio is best used for vocabulary and concept items.

If used to explain procedures, it should be supplemented with a printed job aid or a practice disk to give learners something to manipulate instead of having to rely on their imaginations.

Learners can do guided-practice exercises with an audiotape if you calculate the time required for each procedure and build in pauses accordingly. A tape can suggest unguided-practice exercises but doesn't provide a way to check learners' accomplishments. Similarly, a tape can't check for confusion. By providing the right answers to practice questions, a tape can help learners do their own checks for understanding.

Production and duplication of audio-based training materials are equally inexpensive. A professional sound studio, which is not even required, can be rented for between $50 and $150 per hour at a local radio station. (Rental of a video studio, by comparison, costs at least $300 per hour.) Duplication costs can be as low as $1 for a 60-minute cassette.

You can cut overall training costs by using audio instead of lecture or video for the anticipatory set, information transfer, and guided practice. This allows you to save more expensive instructor time for the components of training that audio can't provide. Be aware, though, that it can be difficult to monitor learners' participation and progress in self-study activities like audio learning.

Although audio training requires a minimal investment in technology, management must make a commitment to maintaining that investment. An extensive tape library is useless if there are no batteries for the portable cassette player. Movable technologies, such as cassette players, also present some tracking/security concerns.

If audio is used as the predominant method of training, many learners may not listen, causing demand for support to be high. However, widely distributed audiotapes can encourage consistent vocabulary throughout the organization. Ensuring that the support group has access to the audio scripts will enable them to help learners more effectively by using the same vocabulary.

Advantages

Lack of visual competition. Audiotapes allow learners to concentrate on their computer monitors without videotapes or demonstrations competing for their attention.

Affordability. Audiotapes are one of the lowest-cost-per-learner methods of training.

Availability. If an organization or department doesn't already have tape players in its possession, they are not a major purchase.

Portability. Small tape players can be moved from one part of the organization to another, and learners can easily take them home. Learners with cassette decks in their cars can even listen to tapes containing conceptual content on the way home from class.

Office use. With headphones, learners can concentrate on audiotapes even amid office distractions.

Self-pacing. Learners can stop, start, rewind, and repeat audio training at will.

Quality. Learners don't impose the same expectations of quality on audio productions as on video, which has inherited a critical, TV-influenced audience. "Homegrown" audiotapes are quite acceptable to listeners who might be critical of equivalent video productions.

Ease of production. Audio production is inexpensive and quick. After writing or outlining a script, you can record an hour-long training tape in a couple of hours. Nor does playing the average tape require highly sophisticated, expensive equipment.

Ease of alteration. Revisions to accommodate system changes are as easy and inexpensive as initial production.

Alternative to reading. Audio can't replace reading altogether, but learners who don't like to read welcome it as a substitute for some written instructional material.

Disadvantages

Generic nature and inflexibility. Like any fixed method of information transfer, audio doesn't give learners a chance to ask questions. If they can't grasp material as it's presented on tape, they're out of luck.

Risk of layered confusion. Like low-participation lecture, tapes provide no opportunity for instructors to detect learners' confusion. This leaves room for learners who misunderstand the first in a series of concepts or steps to remain confused throughout.

Lack of visual input. Some learners need, or at least prefer, to see some visual representation in addition to listening.

Assumptive needs assessment. Like other training materials produced for wide-scale distribution, tapes aren't based on a first-hand assessment of learners' needs.

Visibility. Some learners may be self-conscious about sitting in their offices listening to an audiotape.

Pacing. A learner can become uncomfortable with a tape that delivers content at a speed other than he or she is accustomed to working.

Limited shelf life. Like all technology-related training materials, audiotapes become obsolete rather quickly. And despite the ease and low cost of updating, many trainers seem to think that the initial effort is sufficient.

Tips

■ The development of the compact disk provides a unique ability to present audio in a more random-access mode than analog tape can. There are a few pioneers in this medium that are developing audio training components to match books or computer-based learning modules.

■ Professional actors aren't needed to make training tapes, but try to find people whose voices, on tape, are relatively pleasant and non-grating.

■ Consider using audiotapes as a postclass "present" to learners. I give a 10-minute tape to everyone who attends one of my seminars. The tape is titled "Now That the Seminar Is Over." It is a simple message advising learners to proceed slowly when they get back to the office. I also remind them to practice their newly learned skills the first day back to work.

22

On-line and Internet-Based Learning

(AKA: the use of on-line services such as CompuServe, America Online, Prodigy, or the Internet for learning and training)

> **This is the most temporary chapter in this book. I guarantee that 10 percent of its content will be out of date by the time the ink dries at the print shop. Twenty percent will be obsolete within a few months, and at least 60 percent will seem passé by the time you've had this book a year. And that always-changing quality is what makes the topic of on-line and Internet-based learning so exciting!**

Let's start with a few simple definitions for readers unfamiliar with this emerging field. *On-line learning* is the use of a computer network connection to disseminate and receive knowledge and information. The connection may be from a *stand-alone personal computer* (PC) through a *modem* to a *local bulletin board* (BBS). Or, it may be a corporate *LAN* or *WAN* connection to a central server with content. It can also be a dial-up connection to a commercial service like *CompuServe* or *America Online*. For many, it is their ability to hook up to the global "digital superhighway" we call the *Internet*. On-line learning is the ability to electronically "reach out and touch" knowledge and learning materials.

There are several models for on-line learning. Each has a unique level of learner interaction and offers a training experience with specific learner options.

Bulletin Board Models

Bulletin boards are computer programs that allow users to leave, read, and receive messages. They provide access to data files (and sometimes specific screens) and permit on-line, real-time conferences between two or more users. All three functions of the BBS — messaging, data access, and conferencing — can be used for both formal and informal support and training.

Response time to requests for bulletin-board support varies from immediate to longer term. (Depending on how long a message is left on the bulletin board, a response could be received months later.) There is usually some delay after users leave support requests, although some systems have an "SOS" feature that allows users to indicate emergencies. These emergency messages are read immediately, and the user and support provider communicate directly by typing. Otherwise, the support staff leaves messages in response to requests, usually in order of urgency.

Bulletin-board setups used for support generally fall into one of these three categories:

1. Organizations with multiple sites equip a PC at a central location with bulletin-board software and an incoming modem. This allows

users at all sites to receive help from the support staff at the central location.

2. Organizations with mainframe electronic-mail systems can use these systems as bulletin boards. These systems also can be used to broadcast messages about overall system changes.

3. Many software vendors have established customer-access bulletin boards for training and support. User groups and other membership organizations are doing the same for their members. Vendors' bulletin boards are usually electronic versions of the telephone-support hot line, while user groups' bulletin boards are more like electronic meeting places for conferences and even formal courses.

E-mail Broadcast List Models

This is a form of "nonjunk" third-class mail. Learners subscribe to a mailing list accessible via the training department's E-mail system or a global mailing list that uses the Internet to deliver messages to dozens of countries. The mailing list provides learners with a regular "feed" of E-mail messages focused on a specific topic.

Broadcast models can be used as structured or nonfacilitated communication vehicles. In the structured model, the learner gets an E-mail packet of lessons, each containing text, graphics, and even multimedia. In the nonfacilitated model, any list member can broadcast a message to the entire list. This is used as a virtual bulletin board for those without BBS access.

I recently offered a training-skills course via a few Internet bulletin boards, hoping to structure a 12-week class for a few dozen learners. By the time the class started, there were more than 4,000 participants in 26 countries. Incredible!

The major software publishers are increasing their use of mailing-list models to disseminate updates and learning materials to their user communities across the globe.

Newsgroups and Agents

The problem with bulletin boards and mailing lists is the volume of data a learner must sort through to get a few nuggets. On-line learning is gravitating toward the use of a highly personalized filtering capacity. As I typed this paragraph, my fax machine spit out a one-page daily summary of technology news based on my request of eight topics I want to track. I can also receive this update via my E-mail.

These filters, or "agents," have enormous potential for assisting learning. The Internet has thousands of newsgroups that will be filterable by learners expressing very precise knowledge interests. For example, a new user of Powersoft could launch a request for information about client-server models using Powersoft and Oracle in financial services companies. As soon as information appeared on thousands of bulletin boards, newsgroups, or mailing lists, the requesting user would be notified.

Bigger Bandwidth

Computer users have a temporary "plumbing problem." The current structure of the digital superhighway is a very small pipe, through which most users can shove only a bit of text. Most training developers are anxious to ship high-density packets with multimedia and graphical/video components via the superhighway. The capacity for this will appear in 1995 and beyond; for now, however, we are constricted to a mainly text and graphical model.

Advantages

Wide audience. Bulletin boards give users almost immediate access to the best aspects of user groups, including the potential for a broad base of expertise. Public-access bulletin boards and Internet linkages are potential vehicles for the growth of a vast collection of public-domain courseware.

System-change notices. In large organizations with fast-changing mainframe systems, it's impractical, or even impossible, to provide all users with training on every minor system change. It's even costly to send out memos describing these changes. A cost-saving alternative is the use of electronic mail to broadcast these changes via announcements that appear automatically when a user logs on to the system.

User involvement. Bulletin boards give users the opportunity to help each other, reinforcing their own skills and raising their self-confidence.

Customization. Bulletin-board help combines the immediacy and individuality of a phone call with the convenience of on-line help.

Efficiency. Bulletin-board support eliminates endless rounds of "telephone tag" and long waits on hold. Support providers control their time by determining the urgency of the messages and limiting immediate responses to emergencies. In the "SOS" mode described earlier, users are forced by the demands of written language to be more succinct than they need to be on the phone. Bulletin-board support providers can save time responding to common questions by plugging in prepared message macros when those questions arise.

Disadvantages

Security threats. There is some anxiety that the use of networks presents a threat to system security, especially among organizations with substantial internal networks. Therefore, some companies limit employee access to the Internet and bulletin boards.

Limited appeal. Not all users feel comfortable with the relatively impersonal nature of electronic communication. On the other hand, some prefer it to in-person contact — in fact, computer bulletin boards have become a form of social activity for some users. These people may use bulletin boards more for social interaction than for actual training or support needs.

Lack of enforcement. The use of electronic-mail systems to broadcast announcements of system changes does not guarantee users will read the announcements, especially if they appear frequently. Many users will even discover shortcuts for bypassing messages when they log on.

Costs. With long-distance telephone costs, hardware-modem connections tend to incur greater costs than mainframe networks do. Connections to commercial services range from $3 to $12 per hour. Internet access, often free through a university or Freenet, may require additional software and high-speed modems.

23 TECHNOLOGIES

Cheat Sheets

(AKA: job aids, keyboard templates, prompt cards, quick-reference cards, keystroke guides)

> *A "cheat sheet" is a concise, task-specific guide to some subset of a system or software package's features and procedures. It is kept close to a user's desktop computer for immediate reference. Used on the job as concise forms of documentation, cheat sheets play a major role in supporting computer use. They also have various training applications.*

Learners can create their own job aids during training, either from scratch or from a menu-like text file of system features provided by the instructor. Instructors should check all learner-generated job aids to make sure they are accurate. In a navigationally oriented class, you might hand out job aids to learners having particular difficulty.

Cheat sheets can be used for a kind of minimalist information transfer. They can also be used as tools in guided- and unguided-practice exercises. The cost of producing cheat sheets is minimal to moderate; the payback in proficiency and reduced support can be enormous.

Good job aids can reduce users' dependence on support. They can also eliminate the need for users to have full-reference manuals at their terminals. When centrally created, job aids advance standardization of input style and format. They can also be used as tools in on-the-job training and support. When repeated calls for help demand, the information center or support center can issue job aids on particular procedures. Dependence on cheat sheets is a sure sign of a procedural user, one who will be equally dependent on support staff during tasks beyond the scope of the job aid.

Advantages

No memorization. Providing job aids during training eliminates the need for learners to memorize procedures, thereby eliminating the memorization anxiety common among adult learners.

No transcription. The use of job aids during training also lessens learners' tendency to write down every keystroke — a process that interferes with information assimilation and often yields inaccurate data. (Learners typically make at least one error for every 10 or 20 keystrokes transcribed.)

Disadvantages

Dependence. Reliance on job aids can lead to false confidence, with users blindly heeding the job aids and forgetting to check the results of their input or the screen for validation. The outcome of such a situation can be disastrous. Suppose a user is looking at the wrong line on the cheat sheet or the wrong card in a stack of help cards, enters a delete command instead of an add command, and executes without checking the screen. It's extremely important for instructors to warn learners of this hazard.

Compulsive behavior. For some learners, this tool becomes the sole focus of their attention. Their tendency is to spend too much time checking the cheat sheet instead of following the instructional pathways of the class.

Tips

■ Job aids should be dated and should visually resemble the current version of the system or software they support. They should be designed for specific job functions and, if possible, specific employees.

■ Job aids are compact and concise by definition. A job aid overloaded with information defeats its purpose and sends users hunting for a magnifying glass. Conceptual thinkers do prefer cheat sheets cross-referenced with more substantial documentation, however.

■ Accommodate users' styles and needs. A British brokerage house encouraged its stockbrokers to use a new system by distributing desk blotters printed with procedures.

■ Don't refrain from spending a little money on job aids. These single pages will probably get many more hours of use than a hefty manual, so it's worth having them typeset and even laminated for durability. One company printed mini job aids on Post-it™ notes to encourage users to keep them close to their terminal.

■ Consider building a cheat-sheet generator as part of a computer-based product. The learner could have the option of printing cheat sheets as a postlearning experience.

Note: Learners should select the cheat sheets they need based on the types of work tasks they will be performing.

24

Computer-Based Training

(AKA: CBT, computer-assisted instruction [CAI], computer-based instruction [CBI], computer-aided instruction [CAI], computer-based education [CBE], computer-based tutorials, interactive tutorials, technology-delivered instruction [TDI])

From the first days of computers — featuring the pioneering vacuum-tube data-processing machines — there has been talk of using the computer as a teacher. The obvious task on the minds of futurists was to have the computer teach people how to use computers. Hence, the first vision of computer-based training.

One of my early programming experiences involved a professor informing my class that we would be learning to program in APL. He proceeded to tell us that there would be no classes on APL programming but that we could log on to our SUNY Binghamton computers via teletype terminals and type the words: TEACH ME APL. What followed was a long, sometimes helpful, often confusing, typo-laden attempt to walk us through the APL learning process. Wonder of wonders, I mastered APL enough to write a program resembling Monopoly in 1968.

Recently, I decided I wanted to learn Visual Basic. This time, the decision not to take a class was mine. I purchased a self-paced learning disk and got the hang of VB programming without too much struggle. A few days ago, I sat in my office and previewed a full-motion video CBT program that featured every bell and whistle the original futurists and all CBT learners hoped would be possible.

Computer-based training is a hot topic that's getting hotter. Micro-, mini-, mainframe, and networked computers all can be used as vehicles for the various stages of the instructional process. Information can be delivered on screen, questions can be posed, and the computer can be programmed to provide feedback on learner responses.

CBT is often touted for the interactivity inherent in this question-response-feedback process. The sophistication of both learner actions and computer feedback, however, varies widely. In the simplest tutorials, learners respond to multiple-choice questions, are told whether their answers are right or wrong, and have an opportunity to review the information and try again. With more sophisticated designs, system feedback sends learners down several branches of instruction, depending on their responses. The computer may even store information on learner performance, selecting the instructional sequence accordingly.

CBT is most often thought of as a self-study medium, delivering complete lessons or courses. But it can also be used in conjunction with other forms of training — for information transfer, testing, drill-and-practice exercises, or simulations. A range of basic training structures — such as information-delivery screens, various question formats, response analysis, feedback, and branching — is preprogrammed. The author selects the desired structures, usually from menus, then fills them in with the relevant content.

CBT courses written on certain microcomputer authoring systems can be used only in conjunction with separate presentation software, which serves as a kind of translator between the course and the computer. In some cases, though, the necessary presentation code is included on the course diskette. CBT written on most mainframe authoring systems requires the installation of a presentation system.

Developing CBT is very expensive. Industry experts' estimates range from $10,000 to $100,000 per hour of training. CBT is also very expensive to keep current, not lending itself to applications in flux. However, if your application is stable, an investment in CBT is a one-time, worthwhile investment. Distribution costs are minimal, as is the cost of each use of a lesson or course. Off-the-shelf courses are clearly much cheaper, available for as low as $29 and as high as $5,000.

In terms of the Sagamore Design Model, CBT conveys objectives and context most satisfactorily of the three-part set. Because motivation is intrinsically personal, it is less effectively achieved at the screen. CBT can accomplish most information transfer quite effectively, although lessons may need to be more complex to teach concepts. Because it determines mastery, CBT can check for understanding more accurately than for confusion. And while it is a good vehicle for guided practice, CBT is less successful in providing unguided practice. Conceptual thinkers seem most responsive to CBT, although it also appeals to practical thinkers if it incorporates lots of practice.

Advantages

Cost-efficiency. If a large audience needs training on a stable application, one-time CBT development costs can be lower than those for repeated classroom training. This is especially true when the training need is a recurring one.

Self-pacing. CBT is designed to accommodate the pace and comprehension of individual learners.

Convenience. Because CBT is easily distributed and doesn't require an instructor, a classroom, or a minimum number of participants, it's a good way to deliver training to employees who work on different shifts or need training at different times. It's also a good way to provide fill-in training for participants who have missed part or all of an instructor-led class.

Ease of distribution. CBT eliminates the need for travel and lodging when an organization needs to train large numbers of employees at geographically dispersed sites.

Mastery. Most CBT ensures the mastery of each instructional segment before a learner can progress to the next section.

Standardization. When offering a CBT course, you can be confident that all learners will have basically the same learning experience.

Disadvantages

Untapped potential. So far, much CBT uses fairly unsophisticated design that doesn't begin to tap the medium's potential for learner involvement, simulation, and individualization. Many courses are little more than opportunities for electronic page-turning. Despite the evolution of computer-graphics capabilities, most CBT is still heavy on text, and reading isn't the preferred way of learning for many adults.

Generic content. Although CBT is self-paced, it's rarely equipped to offer learner-specific, job-related examples, or to address learners' questions.

The worst of classroom instruction. While the excitement and potential of CBT lie in its promise to be more personal and innovative than classroom instruction, a good deal of the existing CBT emulates the classroom experience. It involves too much focus on controlling the learning process and too many quizzes and tests.

CD-ROM Technology

The CD-ROM has created a revolution in the CBT industry. It provides the following capabilities for the learning and knowledge disseminator:

■ More information. CBT can now contain an almost unlimited amount of data, text, graphics, animation, sound, and even video.

■ Random access. The CD-ROM allows for quick and instant random access to any point in the knowledge repository.

■ Low cost of distribution. The CD-ROM is an extremely low-cost distribution method for CBT. After mastering costs of a few thousand dollars (the price drops monthly), the duplication and manufacturing costs of a CD-ROM are just a few dollars per disk.

Skills for CBT Development

I often receive calls from trainers and others asking which knowledge and skills are needed for a career in CBT development and other technology-delivered instructional media. This is a difficult question to answer. While it was not uncommon for an individual to write a CBT program in the days of text-only authoring systems, the new multimedia authoring platforms require a broader skill set than is usually found in one person. Here is a list of skills required by a successful CBT-development team:

■ Instructional skills
■ Instructional design skills
■ Testing and remediation skills
■ Knowledge of reinforcement
■ Knowledge of Adult Learning Theory
■ Skills with authoring language
■ Skills with technology
■ Graphical skills and tastes

■ Screen design
■ Bug testing
■ Audio and/or video skills and tastes
■ Business knowledge

It's unlikely that all of these skills would exist in a single individual. Most major CBT and TDI development projects are now in the hands of teams, with these skills spread out among two to ten people. So, while CBT and multimedia are growing career areas, one needs to look beyond a single job role or function.

CBT and Interactive Video

The chapters titled "Interactive Video" and "Performance-Support Systems" are important companions to this chapter. CBT is transforming and extending the task of helping workers do their daily jobs and learn with the widest possible range of media forms. The goal is to offer learners the chance to acquire knowledge in the ways they prefer, at their desktops, when they want it.

25

Flipcharts, Blackboards, and Whiteboards

The blackboard is an integral part of our culture's educational history, and the flipchart (a large pad of paper on an easel) is nearly a trademark of the stand-up training profession. All the same, these tools have been replaced in many computer-training classrooms by overhead projectors and a range of video-projection systems for large-scale display of the computer screen. Granted, these devices enable trainers to do things that can't be done on a blackboard. But a blackboard, whiteboard, or flipchart is essential for spontaneous explanations and diagrams — or for the *appearance* of spontaneity.

Advantages

Spontaneity. The ability to record ideas as they are proposed helps stimulate brainstorming.

Learner involvement. When learners see their comments written down, they become more invested in participation. Using learners' own words, rather than translating them into your own, increases learners' chances of grasping and retaining the material.

Low cost. None of these devices is expensive. Whiteboards cost slightly less than flipcharts because they don't require paper refills.

Disadvantages

Legibility. The quality of the instructor's handwriting determines the legibility of flipchart notes. Plus, learners' distance from the chart or board can affect their ability to read what's been written.

Instructor distraction. An instructor who's writing on a flipchart temporarily loses his or her focus on the class. This can slow down the progress of the class and make any unruly learners harder to control.

Tips

■ Use the blackboard and flipchart selectively, when they will have the greatest impact. Overusing them will cost you learners' attention. For material that must be generated repeatedly, use an overhead-projector transparency.

■ Don't spend so much time writing on the board or flipchart that you slow down the pace of the class.

■ Ensure that your writing is large and legible, checking its visibility and clarity from all parts of the room before beginning a class.

■ Take advantage of color for highlighting important information and helping learners organize it appropriately.

■ Using two flipcharts will add to your flexibility.

■ If a learner or group of learners has difficulty with a concept as presented on the overhead projector, try generating a new explanation on the board or flipchart instead of echoing the original explanation.

■ Incorporate the board or flipchart into practice activities by asking learners to come up and write answers or draw explanatory graphics. You can also ask a learner or learners to take notes on the board or flipchart during class discussions to free yourself up to focus on the class.

■ Whiteboards tend to be more popular than blackboards because there's no squeaking chalk, and they're often easier to read. But the decision between a whiteboard and a flipchart tends to be a matter of personal preference.

For the spontaneous creation of handouts, several audiovisual companies have developed a process for printing the contents of a whiteboard on a fax or laser printer. This technology is available from Sharp, Panasonic, and Gestetner.

26 TECHNOLOGIES

Handouts

Even when the bulk of instruction is delivered by an instructor or some other medium, printed material is usually distributed to participants for visual reinforcement. Handouts can include class agendas, lists of key concepts, procedural cheat sheets, trouble-shooting suggestions for learners to take back to the job, or supplemental material to be read later. They can also be examples of screens or reports, the latter being particularly helpful for training on systems that do overnight reporting. In addition, trainers often distribute printed versions of overhead transparencies. This practice makes it easier for learners to follow a lecture and allows them to annotate what they see on the screen. Not all transparencies make useful handouts, however. This technique should be used only when appropriate rather than as a matter of course.

Increasingly, software publishers are foregoing the practice of providing print documentation with their programs. As CD-ROMs become more available, and as networks evolve as a distribution method, we can no longer assume that new users will receive formal manuals. Often, classroom handouts will be the only printed materials provided to learners.

Advantages

Reduction in note taking. If possible, note taking should be eliminated entirely when procedures are being taught, since 100-percent accuracy is very rare.

Anticipation and orientation. A handout listing several items not only gives learners a sense of what's coming but also helps them pinpoint where they are in the sequence.

Replacement for memorization. Thorough handouts can help eliminate memorization anxiety.

Disadvantages

Reduced learner attention. If handouts contain most of the content of a lecture, participants may think it's unnecessary to listen carefully.

Replacement of classroom lecture and practice. Some instructors assume that any material covered in take-home handouts need not be covered in class. This is a mistaken assumption; often, take-home handouts aren't even read.

Ritualization. The use of handouts created from overhead transparencies has become almost ritualized. While these handouts make it easier for learners to follow a lecture and allow them to annotate what they've seen on the screen, not every transparency makes a useful handout.

Tips

■ Handouts should not only be easily annotated, they should elicit annotation and, therefore, more active learner involvement. A handout with lots of white space and an outline format (rather than a solid block of text) is conducive to annotation. A handout with blanks for the learner to fill in invites it. Instructors can further encourage note taking on handouts by mentioning appropriate times to do so.

■ Handouts should be given out one at a time, as they are needed, rather than in a stack at the beginning of class. True, it's easier to hand them all out in advance, but you'll find participants receive them more enthusiastically if they are distributed gradually. This also prevents learners from jumping ahead in the instruction and allows them to get more out of each handout.

■ If possible, handouts should be produced so they can be added to and interleaved with system documentation.

■ Keep in mind that learners may become trainers shortly after completing your class. Many managers ask recent graduates of training programs to act as on-the-job trainers within their work groups. Their class notes may have a life far beyond the current seminar. Consider providing additional reference materials and activity suggestions for graduates' possible on-the-job training sessions.

27 TECHNOLOGIES

Interactive Video

(AKA: interactive-video instruction, IVI)

The evolution of interactive-video-based training is at a crossroads as the second edition of this book goes to print. The theory, model, delivery systems, costs, and usage of this medium are undergoing radical change. I'll do my best to provide a brief overview of this "moving target" of a training technology.

The term *interactive video* can be defined as the use of video images and sound, with a modicum of learner control, to facilitate instruction. Interactive video hit the scene in the 1960s, shortly after the introduction of videotape. The first interactive-video system was linked to a control panel for a videotape. The learner would watch a segment of linear video, answer a question posed on the computer screen, then the tape would stop. If the learner's answer, entered on a push-button box, was correct, the video would proceed; if not, the tape would rewind and the instruction would start over.

The next stage of interactive video was its linkage to a computer system — first mainframe, then desktop. At first, the authors' and learners' choices weren't much more sophisticated than those just described. The questions were delivered via the computer screen, the instruction via the video monitor. Around this time, IBM developed a monitor capable of displaying the output of both the computer and the video device, thus eliminating the need for two desktop monitors.

The advent of laser-disc technology took interactive video to its next stage of development. By permitting easier access to specific points on the disc, this technology enabled authors to develop courseware with more layers of instruction and remediation. However, a lack of standards slowed expansion of this instructional mode, and laser-disc players remain a rarity in the corporate world.

In 1994, video and CD-ROM started being merged. The ability to compress full-motion video images onto a CD-ROM and display them on a standard desktop PC has lowered the cost and threshold of using this technology for learning. Each month brings an announcement of a better compression technique, enabling authors to add more content with clearer and larger video chunks.

Nineteen-ninety-five will be the year of the video server. The storage of an enormous amount of video content on a central server and its distribution through a cable or even a LAN network holds incredible promise for both the work and home markets. The concept of interactive TV has captured the interest of major investors wagering on the future of media markets. But what will all of this mean to the corporate marketplace?

Since it's impossible to answer that question with any degree of certainty, let's back up and look at the reality of the marketplace going into 1995. It offers:

- Dedicated laser-disc interactive-video systems
- Dedicated CD-ROM interactive-video systems
- CBT titles with interactive-video segments
- High-end simulator models

The number of off-the-shelf interactive video courses available on computer-related topics is around 200. In spite of the fact that a major strength of interactive video is its potential for customization and specificity, these courses are by necessity generic. Users trained with off-the-shelf courseware may need more follow-up support than those who used custom courseware. However, generic interactive-video courseware can be augmented with text or video focusing on organization-specific uses of the application being taught.

Because it allows courseware developers to enhance computer-based training with photographic images and sounds, interactive video appears to be the ultimate training medium. Engaging learners through three senses — sight, sound, and touch — it enables developers to apply more of the current knowledge about how people learn than either of its component technologies, computer-based training and video.

Like CBT, interactive video can fulfill the goals of all stages in the Sagamore Design Model except the anticipatory set. The random-access speed of video technology makes it easy to provide multiple pathways that correspond to learners' different styles and responses.

Advantages

Authenticity. While CBT displays are limited to text and computer-generated graphics, the video component of interactive video allows developers to include self-selected photographic images in their courses. This feature gives courses an extremely job-specific feel. With the addition of touch-screen technology, it's especially useful for training on computer equipment with a user interface other than the keyboard — control panels, CAD/CAM systems, and so forth. Learners can work directly with simulated versions of these interfaces, recreated realistically on the screen, instead of pressing keys to select multiple-choice answers. (See Disadvantages.)

Sound. With the addition of sound, interactive video depends far less than CBT on the learner's inclination to read.

Activity. The opportunities for learner involvement offered by the computer solve the passivity problem of linear video.

Learner focus. Most interactive-video setups are equipped with a monitor that accepts both computer and video inputs, thus eliminating competition between the computer and video screens for learners' attention.

Flexibility. The high-volume storage and high-speed random access of laser-disc video allow developers to store a variety of scenarios on a single disc. Individual learners can select specific scenarios that correspond to their jobs, work sites, or other personal requirements. With the addition of artificial-intelligence techniques, a course can be programmed to display certain frames in response to an analysis of learner inputs.

Disadvantages

Authenticity. Realistic visuals have a flip side: they are just as powerful when learners *can't* relate to them as when they *can*. An executive will quickly "tune out" an interactive video course whose visuals show only secretaries, and the reverse is just as likely to be true.

Cost. The prices of multimedia-ready computer systems have been dropping. However, there is still a need to upgrade most PCs with additional memory, video cards, speakers, and better monitors. Off-the-shelf courseware varies widely in cost, depending in part on the length of the course and vendors' purchase or rental agreements. It is, however, predictably expensive. Interactive-video development is extremely time-consuming and even more expensive than CBT development. It is likely to be prohibitively expensive for small organizations or for teaching courses needed by a small number of people. The costs of revising existing custom courseware to accommodate system changes are also high, making interactive-video training most suitable for stable systems.

Future Trends

As stated earlier, interactive video is expected to change dramatically in the coming months and years. We will witness new capabilities as corporate video servers are added to the computer-training mix. In addition, national and global interactive-video networks will be developed. You may one day be able to buy access to hundreds of thousands of titles on a pay-per-view training network. Until then, stay tuned!

28 TECHNOLOGIES

Large-Screen Projection

(AKA: LCD panels, large-screen projection devices, television)

Large-scale displays of real-time computer screens are desirable in any classroom-based computer training for two or more learners. Trainers need to refer to specific, changing screens during initial demonstrations and subsequent question-and-answer sessions, and participants should be able to see these screens as they are discussed. After all, using computer software is a process in which users constantly look at the screen, responding to visual prompts and confirming the results of their actions. Any individual monitor is too small for more than a couple learners to look at simultaneously.

There are two basic techniques for making a computer display visible to a class. You can send the content of the "teaching" screen through a network so that it appears on each learner's display (see the minichapter titled "Classroom Network and Mirroring"). Or, you can create a large-screen projection, linking the computer directly to some form of projection technology — an overhead projector, a video-projection system, or a television — to give learners a common focus.

One of the most common devices for large-screen projection is a liquid-crystal display (LCD) panel, which acts as a duplicate of the monitor when connected to the computer. Light shines through the display as it sits on top of an overhead projector, and a facsimile of the computer screen appears on the projector screen.

Video-projection systems that accept computer input are more expensive than LCD panels, but competition has driven down their costs over the last two years, and the use of both types of projection is on the rise.

A third alternative is the good old-fashioned television, which can accept a converted computer signal. (Digital sets accept computer input directly.)

Remote-control devices are available for versions of all these systems, allowing you to move a cursor or pointer arrow from across the room. Some systems' remotes even allow advancing or backing up to previous screens.

By now, projection setups of one kind or another are standard equipment for most computer-training vendors. They are especially common in organizations with formally structured computer-training programs and training budgets of $100,000 or more annually. For smaller companies and those offering less formal computer training, more traditional forms of presentation — such as overhead transparencies, slides, and flipcharts — can be adapted to meet organizational needs.

Whether you choose an LCD panel, a video-projection system, or a television, large-screen projection has certain advantages and drawbacks as an instructional tool. The pros and cons of each of these three technologies are covered following this general discussion.

Advantages

Size. Allows a large group of learners to view the same image simultaneously, encouraging group synthesis of information, questions, and discussion.

Visibility. Reduces amount of instructor explanation needed; viewers can see what's happening on the screen.

Enhancing teaching possibilities. Allows instructors to use individual learners' problems as "teachable moments" for the whole class. Instead of handling questions individually, an instructor can project problem screens and respond to learners' questions in front of the whole class.

Common focus. Provides a focal point for both the trainer and learners.

Disadvantages

Potential for eyestrain. It's not unusual for complex corporate applications to contain up to 80 fields per screen. No matter how large the screen is, that's a lot for adults with less-than-perfect eyesight (almost all of them) to read from the back of the room.

Competition for attention. Participants may not know when to look up at the big screen or down at their monitors.

Tips

■ Avoid "choral typing" sessions. If you act like Mitch Miller, conducting participants through a series of specific movements, they'll learn to copy instead of understanding the relationship between tasks and keystrokes. They won't bother reading the prompts at the top or bottom of the screen, and back on the job, they'll be lost.

■ Instead of doing all the work yourself, involve participants in the procedures you demonstrate. If you're teaching data-entry learners to fill in a multifield screen, for example, solicit their suggestions for entries. Ask individual learners to make entries at your keyboard, or, if you have a master-selection device, select individual learners' screens for the large projection.

■ To relieve participants' eyestrain when using an LCD device, try covering up parts of the panel with a piece of paper, or shift to non-computer transparencies by moving the LCD panel. If you're using a video-projection system that allows toggling back and forth between two software programs, use storyboard software to create partial screens. Distributing printed versions of important screens is another solution to the eyestrain problem.

■ To prevent confusion about which screen learners should watch — their own or the big one — establish clear guidelines and direct participants' focus with a pointer or even your position. A slightly more elaborate solution involves deactivating learners' monitors, using a master fuse or control panel, when they should focus on the big screen.

■ If you intend to use a projection system to show displays from a variety of computers, make sure its computer interface meets the compatibility requirements of your equipment.

Choosing a Projection Technology

The basic differences between projection technologies concern their display capacity, multimedia capability, cost, portability, and setup requirements. Your decision to use a particular type may be affected by other factors as well.

LCD Projection Panels

Cost: Approximately $800 to $5,000

Portability: LCD panels weigh about five pounds.

Setup: Attach cable to computer and place unit on overhead projector; easy to set up and disassemble. The overhead projector needs a powerful bulb and high-intensity mirroring system to generate enough illumination to display images clearly.

Advantages

Convenience. You can use LCD panels wherever there's an overhead projector. If you carry a laptop computer and an LCD panel, you can do a training session just about anywhere.

Lighting. If room lighting is directional, you should get a crisp image without having to darken the room.

Multimedia capacity. Many of the LCD panels currently on the market are able to display full-motion video. These panels can be used to project video images from a tape or CD-ROM onto the screen and also provide accompanying sound.

Remote controls. New LCD panels have a range of remote-pointing and -selecting devices that give the trainer full mobility throughout the classroom.

Disadvantages

Lighting. If the room has full-coverage diffused lighting, overhead projection tends to wash out.

Overhead-projector phobia. Because overhead projectors are often overused or poorly used for corporate training, some participants shut down as soon as they see a projector in the room.

Heat-sensitivity. LCDs can fade and blur due to prolonged proximity to the heat from an overhead projector's high-wattage bulb. Newer models include their own fans, and newer overhead projectors run much cooler than the old ones did. If you're not working with the latest equipment, however, consider raising the panel slightly, using a weaker bulb, or turning the projector off periodically during use.

Resolution. LCD projections are as readable as any projection device except high-priced video projectors. They are also more easily adjusted than other devices, but some learners complain that any overhead projection is difficult to look at for long periods of time.

Noise. Before the recent models, the fans on most overhead projectors were distractingly noisy.

Video-Projection Devices

Cost: $2,000 to $20,000

Portability: They weigh anywhere from 5 to 100 pounds; even the so-called portables are more "luggable" than portable. Usually mounted on ceiling or floorstand.

Setup: Requires mounting of projection device and cabling to computer. This isn't a problem if you consistently teach the same system in the same classroom in a stable configuration; you can keep the system in place and simply turn it on.

Advantages

Transparent technology. If a projection device is ceiling-mounted and doesn't have a noisy fan, viewers can focus on its image without distraction. Rear projection keeps the technology even farther out of the way, but it requires a major construction project to install.

Versatility. Some projection systems can be used for video, slides, or software other than the application you're teaching. This provides an alternative to the overhead projector for graphics or notes you want to include in your presentation. If your learners will run the same application on various types of computers, you can use storyboard software to create graphic versions of how screens appear on the different computers.

Disadvantages

Lighting. To get a truly crisp image, you need to diminish the lighting in the room or use rear projection. It's hard enough for learners to stay awake — much less alert — in a darkened classroom.

Seating limitations. Video projection is most effective with a curved screen, which may not be visible from every seat in the room. In some classrooms, you may have to give up several seats if you want everyone to see the whole screen.

Resolution. Somewhat coarse, especially if you want to show desktop-publishing-quality graphics.

Television

Cost: Varies from around $600 for a 28-inch screen that's suitable for small groups to $1,000 up to $6,000 for large digital equipment

Portability: Varies with size.

Advantages

Multimedia. You can combine computer input and footage from a video camera with audio to create stand-alone demos or a videotaped class for learners unable to attend the live presentation.

Color. With color available on IBM and Omega computers, you can take advantage of a TV's entire spectrum.

Resolution. Can be very high, depending on quality of equipment; declines slightly with RF conversion of computer signal.

Flexibility. Displays a screen within a screen; the digital models have memory.

Disadvantage

Size limitations. Even the largest TV screen can't match the size of a large overhead projection. But in a huge lecture hall, 20 TV monitors hanging from the ceiling throughout the room may be visible to more learners than one 12' x 12' projection. (Some facilities use both methods and even place mini-televisions at every seat.)

29 | TECHNOLOGIES

Classroom Networking and Mirroring

(AKA: slave systems)

All instructors could use 15 pairs of eyes. When training, I always want to know what's going on at each learning workstation. Every instructor wishes for 15 mouths and 15 pairs of hands, too. I want to be able to coach all learners at the same time. What genetics has denied trainers, technology has supplied. It's called mirroring.

Mirroring techniques allow instructors to control the displays that appear on learners' monitors. They can be used as an alternative to large-screen projection or in conjunction with it. Learners' monitors are connected with the instructor's computer through various combinations of hardwiring and networking, and the instructor has a master-selection device, like a central switchboard, for directing input between the instructional computer and participants' screens. This can mean sending a master screen to the whole class or to one class member. Or, it can mean calling an individual learner's screen forward for projection from the instructor's monitor or distribution to other learners.

The versions of this technology that work with Windows feature a learner's screen in one window, the instructor's in another. And a PC or mainframe terminal with five or six monitors for learner viewing functions as a simple, homegrown mirroring system. This last technique is more useful for demonstration than for guided practice, though, since learners don't have their own keyboards .

Advantages

Instructor control. An instructor can determine what appears on every learner's screen at a given time.

Keyboard locking. Mirroring systems can be set up so that the keyboards lock when learners are looking at external screens. This forces learners to observe what's being demonstrated and makes it easier to separate demonstration from practice. It also reduces the incidence of "choral typing" (keyboarding in unison with the instructor), which doesn't help learners understand the relationship between tasks and keystrokes.

Convenience. The instructor can see learners' screens without moving around the room.

Visual content. Instructors can answer learners' questions without having to reconstruct each screen using words.

Enhanced teaching possibilities. The opportunity for a large group to see an image simultaneously encourages synthesis of information, questions, and discussion. Because individual learners' screens are visible to the whole class, "teachable moments" often involve learners providing tutoring and support to each other. The instructor is not the sole source of information.

Disadvantages

Learner intimidation. Mirroring causes some learners to feel uncomfortable about exposing their work — and their errors — to others.

Trainer attitude. Trainers need to be careful not to "go over the line" with this technology and risk being seen as intrusive or nosy. They should explain their intended use of mirroring and position it as a plan for helping each learner achieve his or her instructional goals.

Future Trends

The capabilities of mirroring technology, enhanced by increasingly sophisticated networks, may soon include delivery of multiple-media formats to the desktop. At least one college is working on a system that will present either a live video of the instructor or a replay of a previous lesson as a window on each learner's screen.

Be prepared for more distance-learning versions of mirroring, especially those that bring additional training resources — including peer and help-desk assistance — into the classroom. These options will improve our ability to put unlimited instructional control at learners' fingertips.

30 ~~TECHNOLOGIES~~ TECHNOLOGIES

 # Overhead Projectors

The first training tool I look for upon entering a classroom is the overhead projector. I know I'm in the right room when I see one of those weird-looking devices. Despite the rising popularity of large-screen projection systems for showing real-time computer screens, the overhead projector still has a place in the trainer's supply closet and the computer-training classroom. In fact, this device is a requirement for one large-screen projection technology, the LCD panel. Overhead projectors also provide wider visibility than either flipcharts or blackboards in a very large room, and they're a good way to shift learners' focus away from the trainer.

Not all computer-training topics require real-time projection. For programming and other conceptual, non-screen-based topics, overhead projectors are usually sufficient. But what if you need to show real-time computer screens and don't have the room or the budget for a projection system? Try converting screen printouts into overhead transparencies and simulating real-time procedures via a series of screen images that change one field at a time. You can also draw screens on an overhead transparency or a flipchart.

Advantages

Availability. Overhead projectors are abundant in the corporate environment.

Flexibility. Instructors can easily control image sequences using this device.

Portability. Of all audiovisual equipment, overhead projectors are among the easiest to move from one location to another.

Low cost. Overhead projectors range from $250 to $2,000 in price, depending on size and capabilities.

Disadvantages

Excessive use. Too many instructors make the mistake of letting their courses become transparency-driven. After handing out copies of the transparencies and projecting the material on the screen, they assume their work is done. If you abdicate to the overhead projector this way, you're likely to have more than a little trouble keeping participants focused.

Noise. Until recently, projectors' cooling fans were noisy, making it difficult for learners sitting near the projector to hear the instructor. The latest models are much quieter.

Tips

■ Stand away from the projector when lecturing so your voice isn't obliterated by noise from the fan.

■ To cut down on noise and avoid a hypnotic effect, turn the projector off when it's not in use. You want learners to notice the projected image when it's being discussed; if the image appears on the screen too long, they may begin to ignore it.

■ Use a flipchart for making notations while discussing transparencies.

■ Always carry extra overhead-projector bulbs.

■ A master of the creative use of overhead-projector tools is Bob Pike. The president of Creative Training Techniques International, Inc., Bob has written a series of books that provide tips on improving instructor-led training. I highly recommend his book titled *The Creative Training Techniques Handbook*, which contains practical tips on making the most of your overhead projector.

31

TECHNOLOGIES

 ## Slides

Trainers have traditionally used slides as an alternative to overhead-projector transparencies. The rising popularity of large-screen, real-time projection of computer screens has overshadowed both technologies somewhat, but the slide projector is by no means obsolete. It is particularly useful for benefit selling, conceptual explanations, and other training tasks that aren't screen-based. If you don't have the room or budget for a large-screen projection system, you can simulate real-time projection by making slides of computer screens and showing them in rapid succession.

Most presentation packages provide an interface to a slide-production service. After finalizing the presentation, just send it — via modem — to the 800 number listed, and you'll receive a set of slides by overnight mail.

Advantages

Aesthetics. A well-designed slide tends to be more attractive than the average transparency.

Authenticity. In many training situations, it's desirable to show photographic images of people using the system being taught.

Compatibility with laser-disc and CD-ROM technology. Up to 36,000 slides can be stored on a laser disc, providing high-speed random access of still images and making it easy to mix slides with other media. Replication of laser discs is inexpensive, and a disc containing a variety of examples can be used for training multiple audiences.

Disadvantage

Lighting. Slide projection requires a darkened room, which can put learners to sleep or cramp their note-taking style.

32 TECHNOLOGIES

 **Video
Teleconferencing**

Gone are the days of the wrist-radio/walkie-talkie as a cartoon symbol of a high-tech era. Today's Dick Tracy sits at a PC, using full-motion video and audio to communicate with people all over the world. Times change!

There you have a brief description of the hot technology known as desktop video teleconferencing. The development of a small-scale, PC-based unit capable of supporting video teleconferencing right at the desktop will have profound effects, especially on the worlds of learning and business meetings. In 1995, the technology to support this process will enter the computing environment with a bang. Research reports are projecting a per-unit cost below $500. The telephone companies are offering ISDN service for a pittance. And the bridges for linking users from diverse locations into one video teleconference are under construction.

What's driving the development of desktop video teleconferencing? For one thing, the desire to conduct meetings without regard for participants' locations and without the need for travel. For another, to provide a network of "virtual" bridges that link workers, colleagues, customers, and friends. Content providers see desktop video teleconferencing as the next superhighway for delivering knowledge and entertainment. Finally, multinational companies view this technology as a tool for implementing enterprise-wide coordination.

This medium is not without its challenges, however. Here are a few that desktop video teleconferencing is likely to present.

- What if someone's having a "bad hair day" and wants to go audio only?
- What's protocol when someone is conducting a desktop video teleconferencing session and a coworker stops by with a question?
- What are the maximum time frames for learning via this method based on topic and style of instruction?
- Are certain learning styles "allergic" to this process?

Desktop video teleconferencing is still in its infancy. Fewer than 8,000 units were active worldwide at the beginning of 1995. The unit in my home office required the installation of a special ISDN line and many hours talking and working with technicians. The picture is limited to 15 frames per second, which is a bit jumpy. But these hurdles will disappear. The compression ratios will get better, and forecasts predict a million new units in use by 1996.

Corporate networks also will be developed to handle this new technology. The MASIE Center is developing materials for training departments starting down the path to desktop video teleconferencing. We are conducting research on the most effective uses of this exciting technology.

Satellite-Delivered Video Teleconferencing

Satellite-delivered video teleconferencing combines telecommunications, video, audio, and computer networks to broadcast training to geographically dispersed audiences. A lecture is delivered live at a central location and is then relayed by satellite or landline to other sites. Participants can phone in their comments and questions for the instructor or send them on-line if the sites are networked. These comments and the instructor's responses are then broadcast, like the original lecture, to all participating sites. Live, postlecture discussion can take place at individual sites or in peer groups; it also can be facilitated by a local expert or instructor.

Some companies are using video teleconferencing experimentally for large-scale systems installation training. But its most suitable applications are the benefit-selling aspects of new feature rollouts, management briefings, and other training tasks that don't involve measurable skills.

Audio teleconferencing — which, as its name implies, lacks the video component — is widely used. Organizations without satellite dishes can have access to the Holiday Inn chain's HiNet program. Through HiNet, they can rent conference rooms and use satellite dishes that have been installed for the in-room movie channel.

Regarding the Sagamore Design Model, video teleconferencing can accomplish the anticipatory set and information transfer. All other stages of the model are more effective with the help of local experts or on-site trainers, although this assistance can be provided by the video hosts/trainers.

Advantages

Range. Video teleconferencing makes it possible to reach a large, widely dispersed audience with a single training event.

Just-in-time and at-your-desk training. This technology provides the ability to deliver instruction when needed, without travel or major disruption to the workday.

Disadvantages

Limited participation. Theoretically, video teleconferencing allows as much audience participation as live lectures (varying, of course, with the instructor's style), but this can be an illusion. The larger the total audience, the less opportunity each participant has to speak. Plus, it's likely that only a small percentage of learners will be fully comfortable with this technology at first. Video teleconferences with a smaller number of participants — and fewer at each location — are more likely to achieve their instructional objectives.

Limited procedural training. Regardless of audience size, video teleconferencing may not be the best way to teach procedures. It does not allow the instructor at the main site to see participants' computer screens when answering their questions. Unless each site has a resident expert, conceptual questions are more easily and effectively handled than procedural ones.

33 TECHNOLOGIES

User Groups

(AKA: SIGS, special-interest groups, support groups)

User groups are forums for discussion of system uses and improvements, sometimes organized specifically to provide training or support. Membership can be based on users' hardware, software, profession, industry, or special interests.

User groups are sponsored and administered in several ways.

■ One type of in-house user group is created and sponsored by the organization.

■ Another type of in-house user group is created and administered by users themselves.

■ The external, cross-organization user group is created and administered by vendors or users. Along with international, well-known groups like IBM's Share and the Boston Computer Society, thousands of local groups have grown and flourished.

■ The occasional user group is sponsored by vendors or organizations. These groups meet as infrequently as once a year to receive information and training on system updates, new releases, and so on.

■ User events are sponsored by organizations and open to all employees. These meetings are held several times a year, on company time, for discussion of system-related topics or to function as informational clearinghouses.

User groups provide a vehicle for assembling users for training. They can also function as large-scale cooperative learning situations, with users providing training and support to each other. This can happen spontaneously and informally or in a more structured format. In the early days of microcomputers, an enormous amount of training occurred in user groups of all types.

Advantage

Conviviality. Well-managed, organizationally licensed user groups can be the basis of a mentor or buddy system for on-the-job training and support.

Disadvantages

Loss of enthusiasm. As the novelty of computing has subsided, users are less willing to participate in user-group activities on their own time.

Attrition. Most user groups begin with high enthusiasm and high membership, both of which tend to decline as experienced users lose interest in helping less experienced users. Often, the only remaining members are those with high support or social needs. User groups that schedule meetings too frequently are particularly vulnerable to attrition.

Political awkwardness. In-house user groups can become breeding grounds for unofficial "wizards," whose strong attitudes and opinions about computing often contradict MIS standards and policies. Such groups can become political trouble spots, especially if they began with management support.

Overgrowth. Some user groups become unmanageably large as more and more people in the organization begin using a package initially limited to a few users.

Administrative distraction. A user-sponsored group can get sidetracked by questions about the group's administrative structure, naming the group, and planned activities. Organizational sponsorship tends to provide clarity and definition, thereby preventing these types of questions.

Tip

Ensure that a user group's purpose, membership, and mode of operation are clearly defined from the start. If a group is expected to serve as a primary source of training and support, management should monitor its activities to ensure it is accomplishing that purpose.

34 TECHNOLOGIES

Video Learning

(AKA: films, videotapes, video cassettes)

Video, as a sequential or linear media, has become a major component of our home lives. An amazing percentage of households rent or buy a prerecorded videotape every week. As a training tool in the business environment, video is an important yet minor player. It's used most often as an alternative to classroom training — when there are too few enrollees to conduct a class, when learners can't get to class, or when resources (financial or staff) aren't available for classroom training. Computer-training videos are also becoming available for rental at video outlets, providing home-computer users with a less expensive alternative to formal classes.

Video's reputation as a cost-effective, trainerless approach to delivering repetitive training makes it the most-used technology in computer training. But it also can be the most *misused* technology when it's the only source of training provided.

One of the drawbacks of video is that it doesn't allow learners to ask questions. Its coordination with practice is also problematic. In the past, computer terminals and VCRs were occasionally placed together in learning carrels. This setup is less common now that interactive video accomplishes the same purpose. If learners have access to a keyboard while watching a video, their attention will be divided; plus, the pace of the video may not match their keying speed. Because of its limited opportunities for experimentation, video training tends to produce procedural users who have frequent procedure-related questions for support.

Regarding the stages of the Sagamore Design Model, video can deliver the set and information transfer on its own. With built-in pauses, very simple guided practice is also possible. Training of any complexity requires supplementary material, such as a practice disk.

Consequently, video is best suited for informational briefings on new technology and other training geared toward knowledge rather than performance. For skills training, video can be used for benefit selling or information transfer and then be followed by other activities.

The equipment required for viewing videos ranges in price from $100 to $40,000, depending on whether simple TV monitors or large-screen projections are used. The cost of development depends on the production quality desired. A few hundred dollars will pay for the production of a fairly unpolished, homegrown videotape. Professional production is required to ensure the stability and readability of computer-screen images, and a half-hour, professionally produced tape can cost $5,000 or more. Off-the-shelf videos can cost from $19.95 to several thousand dollars. The cost of altering videos to accommodate system changes can be high, and a commitment to video training requires an investment in viewing equipment not present in today's average office.

Video is being used by corporate and government training departments in a wide range of formats. For example, it's being used as:

■ A stand-alone training option. Learners are provided a videotape, a practice disk, and a course book. Often, the help desk provides support to learners during their ramp-up stage.

■ A preclass or postclass training supplement. Prior to class, learners are given a videotape covering concepts or elementary procedures. Learners unable to attend the introductory class can use the tape to catch up. Likewise, the tape can be used as a follow-up to the course, addressing advanced or specialized content.

■ A take-home learning extender. Learners are provided with a tape to view at home as reinforcement of newly presented content.

■ An in-class tool. Video can be used to introduce new faces, new computer context material, or new metaphors to learners. It also can present information beyond the technical level of the instructor.

■ A visual teaching aid. The trainer can make a point more dramatically by showing a video featuring the workplace where the training is happening. One bank provided a videotape showing typical customer requests to a trainer preparing to teach a teller-training course. When it came time for guided and unguided practice, the trainer could show clips of real customers making real requests. This was a great motivator for the learners.

There are also ways in which video can be used as a recording device. Some trainers videotape the lecture segments of their courses or class-discussion sessions. This allows learners who miss a class to view the video later. One caution: Few learners actually take advantage of the chance to view taped class sessions.

Video is a powerful and familiar tool. The computer-training industry is expanding its flexibility in using this technology.

Advantages

Standardization. When a video is used for benefit selling and information transfer, there's little doubt that all participants have received the same message.

Relevance. Homegrown and industry-specific off-the-shelf videos allow learners to see class content applied to their own work environment.

Convenience. Videos can be distributed to multiple sites and used by individual learners at any time.

One-time investment. A single filming session can yield a videotape that's good for an infinite number of training sessions.

Disadvantages

Expectations. Television has raised audiences' expectations of video-production quality. Unless training videos meet viewers' standards, they will be judged critically.

Poor screen display. Unless the computer signal is run directly into the video, high-quality reproduction of computer screens is difficult to achieve. High-end television-studio cameras are beginning to include a tracking adjustment that yields flicker-free reproduction of computer screens.

Limited practice. Training is most effective when it provides opportunities for learners' active involvement and experimentation. Video provides limited practice opportunities, which may be paced too fast or too slow for the learners.

Inflexibility. Video alteration to accommodate system changes is costly and inconvenient.

Tip

When showing a video to a class, use a large-screen projection system or place multiple small screens throughout the room whenever possible.

Future Trends

As video technology continues to permeate our lives, its use in training will continue to grow, especially in organizations that don't want to invest in interactive video. Video production quality is likely to increase, especially for the display of computer screens. Developments in computer-graphics technology also may encourage greater use of animation in training videos.

35

PSs Performance-Support Systems

(AKA: PSS, electronic performance-support systems, performance-support models, wizards, work front-ends, learning and performance shells)

Performance-support systems (PSS) are applications or application features designed to improve employees' productivity when using computer systems. These systems have the common goal of bringing employees to a highly effective and productive state with a minimal amount of training by providing information, communication, guidance, and support on their desktop screens.

My good friend Bob Frankston, one of the developers of the spreadsheet, has a controversial view of the computer-training industry. Bob believes that our profession exists because programmers don't finish their job. He argues that a program is not done until it allows an individual to perform a complex work task easily.

Performance-support systems fill in the gap between technology and the need for worker productivity. In its broadest definition, PSS includes the following systems and features.

- On-line help
- Work wizards, coaches, and macros
- Monitoring capacities of applications focusing on prompting employees
- Groupware functionality for knowledge sharing
- Just-in-time computer-based-training modules
- Highly interactive expert systems

The concept of performance support as a technological category was pioneered by Gloria Gery. Gloria believes that performance development is a process, not an event — that organizations accumulate events, activities, and other interventions over time to spur performance development. Gloria's clients and colleagues have evolved the development of instructionally based CBT into a tool for managing performance. Her research concentrates on ways in which users can be prompted and encouraged for performance rather than focusing on learning events.

What are some examples of performance support? Microsoft's Wizards and Novell's Coaches are user-assistance features of these applications designed to help new users accomplish tasks. Microsoft's Publisher offers a Newsletter Wizard, which asks a few questions, then lets the user design a publication according to the specifications provided. Rather than taking a tutorial, users accomplish a task.

Another example of PSS is a trucking company's use of a series of customer-service prompting screens to adjust its level of service to a wide range of clients. For each call received, the computer identifies the organization that's calling through a link with ISDN code. Next, that client's history is displayed, as is a customer strategy. A high-volume customer will receive a gold-level set of responses and services. An occasional customer will get good service, but the customer-strategy screen will suggest an average-level response time of several hours.

A final PSS example involves a reservation center for a major travel organization that wanted to reduce its training time. The organization installed a PSS that allowed call-center employees to use the reservation system with a minimum of training. As employees improved, the screens offered less on-line prompting. The center was able to reduce its ten-day training cycle to three days while maintaining its normal rate of customer service and satisfaction.

Performance-support systems are expensive to develop. They require a reengineering approach to the work elements of a business unit or job task. However, the expense of developing a PSS may seem reasonable in light of the savings in training and support costs.

Performance-support systems come in all shapes, styles, and sizes. One MIS manager's response to the issue of PSS was that he's been trying to include these features in his design and development for the past 10 years. PSS purists would claim he was only adding learning-and-support bits and pieces. Others would say that, to one degree or another, performance support is the goal of all instructional development.

Performance-support systems offer a new angle for marketing training and support services. Most of the leading CBT-development outfits offer PSS services, extending their involvement beyond the instructional-design phase. This is an exciting opportunity for designers and developers to influence employees' performance improvement.

For a full description of performance-support systems, I strongly recommend Gloria Gery's books, published by Softbank Institute.

36

Evaluation

The trainer (Beth): *"I think this class went very well. Based on the end-of-class evaluations and learners' comments during breaks, I'd say it was a success. But who knows for sure?"*

The trainer's manager: *"Beth is one of our top trainers. I know she does a super job. The class evaluations are always top-notch. But I can't understand why calls to the help desk from learners in her classes are up."*

The learner (Pat): *"That was a tough class. Beth worked really hard, and I like her. We must have been a tough group. It seemed like we covered everything on the agenda. But I'm still not sure I'll be able to use this software without lots of questions on Monday morning."*

The learner's manager: *"I'm glad Pat's back from class. I had mixed feelings about approving her attendance. We're so busy, it's hard to have a person*

out for a day. It'll be interesting to see if this class
really was a good idea. I'll have to talk with Pat on
Monday morning."

Each of these four players in the "learning-about-computers game" has a vested interest in training evaluation. Each wants to know the outcome of Pat's participation in Beth's class. Each wants to test the effectiveness of the instruction. Each wants an evaluation that goes beyond an end-of-class "smile sheet." Will all four get what they want?

Few organizations can afford to spend money or excuse employees from their jobs without adequate justification. But that's exactly what most training requires — taking people away from their jobs and spending money to do it. So, in many organizations, justification is as much a part of the training process as the instruction itself. Justifying most organizational activity means evaluating its effectiveness and cost-effectiveness — asking, "Has it accomplished what it was intended to, at a reasonable cost?"

The pressure to justify computer training — and, therefore, evaluate it — is particularly high. The training that has accompanied the introduction of new technologies over the past 10 or so years has been extensive and visible, and the spotlight is already focused on huge computer-related expenditures.

Unfortunately, evaluating computer training is complicated for two main reasons. First, it's difficult to determine how effectively an activity has accomplished a mission that hasn't been clearly defined, which is frequently the case with computer training. And second, consider how often you've heard managers request "Lotus training" without specifying whether the training goal is knowledge or performance — and if it's performance, what they want their employees to be able to do with the software at training's end.

The first step in evaluation is to define what you're evaluating. If the goal of computer training is computer use, then users' performance should be the ultimate target of evaluation. But if you want to

understand the relationship between training and performance —
to make the most of training — you need information on these five
factors: learner performance, instructor performance, the course
itself, the software, and related managerial and environmental factors.
It's critical that you separate these factors into five distinct areas when
setting up your evaluation process.

Evaluating Learner Performance

Evaluation of participants encompasses their performance first as
learners and later as users. Learner performance is important mostly
for what it reveals about the class; user performance is the major indicator of training success.

It's crucial not to limit the evaluation of learner performance to one
incident. (Just as no single evaluation technique described here is
particularly useful on its own.) Without a pretest or precourse evaluation, you have no way of knowing where each learner began or,
therefore, how much progress has been made. And for many people,
learning is a gradual process that continues to cement itself. Many
learners master new skills only after using them on the job, so judg-
ing their performance as users based on their performance as learners is premature. Likewise, signs of confusion immediately following
training are not necessarily cause for concern. Some confusion is
inevitable until learners have had a chance to practice their new skills
on the job.

During Training

Learners' contributions during training can be used in evaluation, as
can instructors' impressions of them. If you follow the Sagamore
Design Model, checks for understanding are an informal indication of
learner progress. You can also tabulate the results of guided and
unguided practice if you need written documentation of learner performance. Or, you may assign a summary project that serves as a sort

of final exam. Pretests make this information even more meaningful by providing a baseline for comparison.

After Training

■ Require users who have completed training to pass a competency test before issuing their passwords and licensed software. Results of this "checkout" test provide an indication of learner performance.

■ Ask managers — by written survey, on the phone, or in person — how they think the training "graduates" are doing on the system.

■ Look at reports of system use. Some firms conduct regular audits of microcomputer use through random inspection of users' disk directories. With mainframe systems, it's easy to track employee productivity by recording numbers of keystrokes and frequency of file updates. However, system monitoring calls for caution. Its legal ramifications are unclear, and it's become a controversial topic in labor-management negotiations. Legality aside, system monitoring may become less and less accurate as skeptical users undermine it by making random keystrokes during personal telephone conversations or creating autoexec files that automatically update their directories.

■ Find out what kinds of calls the help desk is getting, in general and from individual users. By written survey, on the phone, or in person, ask users themselves about their use of the system.

Sample Postcourse Telephone Survey

"Hello, this is Rita Schwartz from the training division. Our records show you as a new user of Lotus Notes. May I ask you a few questions about your experience with this software?"

"In the five weeks since you started using Notes, how has it been going?"

"What aspect of using this software has given you the most difficulty?"

"What types of notes or messages have you created using Notes?"

"Describe the most difficult project you've undertaken with Notes. How did that go?"

"Are there aspects of Notes that you've found chronically difficult or impossible to use?"

"When you get stuck, where do you go for help?"

"How helpful has the documentation been?"

"What role did the training course play in your mastery of Notes?"

"Knowing what you do now, how would you suggest we modify the training?"

"Do you feel you need or want additional support?"

Evaluating Instructor Performance

Although they're often associated, learner performance is not necessarily a reflection of instructor performance. A learner willing to experiment can learn even from an ineffective instructor. And depending on factors like learner motivation, opportunities for use, and timing, even the most effective instructor may fail to produce skilled users.

Follow-up interviews with users are one source of evaluation data on instructors. Waiting at least two weeks after training ends to conduct these interviews gives users a chance to test their learning on the job and yields information beyond their initial, subjective reactions. If you wait longer than six weeks, however, users' impressions of training and its impact may have faded.

When consulting users for evaluation data, ask open-ended questions about the software and their use of it rather than questions about the specific course or instructor. You'll find they have plenty to say on those topics regardless, and you want to avoid shaping their answers.

Observation by managers or fellow instructors provides another perspective on instructor performance. For example, if you were evaluating the work of a heart surgeon, you wouldn't ask patients in the recovery room how they liked surgery. Of course, patient recovery rates would be indicative of competence, but you'd likely seek the opinions of other respected heart surgeons for the fine points.

Peer observation fills out the instructor performance evaluation in the same way. If instructors in your organization are licensed to deliver vendors' courses, you might bring in vendor representatives to observe them. Some companies also have set up reciprocal observation plans among their training staffs. Observation is most constructive when based on a set of specific performance criteria such as those listed next.

A Sample List of Observation Criteria

The trainer:

– Is comfortable in the role of instructional leader
– Is in control of the classroom environment
– Has planned well
– Uses lesson plans or outlines
– States objectives in practical terms
– Checks for learner resistance
– Handles learner resistance appropriately
– Uses a variety of handouts and materials
– Distributes handouts in a timely fashion
– Provides motivational elements
– Uses work-appropriate examples
– Praises learner success
– Solicits active participation
– Models enthusiasm for software and system
– Models the use of documentation for reference
– Models the use of on-line help for reference
– Models the use of support services and help desk
– Provides information transfer in varied fashion
– Is open to interruption
– Handles off-topic questions appropriately
– Provides examples above and below mean skill level
– Avoids pressing keys on learners' keyboards
– Avoids "choral typing"
– Circulates throughout room during practice
– Provides practice in verbal and written form
– Allocates appropriate time for practice
– Addresses needs of wizards and experts
– Uses cooperative learning groups when appropriate
– Cites references providing further information
– Models how to obtain support after course
– Provides postcourse feedback to managers
– Has an accurate perspective on the success or failure of the class

Observers should be trained in observation techniques, and a structure should be established for conducting the observation. As an example, University of Massachusetts educational philosopher Sid Simon suggests beginning an observation assessment by asking the instructor the following series of questions.

■ What did you like about the class?
■ If you had to do it over and all external circumstances were the same, what would you do differently?
■ In order to do that, would you need additional support? What information or feedback would you like from me?

Evaluating the Course

To distinguish the course itself from the instructor's presentation of it, look at the written course materials — the vocabulary, concepts, and procedures list, if there is one (see also Chapter 10, "Vocabulary, Concepts, and Procedures"), the outline, and the handouts. To determine whether the content, length, sequence, materials, and practice activities are appropriate, look at the actual use of the course contents following training. Are users applying all functions taught, or have some turned out to be superfluous? Once more, gather data from the support center or help desk. What do users' call patterns reveal about missing course information or concepts not being taught effectively?

Observation is also useful for course evaluation, since the course design itself may be responsible for the amount of remediation needed. Observers should note the frequency with which an instructor jumps back and forth in the subject matter, since poor sequencing is often the result of bad design decisions rather than poor instruction.

Evaluating the Software or System

User performance is affected by the features and idiosyncrasies of software and systems, and so is the effectiveness of training. Any training evaluation, then, should include a look at the software or system being taught and its documentation and other peripheral materials.

This evaluation sometimes points up the need to change the system, not the training. Indeed, software modification can solve users' problems. For example, an accounting firm having difficulty teaching clients how to enter data on a complex set of screens approached The MASIE Center for ideas on innovative teaching strategies. But even with new approaches, the amount of time clients would spend trying to master the screens far exceeded the resources needed to modify them.

Following are some questions to ask during software evaluation.

- Are navigational commands consistent throughout the program?
- Are inputs and their consequences logical? Or is it a difficult package to teach and learn?
- Does the instructor have to work around bugs or glitches in the system?
- Is the software appropriate for users' needs? (If users aren't using all available functions, the problem simply may be that the software is too sophisticated for their needs.)
- Is the documentation — on-line or print — helpful or burdensome?

Evaluating Environmental Factors

Training doesn't occur in a vacuum. Motivated learners, skilled instructors, and well-designed course materials are, of course, essential. But they don't guarantee effective learning or, later, effective computer use. Physical and organizational conditions are just as important, and learners' supervisors or managers are equally important players in the training process.

During Training

Is a classroom available, or does training take place in a freight elevator, in a supply closet, or at the user's desk, with telephones ringing in the background?

After Training

The following list of questions should be considered by managers of computer users completing training.

- Do users have terminals to return to?
- Are they given sufficient practice time upon returning to work? (New skills are quickly lost without the opportunity to practice them within 10 to 14 days of learning. Ideally, practice begins immediately following training.)
- Have the right people been sent to training?
- Have they been sent to the right training?
- How well does the timing of training coincide with job requirements?
- How much managerial support or encouragement have learners received?
- Are learners able to focus on training, or do they feel obliged to spend much of the day on the phone to the office?
- Will learners' initial low productivity be tolerated?
- Are there manuals in learners' offices?

Such management-related issues are rarely acknowledged or evaluated in a systematic fashion. They are, however, critical factors in the success of training, and relevant information is available if organizations are interested in looking at it. Users' managers might be surprised to learn how quickly they acquire reputations among the training staff for their participation in the training process — their support (or lack of it), their expectations (realistic or not) of new users, their tendency to send the right (or wrong) people to training, and their policy of explaining (or saying nothing about) why employees are being trained.

Trainers also can collect some information systematically during class, polling learners about why they're there and noting which ones have been sent to training with clear expectations and goals.

Here again, the support function is a source of valuable information. Do system crashes, confusion patterns, or specific kinds of questions repeatedly come from certain departments?

Tips on Evaluation Methods

Forms and Questionnaires

■ Make sure results aren't skewed by questions that require varying amounts of effort for different responses.

■ Numerical scales, although more conducive to statistical analysis than open-ended questions are, yield relatively limited information. Also note that a large response base is needed for truly accurate statistical analysis.

Observation

■ Be aware that an observer's presence can alter the very conditions being observed.

■ Try not to base evaluation on a single observation.

■ Despite its popularity, the use of videotaping for instructor evaluation and self-evaluation can be disruptive. Audiotape is almost as effective and much less distracting.

Interviews

■ To ensure honesty, learners should be interviewed by someone other than the instructor who taught them. Another instructor, the training manager, or a staff assistant can conduct these interviews quite satisfactorily.

■ The interviewer should ask open-ended questions to avoid influencing learners' responses.

The Evaluation Process

Much of the preceding information is readily available, but few organizations have methodical processes for collecting, collating, verifying, and analyzing it. A tool such as the following list is one way to organize an evaluation effort.

Evaluation Clients and Focuses

Evaluation Clients
■ Trainer leading course
■ Other trainers in department
■ Trainer's manager
■ Learners in course
■ Learners' managers
■ Course developers
■ Support or help-desk staff
■ Systems staff

Evaluation Focuses
■ Opinions about course
■ Learning at end of course
■ Learning six weeks after course
■ Course curriculum
■ Postcourse need for support
■ Postcourse system use
■ Managerial support for practice
■ Needs-assessment techniques

How much information should you collect? Granted, this chapter encourages an extremely thorough approach to evaluation. But 100-percent coverage is no more necessary or practical in training evaluation than in any other evaluation effort. A candy factory's quality-control department doesn't cut open every chocolate bar, and you need not interview every training participant. Instead, select a sampling ratio that keeps your evaluation methodology from being prohibitively expensive or cumbersome; a 1-in-5 ratio is common and dependable. Observation is particularly crucial for new instructors and is more important for all instructors than is usually acknowledged.

Evaluation results generally signal some follow-up activity, often course redesign. But they have many other uses as well, and an evaluation process that clearly distinguishes between different types of data can help your organization figure out where to direct its resources to improve computer use. Training managers may decide to use the results of trainers' performance evaluations for improving trainers' skills. Or, if user-performance problems are found to have nothing to do with the trainer or the course but are caused by poor internal system marketing, then that's where extra efforts should be focused.

Notes on "Smile Sheets"

Implementing a thorough evaluation methodology requires an enormous amount of effort. Considering the time and budget pressures that govern organizational life, it might seem easier to evaluate by exception — waiting for managers' complaints before evaluating users' performance or for learners' complaints before evaluating instructors. Unfortunately, some of the most useful evaluation information comes forth only when solicited, so the "exceptional" method of evaluation isn't much better than none at all.

The alternative to an evaluation model like the one we've described is a one-shot, easy-to-administer evaluation tool. In most organizations, that tool is the "smile sheet," or something like it — a brief series of questions that participants respond to at the end of a class. Questions that might be asked include:

- Did the instructor stick to the established objectives and cover the promised material?
- Were the audiovisual materials appropriate?
- Did the instructor demonstrate mastery of the course content?
- Were your expectations met?

There is no question that smile sheets are sources of interesting learner data or that the intentions behind their use are earnest. They can be particularly useful for detecting learners' confusion or frustration. Their problem lies in the questions they ask and how they ask them, neither of which produces the most useful evaluation data or the statistical validity some organizations attribute to them.

Limitations

To understand the limitations of smile sheets, think about taking a single snapshot of a moving subject with an out-of-focus camera when what you really need is a video sequence taken with a perfectly focused telephoto lens. The snapshot will show only a frame of the subject's movement, and that frame will be a blur.

Likewise, most smile sheets ask learners about only one of the five areas a thorough evaluation should cover — the instructor's performance. If participants are asked to comment on the course itself, their insights are usually dependent on the instructor's presentation.

Gathering useful information about student performance using a smile sheet is not likely to happen immediately following training. As discussed in the section on learner performance, there is no "best time" for this. A one-time questionnaire gives no indication of what participants knew before training and what they will learn as they make the transition from learner to user.

Another limitation of smile sheets is their tendency to focus on affective rather than objective information — for example, how participants liked the course. Evaluation should certainly look at participants' learning experiences and attitudes as learners, which affect their later performance. But evaluations that focus solely on the learning process ignore the most important question: Can the learner use the system? And if these affective responses are requested at the end of training, they are colored by learners' states of mind at that time, which can range from relief and euphoria to exhaustion. In fact, studies on course and teacher evaluation show that what smile sheets tend to reveal is the mood set by the instructor at the end of the class.

> The smile sheets from Instructor X's classes always produced the highest possible ratings, and Instructor X consistently received the merit pay increases that accompanied strong evaluations at his company. Just as consistently, Instructor X treated his learners to pizza and beer on the last day of his week-long courses, finishing the week off with a party of sorts. He might have gotten ratings of 9 and 10 anyway, but how can we know?

Just as smile sheets don't always reveal the reasons behind positive responses, they may not reveal negative responses at all. Participants are often reluctant to report dissatisfaction, especially in writing and especially when they will continue to have a collegial relationship with the instructor after training. They don't want to cause the instructor harm, nor do they want to jeopardize their relationships with their colleagues. Although smile sheets are always anonymous, they may not seem that way when learners know instructors can recognize their handwriting or even trace their responses to their in-class performance.

Some organizations perform elaborate statistical analyses based on smile-sheet results, yet few have tested their questionnaires for the validity and reliability usually required of any serious testing activity. In fact, the results of all write-in questionnaires are naturally skewed by the unequal response effort that different questions require. Think, for example, about a question like this: "Did the instructor accomplish the course objectives? If not, explain why not." How can you be sure respondents haven't answered yes simply to avoid explaining why not?

One might also question how seriously participants themselves take smile sheets. The more questionnaires people fill out without awareness of their impact, the more meaningless they become.

A lack of appropriate contextual information can also make smile-sheet data misleading. Suppose all but one of the participants give a class a high rating, and the remaining one gives it a very low rating. Without any information on the dissenting person — such as preparation, job requirements, or manager's attitude — the instructor is likely to give the low rating a disproportionate amount of attention, maybe even altering a course that's quite satisfactory.

If the smile sheet is so unreliable, should you get rid of it altogether? Not necessarily, but take care to consider its limitations and supplement it with other forms of evaluation that focus on performance rather than affective responses.

If you decide to eliminate smile sheets, make sure you have a new evaluation methodology in place first. Even if evaluation isn't an explicit management requirement, it's usually an unspoken expectation. Equally important, it gives participants a sense of closure.

Earlier in the handbook, we mentioned the VCP Model of Evaluation Survey. This is a simple format that solicits feedback on learners' perceptions about their level of confusion/confidence at the end of the class. The chart on the next page presents an example of this model. The numbers across the top correspond to the following self-perceptions.

1 = I fully understand and can use this.
2 = I basically understand it and will try to use it.
3 = I am a bit confused but will figure it out.
4 = I am very confused.
5 = I don't plan on using it.
6 = It wasn't covered in class.

VCP Model of Evaluation Survey	1	2	3	4	5	6
Moving a cell						
Creating a new spreadsheet						
Printing a spreadsheet						
3-D graphs						
OLE links						
Importing database items						

Learners can check off their end-of-class status for each of these items. While these ratings may change when learners get back to the office and start to practice, this exercise does produce a good instant check on areas of confusion. I've used this model for more than five years and find it one of the most valuable points of feedback. You can print these forms on two- or three-part paper, allowing both the user and the trainer to have a copy at the end of the class.

Certification

When I was a Cub Scout, I worked hard for my merit badges. That was my first experience with certification. Lately, the topic is one of the hottest issues in computer-training circles. Certification is an attempt to provide a standard measuring stick for skill acquisition and a performance standard for specific job functions.

The most widely attained certification in our field is Novell's CNE and CNA programs. An individual studying Novell's networking software has the option of going through a detailed and structured curriculum and taking tests to become a Certified Novell Engineer. This has created a whole industry for training, testing, and a hot job description in the help-wanted classified ads.

Many of the major software publishers are following Novell's lead in this arena. We soon will see new certification programs from Microsoft, Lotus, IBM, and others. In addition, there are efforts under way to develop non-tool-specific certification programs like Client Service Programming Test.

Certification provides a unique form of evaluation for participants in and buyers of training. The trainer's certification status is considered a prime indicator of the training materials' effectiveness.

Technology for Evaluation

E-mail, Groupware, and Network Interactive Forms are being developed as a delivery system for evaluation surveys. Sylvan Learning has developed the SMART system to communicate evaluation data directly from the learner's terminal to the trainer, training manager, and software company that produced the application just taught. Versions of this type of system are being introduced into corporate learning centers to automate end-of-class assessments.

Summary

Computer training will become an increasingly professional field as trainers open up to and encourage evaluation. Smile sheets certainly hold an appeal for trainers who know they've done a good job. There's nothing more satisfying than a round of applause — or so it seems. But you won't really know if you've done a good job until you find out how your learners use the system and how often they call the help desk. Thorough evaluation can also help prevent trainer burnout by making trainers feel their performance really matters and by sustaining the intrinsic challenge of the job.

Changing the focus of evaluation from the pro forma efforts prevailing in many organizations to an emphasis on performance will not be easy. This change reflects a shift in philosophy and will require managerial support — along with the cooperation of training professionals, supervisors, and users. It will also immerse the training function in the complexities of organizational politics. But with such a change, evaluation has a much better chance of determining how successfully and cost-effectively training is accomplishing its goals.

37

Managing Computer Training

The computer-training function is a volatile one in today's organizations. Most computer-training managers have held their positions for under 18 months. Because of the turnover and change in this area, a question-and-answer format is used here to provide a clear explanation of the issues involved.

Q: Should organizations provide a centralized computer-training function, or is it better to make each major business unit responsible for its own learning?

A: In organizations where a significant amount of computer training takes place, there are real benefits to establishing a centralized department or position to coordinate and manage training. The one caveat here is that centralized training budgets may be more vulnerable to cuts than training allocations "hidden" in departmental budgets. A centralized training group has more visibility and organizational clout than a number of individuals scattered across departments. Centralization also simplifies users' access to training resources, saves trainers from having to reinvent too many wheels, and increases standardization and consistency among courses. (In the absence of a formal centralized function, a central "clearinghouse" can help accomplish these goals.)

Q: Should training be outsourced?

A: There is growing interest in the outsourcing of computer-training services. In the extreme, a corporation subcontracts the entire IS function, including training. Another option is to outsource the computer-training function to a single vendor. There is also the widespread use of external consultants to deliver training. In fact, some of the "safest" training departments are those having a head count of only one or two people, with the rest "borrowed" from other units or obtained from an external provider.

An organization considering outsourcing should look at the ability of the provider to respond quickly to changing training needs and to provide on-site management of the instructional process. Outsource contracts will be used increasingly to address a wide range of learning activities, not just training services.

Q: What is the ideal relationship between the computer-training function and the IS department?

A: When training decisions are made independently of decisions about the acquisition, development, and implementation of computer systems, training professionals must adopt a reactive stance and work within existing structures. Software developed in-house is often subject to changes right up to its release. Unless the training function is in close communication with systems developers, it's virtually impossible to prepare thorough training materials in advance. The sooner trainers know what's happening with systems, the sooner users will get up to speed. When the two functions work together, training can be well timed with implementations and updates.

A common complaint among IS employees is that computer training folks are not "technical" enough. Therefore, it is critical that computer-training managers recruit experienced programmers and other IS colleagues to join or partner with their training efforts.

Q: What is the ideal relationship between the computer-training department and the help-desk/support function?

A: For budgeting reasons, an organization may have separate training and support functions. However, the tasks of these groups are so closely related that some communication — and ideally, coordination — is essential. Trainers decide what to teach based on the kind of support available to users on the job, and they must teach learners how to use that support. To know whether they're doing an adequate job, training departments need to know what kinds of support calls users are making. The support staff, in turn, needs to be familiar with users' training to shape support to their needs. Familiarity with the training function also allows support staff to recommend appropriate training to frequent callers. This cooperation helps organizations make the most of training and keep support costs in line.

If I could make only one management-related recommendation to a CEO, it would be to put the help-desk and computer-training functions under the same line of command. Both are involved in building user competency, and it's critical that they work together on this mission. A combined function also provides greater promotional opportunities and more flexible allocation of staff.

Q: What is the ideal relationship between the computer-training department and individual business units?

A: People don't attend computer training for random knowledge about computers. They attend to acquire specific job-related skills. To understand users' job requirements, trainers need to be in close communication with the people who supervise those jobs — learners' managers. The managers, in turn, must provide the right conditions for users to apply what they have learned. First off, that means acknowledging the importance of training — setting aside assumptions that a program's "user-friendliness" makes training unnecessary or that users can learn by osmosis. Next, it means letting users know what they're expected to learn and how they'll be using their new skills. Finally, after training, it means providing adequate practice time and making sure the training content was appropriate.

Here are a few suggestions for trainers hoping to build better relationships with business units.

■ Coordinate the release of your training schedule with departmental performance reviews. This will help managers schedule their training needs.

■ Appoint an individual in each business unit to serve as liaison between that unit and the training department. This person should sit on an advisory panel that provides guidance and planning.

■ Discover the "covert coaches" and on-the-job trainers in each unit. Try to build them into your plans for disseminating knowledge to the user community.

Q: What would a typical set of computer-training standards include?

A: A typical set of training standards might stipulate that:

■ A schedule of computer-training offerings be developed and published in time for managers to schedule employee training around departmental workloads

■ A thorough needs assessment be conducted before anyone is sent to training

■ All training offerings be accompanied by clear statements of their prerequisites and objectives, ideally stated in terms of vocabulary, concepts, and procedures items and behavioral accomplishments

■ Managers brief all prospective participants on their expectations for posttraining performance

■ Managers be responsible, with some consequences, for no-shows

■ The evaluation process link course effectiveness with actual system use

Some of these standards address the other guidelines explicitly; others implicitly enforce cooperation between the training function and line management. If the preceding standards seem redundant or overlapping, it's because they concern a group of functions characterized in part by their interdependence. What makes the computer-training function successful is the acknowledgment of these mutual relationships and the establishment of cooperation among all players.

The next chapters — "The Computer-Training Staff," "The Cost of Learning," "Marketing the Training Function," and "Purchasing Training" — present in-depth discussion on their respective components of computer-training management, along with some specific guidelines.

38

The Computer-
Training Staff

The task of staffing a computer-training department is laden with difficult choices. Here are a few of the most common questions presented to The MASIE Center.

Q: Describe the computer-training profession.

A: For some people, computer training is a full-time profession; for others, it's one job task among many. Some consider computer training a career, a source of professional identity; others temporarily trade their programming or other hats for training hats. People come to computer training from different backgrounds, they perform different aspects of the job, they are compensated differently, and they move on in different directions. Against this varied backdrop, those responsible for computer training must decide whom to hire and for which particular jobs.

Q: What are the various roles in computer-training departments?

A: There are as many job descriptions for computer trainers as there are organizations with people learning to use computers. But within this broad spectrum, the multiple aspects of computer training are settling into a few job types and levels of responsibility. Following is a list of common categories, in order of increasing responsibility. Keep in mind that one person shoulders all of these responsibilities in some organizations.

Training

Part-time trainers, gurus, or wizards. Often users themselves, these people present short courses to one or two users at a time or simply provide lots of screen-level support. Their training responsibilities are likely to stem from their technical expertise and experience, and probably take only a small amount of their work time.

Instructors or trainers. These people are likely to work full-time in training or training and support. They teach more substantial courses or provide more technical support than the part-time trainers do. They have been selected for training on the basis of both their teaching skill and their content knowledge.

Senior trainers. These individuals teach more advanced courses than the instructors/trainers and offer management briefings. They are likely to be involved in course development, as well, and to have a high level of both training and technical skills.

Course Development

Many organizations have people on staff who develop materials for classroom training, CBT, or other self-study. Course development requires skills in instructional design and writing, along with some subject-matter expertise. It is sometimes included in training positions and sometimes a separate job.

Marketing and Training Consulting

Many training departments have one individual who is responsible for both marketing the department's services externally and consulting with individual business units on internal training needs. These responsibilities also can be distributed among the members of an organization's training staff.

Training Contract Coordinator

As organizations use more and more external training, The MASIE Center has begun tracking the growth of the role of contract coordinator. Involved in bidding and contracting for specific services and products, this individual also may be a trainer or developer, or play a supervisory role within the group.

Management

Depending on the company's organizational chart, ultimate responsibility for computer training may lie with MIS management, corporate training, human-resource development, or some combination of these. But often, an intermediate manager carries out supervisory responsibilities at the local level.

Q: Any advice on hiring computer-training personnel?

A: People come to computer-training positions from many backgrounds — from data processing to corporate or academic education to line departments, where they have used the products being taught. Lawyers take time away from the courtroom to teach their colleagues legal applications for the PC; secretaries become office-automation trainers when their companies go on-line.

The ideal computer trainer combines people skills and teaching skills with content knowledge. (Requirements for technical sophistication vary, depending on the subject matter.) Clearly, the data-processing professional, educator, and experienced user each comes with one part of the needed skill set.

Q: Is it better to hire someone with a training or a technical background?

A: While it's impossible to answer that question with a blanket statement, here's one piece of advice: Think about what you can change in a new employee and what you can't. Lack of experience is easier to remedy than a troublesome personality trait — that is, you're more likely to be successful teaching a new trainer computer skills than social skills. But whatever a candidate's background or whatever position you're hiring for, the following tips should help you select someone with a good balance of skills.

In general, for application-level training, it's usually easier to find people with good training skills (or at least good people skills) and then build their technical skills. The cost of doing that at the high end of technical training, however, is too great. For network and other technical topics, look for people with a strong technical background and the core human-relations skills. These individuals can be developed into better presenters and trainers. I've seen few people move successfully from HR into high-end technical training.

Q: What skill sets are needed for instructors/trainers?

A: The following skill areas should be examined for every training candidate.

Training skills. If you're interviewing people to stand in front of a classroom and train, it's critical that you see them in action before making a hiring decision. There's a range of ways to do that, including observation. If candidates aren't currently employed as trainers or you're unable to observe them in the classroom, ask to see them on videotape. You can also ask candidates to bring a software package to the interview and teach part of it to you. A candidate who has not yet acquired computer skills can choose another skill to demonstrate teaching ability, such as how to plan a party.

Styles and affinities. Ask candidates to describe the kinds of learners with whom they've been most — and least — successful. Compare their descriptions with what you know about the users requiring training.

Courseware-development skills. Consider candidates' ability to create course materials. If they lack experience in this area, examine the way they structure their instruction.

Patience. Try to gauge a candidate's ability to empathize with novice users and to tolerate their confusion and mistakes.

Spelling/handwriting skills. Take a look at spelling and handwriting skills if you're hiring instructors who will be writing on a flipchart, an overhead-projector transparency, or a board.

Social skills. Difficulties with social interaction may be the hardest to overcome in developing trainers.

Q: What do training professionals earn?

A: No national studies have been conducted recently on compensation for computer-training professionals. The MASIE Center will conduct such a study in 1995 and disseminate its findings through various publications. In the meantime, here are current salaries for human-resource trainers and training professionals.

Trainers' Salaries, 1994

Job Category	Overall Average Salary
HRD MANAGER	
Executive-level training/HRD manager (other managers report to me)	$70,650
Manager of a training/HRD department or function (five or more full-time training professionals report to me)	58,731
Manager of a training/HRD department or function (one to four full-time training professionals report to me)	51,121
I am, in effect, a one-person training department	44,341
HRD SPECIALIST	
Classroom instructor	39,336
Instructional designer	43,128
Management development, career development, or organizational development specialist	43,121
OTHER	
Personnel manager	52,482
Line or staff manager/specialist other than training or personnel	54,251

Like most aspects of the computer-training field, compensation standards are still evolving. Compensation also varies according to the employee's responsibilities and background. Trainers with computer backgrounds usually fare quite well, especially if training

is just a temporary stint within a longer-term IS career. Their training salaries are likely to be commensurate with their earning power
in more technical positions. Those who come to training from
lower-paying fields often bear the legacy of their previous salaries
and end up earning less. Such wage discrepancies can create real
friction if salaries are discussed by trainers from different backgrounds.

Q: What career opportunities exist in the computer-training field?

A: The newness of the computer-training field is responsible for its
lack of clearly defined career paths. Outside of a few major corporations with large, consolidated computer-training functions,
not many organizations have made a commitment to the careers
of their computer trainers. One reason for this is the lack of prece-
dent; another is that most organizations can't accurately predict
their manpower needs and are hesitant to develop a training structure that may become expendable.

Due to the field's lack of established career paths, trainers' backgrounds are often predictive of their advancement opportunities
as well as their salaries. IS people usually have jobs to return to
when they come to dead ends in training, as do former users who
have left well-compensated, professional jobs for training positions. While these groups have professional identities to fall back
on, they also share the risk of obsolescence if they're away from
their specialties too long. Some corporate training departments
represent a similar "home" for trainers whose careers originated
there. On the other hand, former teachers who leave the training
field have no obvious destination.

Former users, especially those from clerical positions and those
advancing in the same organization, have the steepest uphill path
in their training careers. An initial shift of employer can increase

the status of users moving into training positions from jobs with little professional status.

One way to overcome the ambiguities of advancement is to formally acknowledge that two or three years seems like a good length of time to spend doing computer training. Some organizations have established their computer-training positions as two- or three-year, midcareer assignments for people whose career paths are kept open in other parts of the organization. Others consider computer training an entry-level position, with the expectation that trainers will move to other positions in the company within three years. But whether these positions are entry-level or midcareer, the key is that they are not perceived as long term.

Q: How can trainers avoid burnout?

A: Burnout is an occupational hazard of the computer-training profession. We are in a giving and helping role on a daily basis, and it takes its toll. The average trainer stays on the job for less than three years, and those who stay longer discover that the job can wear down even the most motivated professional. Yet there are thousands of colleagues in our field with five to twenty years' experience. What is the key to survival? Avoiding the major sources of burnout, including the following.

Lack of feedback. To begin with, training is a "closed-door" job. Trainers are rarely observed or closely supervised, and the little feedback they get is often negative.

Lack of professional identity. Because the computer-training profession is still somewhat undefined, trainers have few role models and little professional context from which to gather encouragement, motivation, and direction. This lack of professional identity can be particularly hard on new trainers from non-professional positions who don't have a professional identity to fall back on to boost their self-esteem.

Sameness. Not only are many trainers assigned to teach the same courses over and over again, they're rarely encouraged — or given time — to improve the quality of these courses. This increases the trainers' chances of boredom and makes it hard for them to maintain personal investment in their work.

The strain of the helping relationship. Training is a social job, one that requires the patience and willingness to help users. This can be exhausting for any trainer, especially one whose "helping nature" goes to extremes, creating dependent users who continue needing help.

Trainers' managers can help prevent burnout in several ways. First, it's critical to limit the number of hours that trainers spend in the classroom every week and to mix instruction with tasks such as support, development, and observation. It's also important for managers to observe trainers, provide feedback, and ensure that trainers' involvement in supporting learners is appropriate.

Monitoring trainers' professional development is another way to motivate them and keep their performance on an upward path. Ideally, managers should establish learning plans when trainers are hired, identifying missing skills and determining ways to remedy those deficits. New trainers should also have an opportunity to observe others' classes and to teach one-on-one before teaching their first class.

Opportunities to do phone support and visit learners' job sites help trainers understand what happens after training and how the systems they teach are used on the job. Exposure to courses learners have taken previously gives them a better sense of their audience. Some course-development work not only gives their jobs variety but also broadens trainers' understanding of the instructional process. Contact with trainers in other subject areas and other organizations is a source of ideas and professional identity. Finally, provide trainers with career-development opportunities.

Those who feel they're in dead-end jobs aren't likely to stay around long.

Q: Any basic advice for computer trainers as they build their careers?

A: If you are considering a computer-training position — or already have one — keep the future in mind. Find out whether your organization has a structure in place to accommodate you a couple of years down the line. You won't be alone if you end up with a nomadic career, switching organizations frequently but doing similar work at all of them. Many computer trainers augment their incomes — and their résumés — by moonlighting in continuing-education programs, adult-education programs, or training programs offered by computer stores.

As for the temptation to go out on your own: Proceed carefully! While many organizations do use contract trainers whose per-diem fees exceed the weekly salaries of in-house trainers, these consultants' fees are as inconsistent as computer trainers' in-house salaries. They range from as low as $35 an hour to the more appealing several thousand dollars a day, with the high end reserved for trainers with specialized knowledge, a well-established image, and a business structure involving more than one person working out of the living room.

Q: Who really succeeds in computer training?

A: Let me answer that with the following list, based on my observations of people in the computer-training field over the last 20 years.

Healthy and Successful Computer Trainers Are People Who . . .

- Really enjoy working with people
- Get excited when a user learns something new
- Have a good dose of hacker in them, but it's under control
- Can draw a readable map on how to get to their home
- Stop and ask for directions when they're lost while driving
- Have a life beyond the classroom
- Have a teacher in their lives that they see as a role model
- Like to read
- Listen well and can control their urge to interrupt
- Are savvy about office politics but don't get too involved
- Can tolerate a high degree of ambiguity
- Laugh a lot
- Can keep a secret
- Are nurturing without becoming maternal or paternal
- Get their ego strokes outside the classroom
- Love to learn and are forever curious

Computer training is a perfect fit for individuals who like people and enjoy technology.

39

The Cost of Learning

"How do we get a feel for the actual cost of learning to use new technology products? It seems to extend beyond the obvious training costs. What does it really cost per new user?"

"We have a few technical wizards in our office. Can't we save training dollars by just having them show everyone else what to do?"

"Should we be using a chargeback system?"

The true cost of learning is always significantly greater than the budgeted cost of training. The challenge is to walk the line between honestly acknowledging the hidden costs of using technology and maintaining training budgets that are within organizational guidelines. As we will discuss, many of the costs of learning and mastering technology never appear in a financial document.

In 1993, a number of studies were released that pegged the total training-and-support cost for a desktop computer at $5,000 to $15,000 per year (excluding hardware and software costs). A large percentage of this amount was driven by the high cost of learning, including multiple uses of support staff instead of formal instruction.

When an organization purchases training externally, calculating costs seems easy; after all, the vendor submits an invoice. Calculating the costs of in-house training seems more complicated, since it includes figuring overhead, development time, and instructors' salaries — or a percentage of users' salaries, if they provide training.

Figuring the cost of training, however, is much more than tallying the costs of the training event itself. You are really calculating what it costs for people to learn to use computers, and this includes all of the time they spend learning, not just classroom time. You must also tag on all costs related to the infrastructure that supports training and new users.

An honest assessment of training costs includes all of the items in this formula:

> **Learners' salaries + Trainer's salary + Developer's salary + Materials + Equipment + Facilities + Travel + Supervision + Support = Total training cost**

Learners' salaries must be figured for the time spent both in training and in informal, independent practice (also called "at-your-desk train-ing time," or AYDTT). This figure might also incorporate any signifi-cant decline in learners' productivity during the early stages of computer use.

The *trainer's salary* must be figured for time spent delivering instruc-tion and doing any related administrative work. If the instructor is also responsible for course development, then the developer's salary is included here.

The *developer's salary* is either included in the trainer's salary or figured separately if someone else is responsible for course development.

Materials costs should include both consumable items (such as books and cheat sheets) and nonconsumable items (such as wall charts and overhead transparencies).

Equipment costs may be incurred for the purchase and maintenance of equipment used specifically for training. If the training function borrows equipment from other departments, the value of the time spent on that equipment should be assessed.

Facilities costs may reflect the costs of rented space or the overhead costs on already owned space.

Travel costs incurred by trainers or learners are often inevitable training expenses in organizations with multiple sites or field offices.

Supervision costs stem from the salaries of those charged with managing and evaluating the training function, along with any related overhead.

Support costs are incurred both formally (for the designated support system) and informally (for the salaried time of users who provide support). The estimated cost of formal support is approximately $25 per support call but depends on the length of the call. That figure increases significantly for untrained users who have difficulty explaining the problem or implementing the solution.

Crunching the Numbers

So, what's the price tag on training? The number of variables makes it impossible to name a specific dollar amount. However, it's generally safe to assume a parallel between training costs and system costs. In other words, the amount you spend bringing each user to proficiency on a given microcomputer software package will be roughly equivalent to the amount you spent on that package in the first place. Software is usually priced according to its complexity; the more complicated it is or the more features it offers, the more it tends to cost — and the more difficult, and costly, it is to learn. Similarly, the total cost of training on mainframe systems usually comes close to the total cost of development.

This cost analysis is complicated even further by the fact that the separate costs are not entirely independent of each other. If you cut costs in one part of the equation, you'll find another part rising. For instance, you may save on instructors' salaries by substituting a video for some classroom training time or by doubling the number of learners in the class. But either action will reduce opportunities to check for learner confusion, and the result is likely to be increased support costs later.

Attempts to save money on training can backfire in other ways as well, since additional costs are incurred whenever training fails to produce competent users. The more class time spent on remedial activity, the less new material learners have a chance to master. When less material is learned per session, the cost of what is learned goes up. And if training is so unsuccessful that users need retraining, costs more than double, since learners may be more resistant and thus harder to teach the second time around. Conversely, the use of class participation and other techniques that enhance learning may give learners more for their money.

Finally, you might want to consider the cost of training relative to the cost of *not* training. Users who aren't trained may not use the hardware and software purchased for them, which costs their organizations not only the purchase price of that equipment but also the value of expected productivity increases. The other possibility for untrained users is to find their own ways of doing the expected tasks on the computer. This can be done, but not without major time expenditures by both the users and their colleagues — time for trial and error, and time for informal support. Stranded users also tend to be extremely dependent on formal support, incurring costs of $25 and up per call.

Who Pays?

In many organizations, the computer-training function is considered a cost center, covered by the MIS budget. In others, some form of chargeback shifts the costs of training and support to the users' departments and their budgets.

There are several chargeback models in common use. In some cases, business units pay a flat per-user fee for training and support. If MIS charges for other computing costs (per PC or per mainframe CPU hour), a surcharge may be added to cover training and support. Finally, some organizations issue a price list for specific training-and-support services. User departments might pay for these services with real dollars, or the costs might be recorded and published annually to heighten organizational awareness of how and where allocated funds are being spent.

Advantages of Chargeback

Awareness. Chargeback can make users more sensitive to the costs of services they use, causing them to use the services more wisely.

Supply and demand. Chargeback creates a market economy for allocating limited training resources. Suppose a training staff has time to train only a limited number of people on a limited number of products. If the price of training goes up, those who want or need it most will pay for it. If everyone is willing to pay more, the training function will be able to afford more staff in order to meet the full demand.

Drawbacks of Chargeback

The risk factor. People are used to paying for specific events, which makes its easier to charge for courses than for nonevent services like assistance or support. Still, some training functions fear — with good reason — that if they charge for training, people won't buy it.

Charging for support. This presents a similar threat to the security of the support function. When users have to pay for support, they're less likely to stay dependent on it. And while independence is one goal of training, too much of it can put the support function out of business.

One remedy for this concern is the practice of charging for "bundles" of support. For a fixed price, often in conjunction with training, a user or department is entitled to a certain number of support calls. By offering a limited amount of support use, this arrangement regulates users' dependence on support.

40

Marketing the Training Function

"Our training department spends an enormous amount of energy organizing and hosting computer classes. Only 32 percent of the workforce attends these seminars, yet we constantly hear employees complain that there aren't any ways for them to learn the corporate technology! How can we get the word out? And how can we get employees to come to class?"

The challenges of running a computer-training department are very similar to those of running a computer-training business. Your colleagues are really prospective customers, and the training department is really a retail operation. And as with a store, all the slick merchandise in the world doesn't mean a thing if no customers come through the door. Advertising and marketing are key!

The training function's marketing efforts may be as understated as the publication and distribution of a course catalog and other descriptive literature. But sometimes, more active measures are needed to spark an interest in training and related services among nonusers, current users who've grown dependent on support, or training graduates who aren't taking advantage of support.

Marketing Is More Than a Catalog

The most common marketing mistake computer-training departments make is assuming their advertising task ends with the publication of a course catalog. The catalog is merely an adjunct to a comprehensive marketing approach. A year-round marketing campaign must be constructed using all of the elements and tools a retail computer-training company would deploy, including:

■ Demonstrations of new software, with a pitch for upcoming courses.

■ Clinics and brown-bag bursts of instruction to get on the "radar screens" of managers and other key decision makers. It's a lot easier to get people to attend a 60-minute briefing and then pitch the longer courses to them.

■ Customer sales and reps. If you were a for-profit business, you'd assign a sales rep to every major customer. Consider using the same approach, with your instructors as account managers. Analyze your customers' needs and plans to determine how to capture a larger share of their business.

■ Regular needs assessments. Find out how various departments and users are — or could be — using computers.

■ User-base skills update. Encourage managers to augment each performance evaluation with a description of the employee's use of any automated tools provided by the organization.

■ Training reminders. Encourage people to think about training even before purchasing new hardware or software. Consider modifying procurement forms to include a question like: "How will the user be trained?"

■ A newsletter update. Publish a regular newsletter, supplementing information on your services with brief articles on new technologies and their use in the organization.

Truth in Packaging

No matter how the training function publicizes its services, its "advertising" must be honest so that learners and managers know exactly what skills a given course will provide. Using the vocabulary, concepts, and procedures analysis as the basis for a course's catalog description is a good way to ensure that content is well represented. Course descriptions should also indicate the specific instructional methods that will be used.

Don't overuse the term *hands-on*. Granted, most users perceive plenty of hands-on time as the mark of a good course; however, the quantity of keyboard time is actually less important than the quality of the course as a whole. Your marketing materials should let learners know how much practice they'll get, whether they'll be working alone or in groups, how much lecture time to expect, how much user participation will be invited, and so on.

Some Marketing Tips and Tricks

Here are a few practical approaches to increasing the visibility of your training services.

Lead time. Make sure your catalog and course announcements get in customers' hands with enough lead time for planning attendance. Allow at least six to eight weeks' advance notice — more for managers and higher-level employees.

Flexible lengths and formats. Don't get stuck on a single format for all courses. There may be a real market for late-afternoon or evening classes. Or, try offering an early-morning session, featuring bagels and coffee, for senior executives.

Ease of registration. How easy is it to get into a class? Identify and eliminate any registration hurdles.

Benefits. Make sure to articulate the benefits of each class to both learners and their departments.

Exclusion. In promoting a class, try including a list of people who would *not* benefit from it. This is a powerful way to show that the course targets specific needs and learners.

Competition copycats. Keep a file of impressive brochures from for-profit training organizations. Integrate appropriate ideas and concepts into your marketing.

41

Purchasing Training

"How do we decide when to buy training and when to develop it with our own resources?"

"What are some tips for checking out the quality of training that's on the market?"

Much of this book has focused on decisions made when designing and delivering your own training. But many organizations purchase external training because they lack the in-house expertise, resources, or time needed to design and deliver their own. Training is also purchased on a supplementary basis by organizations unable to hire a permanent, full-time training staff or those with heavy or special training demands.

Training is available for purchase in a variety of forms. Training companies and individual consultants offer public seminars at their own sites and at public sites. Many of these companies or consultants also tailor their generic courses to the needs of individual organizations — or create custom courses from scratch — and deliver them at those organizations' sites. Other contract trainers deliver courses that have been developed in-house.

Another option is to buy course outlines and materials for your own instructors, along with computer-, video-, or workbook-based self-study materials. Or, you can hire design experts to custom design such materials for your organization.

Using external training vendors doesn't replace the thinking you'll need to do about course design and delivery. Nor does it eliminate your responsibility for managing and evaluating the process. You may even create a vocabulary, concepts, and procedures list and ask the vendor to follow it. That way, you decide what information users need and ensure that the vendor's course design provides it in a form that is specific enough for users to transfer to their jobs. Finally, you must decide how you want users to learn, and select vendors who reflect that philosophy.

The Public Seminar

Public seminars are generic courses with audiences drawn from a variety of organizations.

Costs. Costs can range from a low of about $60 per learner per day — for training offered by a community college or a university continuing-education division — to $500 per day for advanced training offered by a specialized vendor. There are always going to be low-end prices, but you may end up with low-end training at the rock-bottom levels.

Variety and timeliness. If your organization is located in an area with abundant and varied training offerings, or management is willing to pay for travel, public seminars offer enormous flexibility in both timing and subject matter. Users don't need to wait for training until their own organizations have accumulated a quorum of users needing the same training.

Learner appeal. Especially if travel is involved, the opportunity to leave the work site for training offers the inviting possibility of some rest and recreation. Within limits, learners should be allowed to take advantage of those opportunities. Management involvement (as described later) can help establish those limits.

Selecting a Training Vendor

Until you're familiar with the work of a particular vendor, it's essential to check references. Considering the amount of money involved, many organizations are amazingly nonchalant about sending people to external training events. Following are some recommendations for checking references and otherwise screening vendors under consideration.

■ Call the training vendor's offices. If the instructor isn't available to describe the training and answer your questions, talk to someone in a management or supervisory position.

■ If the vendor's descriptive materials don't include information on the instructor, find out who will be teaching the class — and what sort of trainer he or she is. The instructor's approach to the class is just as important as his or her academic and professional qualifications. The larger training vendors use a wide range of trainers. For these organizations, ask for credentials/background information on several instructors who teach the class in question. Check to see if they have passed any industry-level certification exams.

■ When checking references, be aware that most vendors tend to provide names of references who are guaranteed to give them a good word. Specific requests can elicit more objective comments. For instance, try asking for the names of two participants in the vendor's most recent course and two from a course one year ago. You can also request names from a specific company on the vendor's client list or even ask for client names beginning with a random letter of the alphabet. Many local training groups maintain reference files, and colleagues in other companies can be an excellent informal source of vendor information as well.

■ Make sure the vendor offers some form of guarantee so that you can get a refund or a credit if the course doesn't meet your expectations.

■ If time and the vendor permit, sit in on a class taught by the instructor being considered, or send a qualified representative from your organization to observe the instructor and submit a critical report.

Management Involvement

No matter where training takes place or how it's delivered, managers who send users to training have certain responsibilities before, during, and after the training event. Their involvement has a specific emphasis when users leave the office for external training.

Before training, managers should explain to participants why they're attending the class and what they should be able to do with the content when they return to work. Managers can clarify these expectations by describing how the system or software to be learned is used in the organization and by providing company-specific examples on disks or printouts. Some managers give participants a list of questions to be discussed after training or identify tasks — like generating a document, for word-processing users — they'll want them to be able to perform. This makes users active participants in the training process and active consumers as well — learners who hold instructors accountable for providing information they can use and for teaching them to use it.

If the vendor hasn't conducted a pretraining needs assessment, the manager should send a letter describing users' needs. The instructor won't revamp the course based on that information, but it's helpful for selecting the examples and exceptions that will be most relevant.

Managers should request that participants phone the office at some point during training, whatever the length of the course. Training should not be interrupted by learners' office responsibilities, but a quick phone call keeps job awareness foremost in learners' minds. This contact enhances participants' ability to relate training content to the job and is useful if the training isn't meeting their expectations. Employees may feel confused and trapped if they find themselves dissatisfied with training recommended by their managers. A chat with the manager can help put the problem in perspective and help learners figure out what to do.

After training, managers are responsible for providing practice time and for showing interest in what users have learned. Finding out what participants learned and how the course was taught can help a manager decide whether to send people to that course in the future.

Bringing in Training

There are many ways to bring training into an organization. Most often, organizations hire consultants or companies that have developed "packaged" courses that include outlines, handouts, and manuals. Sometimes, these are the same courses vendors teach in public seminars, but you can save money and get some customization by bringing the vendors to your site. Training consultants also can be hired to teach courses developed in-house.

Some organizations contract, or outsource, the entire computer-training function (and sometimes support services as well) to a third-party vendor. This approach, especially popular in government agencies, gives organizations the most flexibility in responding to fluctuating training needs.

Some organizations hire recently retired employees as contract trainers. These people have an intimate knowledge of the organization, know the terms and language that are familiar to users, and are likely to be very capable of helping learners understand new material and how it relates to their jobs.

Costs. Like public-seminar costs, the price of bringing in training varies, as do the methods of setting fees. Some vendors charge by the day for a certain number of participants, with an extra charge for additional learners. By the day, vendors charge from $500 to $5,000. Others charge from $35 to $400 per participant for a day of training. Materials and instructor's travel costs are usually over and above those amounts.

Advantage

Cost savings. Bringing in training instead of sending participants out saves travel costs. Although the organization pays overhead costs on the facilities, out-of-pocket tuition costs are usually less per day, since vendors' fees don't have to cover advertising costs or liability insurance.

Disadvantage

Minimum-audience requirement. Every class needs a certain number of participants to be cost-effective. The cost per learner could grow to unjustifiable rates if you experienced last-minute cancellations or dropouts.

Tips

Checking references. It's just as important to check references when bringing in training as when sending learners out, and the same advice applies. If the vendor you're bringing in also offers public seminars, make sure you know which references you're getting. Some vendors who do a great job with public seminars aren't as effective in-house, and vice versa.

Customization. Be explicit about your expectations for customization. Make sure you know whether the instructor's examples will refer to your business or to the generic "widget" business.

Checking content. It's essential to check the vendor's objectives, but it's necessary to go even further to ensure the training accomplishes your goals and is consistent with other training being done in your organization. Some organizations require vendors to provide a VCP analysis of their course, a description of their strategies, or even a complete course design.

Control. It's important that the training function — or whoever brings in the training — retain a presence throughout the training event. Sure, it's easier to show the trainer to the room and then immerse yourself in paperwork until the course is over. But consultants are not employees or managers, and the presence of someone with internal knowledge and responsibility is essential for everything from helping the consultant find the cafeteria to pointing out organizational applications of the material being taught to handling any problems that come up during the session.

Scheduling. If you have a choice, Tuesday, Wednesday, and Thursday are the best days for in-house training with external trainers. On Monday mornings and Friday afternoons, organizational distractions make it very difficult for learners to focus. And if trainers are willing to provide half-day courses, learners' attention is less likely to lag halfway through the training.

Sneaker-Based Training

Sneaker-based training is on the rise. Rather than hiring a trainer to spend a day in front of a classroom, the company provides a trainer who spends time with individual learners at their desks. This is a blending of instruction and support. Several training companies have started offering this type of instructional service as part of their product mix.

Consortium Training

Many organizations have difficulty filling classrooms with enough participants to justify hiring an outside trainer. One way around this problem is for organizations with similar training needs to join forces. Based on needs assessments of all member organizations, the consortium negotiates with vendors as a single organization, and member organizations take turns hosting the training. This arrangement, usually quite cost-effective, is a middle ground between customized in-house seminars and public seminars. To find out whether there is a consortium in your area, check with your local computer-training association.

Courseware

If your organization employs instructors but lacks sufficient resources for course development, you can buy the tools needed by the instructors to teach their courses — course outlines, overheads, transparencies, workbooks, and learner disks. You also can buy entire self-study courses using video, workbooks, computer-based training, or a combination of these media.

Unless they've been created specifically for your organization (at much greater expense), these materials are generic. And because learners tend to respond poorly to generic materials, it's a good idea to adapt them to make sure the content is applicable to your organization. A quick vocabulary, concepts, and procedures inventory of the generic courseware will reveal whether content should be removed or added. You also may want to modify examples to make them organization-specific, or adjust the quantity of guided and unguided practice.

Recently, courseware companies have started offering "customized engines" that allow users to create personal booklets based on their selection of specific modules and objectives. The internal course designer specifies the learning content, and the "engine" creates a word-processing document that reflects a personalized course.

Evaluation

Externally developed courseware should be thoroughly evaluated before it is purchased, and both users and trainers should be involved in the evaluation process. If possible, do a trial run of the courseware with a potential user who isn't familiar with the content. This will help determine whether examples are appropriate, information is presented in a way that users can index easily, and factors as basic as appearance and tone are appealing or objectionable to users.

Your evaluation of trainers' courseware should answer the following questions.

- Does this material teach the skills I want my users to learn?
- Do the assumptions underlying the training design match our organizational philosophy?
- Does the courseware reflect a training philosophy consistent with ours?
- How much guided and unguided practice is included?

Based on your answers to these questions, you may decide not to purchase the courseware. Or, you may decide to buy it and adapt it to your needs, or supplement it with your own materials. References are also useful when selecting courseware. It's especially important to consult with someone in a similar company or in your industry to find out how successful the material has been.

42

Documentation and Training

"What is the role of documentation with training?"

"Why does documentation get such a bad rap from users and trainers?"

"Is there a way to get users to actually use computer manuals?"

More and more software vendors are claiming that their products don't require manuals, thanks to on-line help and general ease of use. In fact, some vendors use the brevity of their manuals as a selling point. But written documentation of some sort is necessary, even if it's only one page of instructions for activating more in-depth on-line documentation or a computer-based tutorial. Much more than a single page is the norm, however.

This chapter reflects the belief that effective use of documentation plays an essential role in successful computer use. For all but the most restricted procedural user, knowing how to use the system includes knowing how to use the manual, and here's why.

Computer-training courses can't possibly cover every feature of a system. No matter how many commands they learn in training, users are sure to encounter unfamiliar situations on the job and make mistakes that trigger confusing error messages. If every support call costs the organization an estimated $25, users who answer their own questions by referring to documentation can save their organizations a lot of money. Unfortunately, at least half of all computer users who have attended a class never open their manuals after training.

If users are expected to use documentation, then its use should be explained, discussed, and modeled during training. An indispensable tool, documentation is as important an element of training as any system feature or peripheral.

The premise of including documentation in training is a simple one, but the reality is somewhat complicated, even emotionally charged. Affirming the relationship between documentation and training involves more than providing a quick rundown on how the manual is organized or using its table of contents as a lesson plan. There are effective and not-so-effective ways of incorporating documentation into a training design.

Also, because documentation has evolved in parallel with computing in general, it is frequently a source of user confusion and frustration. In fact, it has become the focus of some strong, often negative attitudes. To advance its use, the training function must acknowledge the difficulties documentation presents and work toward overcoming them, whether that means modifying the documentation or changing users' attitudes.

The Evolution of Documentation

A closer look at its evolution will shed some light on the challenges documentation presents to any training effort. Before the days of end-users, when computing was the exclusive province of the MIS department's large mainframe systems, documentation was primarily a record of the programmers' ongoing work. Most systems were in constant evolution, and unless programmers documented their changes, there was no way of tracking a program's features and functions. This early documentation, written by programmers for other programmers, had little or no usefulness to any other audience. End-users — had there been any — wouldn't have known what to do with it.

The demand for user-focused documentation arose when nontechnical people began accessing hardware, software, and systems. For some time, the resources dedicated to documentation development remained disproportionately small. Manuals were poorly written and produced, often confounding users rather than helping them. Technologically unsophisticated and ill-equipped to evaluate the documentation, users figured one manual was as good — or bad — as another. The quality of documentation had little influence on product selection.

In the last few years, users' expectations of documentation have risen. Not only has demand increased, but demand for *usable* documentation is up. One clear sign of this is the enormously and increasingly successful aftermarket for third-party documentation, which accounts for about 90 percent of computer stores' book sales. The IDG *Windows for Dummies* books are an example of the incredible demand for how-to-use-a-computer books. Many purchasers of these materials are software pirates who have illicitly obtained disks but who have no documentation. But just as many are users dissatisfied with vendor-supplied documentation.

Recognizing the value of useful documentation, software and hardware developers have built up their documentation departments, and independent specialists have had little trouble finding audiences for their documentation-related expertise.

Sorting Through the Confusion

Despite the progress that's been made, documentation remains a source of confusion and frustration for computer users. Training still plays a major role in helping users get the most from it. One source of confusion is the lack of industry standards for classifying and labeling different types of documentation. Some manuals are exhaustive catalogs of features and commands; others are technical guides that include program code; still others are designed for instruction. Although these types fall into fairly predictable categories, vendor classification assignments too often seem random. What one vendor calls a "systems guide," another might call a "technical reference." What one calls a "users' guide," another might call a "tutorial." Without standardized classification, it's hard for users to know what to expect from documentation.

Even when the purpose of a document is clear, that document may not satisfy a particular user's needs. As they progress through various stages of learning, users rely on different types of documentation. Each level of skill development calls for different types of information, different degrees of detail, and different methods of access. A cartoon-illustrated booklet instructing new users where to put their diskettes quickly loses its value as users master basic skills and move on to more advanced levels.

Furthermore, despite some real advances, documentation quality remains inconsistent. In too many cases, documentation is still considered a feature of the system rather than a user tool. Illogical formats, inconsistent organization, and poor indexing can make it extremely difficult for users to find the information they need.

While training can provide guidance to users in dealing with these obstacles, these problems can also be tackled closer to the source. With some commitment of resources, you can cut and paste the generic, "one-size-fits-all" manual to create versions for different developmental levels and job requirements. However, vendors' copyrights usually prohibit the replication of manuals, even in a modified format. Plus, producing a completely new set of manuals may require substantial resources. This expense is easier to justify in a large company with a broad distribution of documentation.

Less expense is required for compiling a new index and inserting copies in the front of existing manuals. Issuing tabs or dividers is another simple way of modifying manuals to help users find the information they need more quickly.

Along with simplifying the use of documentation, these modifications make it easier to teach learners how to use it. Less training time will be spent navigating around obstacles and the negative attitudes that tend to accompany them.

Training with Documentation

The amount of attention a trainer gives system documentation depends on the amount users will be expected to give it after training. If users will be expected to rely heavily on their manuals, then teaching manual use may actually be a primary goal of training. Users who are expected to be less dependent on documentation should receive less emphasis on it during training.

Heavy Referencing

When system use involves extensive knowledge of syntax and other specialized information, the only alternative to dependence on a manual is extensive memorization. Many airline reservation systems, for example, are not menu-driven; they rely instead on elaborate combinations of complicated syntax. Reservation agents are expected to refer to the manual for rarely used functions, and their training includes active use of manuals. In fact, a display at the front of some airlines' computer-training classrooms keeps learners constantly notified of the manual page being discussed.

The success of this method depends on the manual. If you expect users to rely heavily on documentation, do your best to make sure the manual's format and organization are easily understood. Manuals allowing easy random access are much more useful than those organized sequentially and lacking detailed indexes.

Light Referencing

In other situations, documentation is not distributed or used until users are further along in training, or even after training. This is appropriate for users who are not expected to rely as heavily on their manuals, or when the manual is organized for random access and the instructor wants the course to follow a developmental sequence. Like all written material, a manual competes for learners' attention. Handing it out after rather than during class is a way for the instructor to maintain control.

Between the extremes of heavy and light referencing is another way of incorporating documentation in training: Focus on manual excerpts developed or reproduced specifically for instructional purposes. This approach exposes learners to relevant sections of the documentation without overwhelming or distracting them with the entire manual.

Ways to Use Documentation

Along with teaching learners when and how to access the information they need, trainers can put manuals to use in various stages of the Sagamore Design Model.

The set. Skimming the manual for references to specific job tasks can be an effective motivator, especially for practical learners.

Information transfer. The manual can provide the structure for a lecture, with readings used to reinforce lecture segments. Readings from the manual can also provide information directly. However, reading assignments should be carefully designed and managed, since many learners object to reading. (See also the minichapter "In-Class Reading" for further guidelines on the use of reading during training.)

Guided and unguided practice. Instead of distributing a list of tips and procedures with every activity assigned, refer learners to certain chapters in the manual for guidance. (Don't cite specific pages, though.)

In addition to its use in explicit instructional tasks, documentation in training implicitly influences learners. The trainer is a role model as well as an instructor in the use of documentation. Once you identify the pattern in a trainer's use of the manual during class, you'll see that learners adopt similar patterns of use. Recognizing this ability to influence users, instructors who want learners to use documentation should introduce it as a peripheral at the beginning of training and refer to it throughout the course.

Intentionally or not, trainers convey their attitudes about documentation to users. Watching a trainer's bored, dutiful expression when picking up a manual is not likely to make learners enthusiastic users of that manual. This is not to say that instructors should ignore or deny a manual's shortfalls. Rather, they should acknowledge them honestly, striving to convey a balance between the manual's value and its limitations.

Documentation Design

There are numerous ways of designing documentation, but certain basic features make manuals easier to use. Trainers should be able to recognize good — and bad — manuals when they see them, and understand what makes each good or bad. This will help them understand and alleviate learners' frustrations with poor documentation, and ensure that any modifications they make are effective. Trainers also can put these criteria to use when asked to evaluate documentation for usability.

Standard Conventions

Consistency of format helps users find the information they need quickly. This may mean providing the same information, in the same sequence, for every major feature or function: name, uses, syntax, examples, an illustration of a screen, a guided-practice exercise, the relevant error messages. If this pattern is repeated throughout a manual, users automatically know where to look for the information they need in each section.

Standards also can be applied to design elements. Used consistently, vertical and horizontal lines, different typefaces, and various layout arrangements can help users differentiate among types of information, and again, find what they need more easily.

Examples

The most effective documentation includes examples that are job- or industry-specific, or generic examples that are easily and widely understood. Users have little patience with examples based on imaginary companies like the ABC Widget Corporation. Unless users can relate to them, examples do little to facilitate the indexing of new information. If the examples in a vendor's manual are inadequate, organizations can create their own and insert them into the existing manual. This creates learner interest while saving the expense of producing a whole new manual.

Volume

A hefty manual may be a thorough manual, but it's also one that's awkward to use and to store near a terminal. Creating quick-reference guides can provide faster, more convenient access to commonly needed information. If a system's main reference manual is issued in several volumes, make sure each volume contains an index referring to all volumes.

Using these criteria to create and customize manuals may seem costly. But poorly designed manuals have their own costs. Confused users with poor navigational skills and little self-confidence require more remedial time in class and ongoing support time. And organizations are less likely to see the return on their hardware and software investments when users can't apply their new knowledge on the job.

On-line Documentation

More and more documentation is provided on-line, for users to access as they need help. On-line documentation already offers some distinct advantages and has the potential to offer more. To begin with, a manual stored on disk is less likely to be misplaced than a printed one. It's also more immediately and easily accessible than a printed manual that has to be taken off a shelf and paged through.

Based on the situation for which the user requested help, context-sensitive help systems provide precise information or a submenu of specific help. If, for example, you're partway into a mail-merge operation and you press the designated help key, a mail-merge menu will appear on the screen.

The more context-sensitive an on-line help system is, the more confident users can be that it will provide the help they need. The existing on-line help is not accessed by a large number of users, and there are several reasons for this. One is the somewhat developmental state of context-sensitivity; if users have to wade through too many levels of submenus, they might as well be leafing through a printed manual.

On-line documentation, like print documentation, must be kept up to date. But most important, it must be used during training if learners are to develop the habit of using it. And so far, few trainers are including on-line help in their courses.

Print Documentation

Printed manuals offer a couple of advantages that on-line help has yet to provide. One is the ability to look at the problem screen and the help suggestions simultaneously. There's no reason on-line documentation can't appear in a movable window, allowing the problem area to be visible, but so far this practice is not standard. The other advantage of hard copy, more difficult if not impossible for developers to simulate on-line, is its physical bulk. Users have expressed that, despite any inconvenience, they like the tactile element of print documentation. Especially when the computer isn't doing what they want, it's a relief to have a familiar, seemingly more trustworthy help option.

Although not always labeled this way, print documentation typically falls into five general categories. Along with enabling you to identify your existing forms of print documentation, the following descriptions outline the challenges each type presents to trainers and learners.

Reference manual. The most comprehensive, encyclopedic description of a product is often called "The Bible." The contents of this official manual may be organized alphabetically, by function, by segments of the system (such as menus), or by job function. Reference manuals tend to be big — too big for convenient storage or access at a user's terminal — and full of more information than users need on a regular basis. Although individual users don't need their own copies of the reference manual, one should be readily available in each office.

User's guide. This is an edited version of the reference manual; its limited contents are selected and arranged (usually by function) with users' needs in mind. To be really useful, user's guides should include syntax and illustrations of common screens. Ideally, a user's guide is small enough to fit on a user's desk, and every user should have one. This not only makes reference convenient; it allows users to make personal annotations.

Technical reference manual (troubleshooting manual). This manual contains information of use and interest to programmers, information-center staff, and perhaps a few very advanced users. It might include in-depth discussions of error statements, file structures, interfaces with other systems, screen configuration, and setup procedures. Technical manuals are rarely found on end-users' desks, although they might be available to these users through a central library.

Tutorials. Tutorials are intended for instruction, and their contents are sequenced accordingly. They often include some practice exercises. Tutorials have limited utility as references after users have learned to use the system. Relying exclusively on printed tutorials for training — self-study or classroom — can be risky. If their authors aren't familiar with the needs of adult learners, information may not be sequenced or presented in a way that helps learners grasp it.

Job aids, or cheat sheets. The most stripped-down, consolidated form of print documentation, job aids (also called "cheat sheets") are intended to remind users of the keystrokes required for specific tasks and don't discuss concepts at all. They are usually no more than one page in length, and can even take the form of a keyboard template. Creating job-specific job aids is a good way to customize documentation for different users.

43

Support

"We're in the process of setting up a help desk. How can we make sure users take advantage of it — but don't take too much advantage of it?"

"Our help desk gets so many questions over and over again. Shouldn't training take care of these common ones?"

"Why are the same people always calling the help desk?"

"What are the advantages — and disadvantages — of having the same staff handle both training and support?"

Effective training takes new computer users a long way down the road toward proficiency, and good documentation can take them even further. But training and documentation aren't enough. Training can't address every situation users will encounter, and documentation can't anticipate every question they might have. Even if that degree of thoroughness were possible, users don't always do what they're taught. Fewer than half of the users in most organizations ever open their manuals after training.

Most people with questions about using computers want to *ask* these questions and have them answered by another person, not search through a manual. Whether the person providing the answers is a trainer, an information-center consultant staffing a help desk, the department software wizard, or the neighbor's teenage computer prodigy, he or she is providing *support* — an essential element in the process of learning to use computers.

Many organizations neglect to make conscious decisions about the way support will be provided and fail to coordinate the training and support functions so that users know who to ask for help and how to ask for it. Organizations that don't make appropriate support available to users don't see the optimum effects of training. The users spend more time trying to get themselves out of hot water than making productive use of their computers. As a result, they're likely to become frustrated and resentful when their expectations aren't met.

Its importance to users and the organization is sufficient reason to make sure that support is well managed, but its cost is another. The average call to a formal help desk costs at least $25 in the user's and support provider's salaried time. (This estimate includes the time the user spends in confusion prior to the call and in any necessary recovery following the call.) That figure increases dramatically when colleagues are drawn into the support effort or when the user isn't able to explain the problem clearly or can't understand the support provider's recommendations. At these costs, it is crucial that the support process be clearly established and communicated to users. To offer the most effective help possible, support providers must be aware of the variety of support needs and users.

Types of Support

The most common support calls fall into one of the following six categories.

System problems. Sometimes users need support because the hardware is malfunctioning or there's a bug in the software. The problem may be obvious (a disk drive continually generating a disk-error message, for example) or subtle (a word-processing program putting hyphens in the wrong places). Some users call because they know the problem lies with the system and they want to get it fixed; others think they are responsible for the error.

Information-recall problems. Users have trouble accessing information they've learned for a variety of reasons. Sometimes, they simply have forgotten it. Other times, they remember vocabulary but not the related concepts or procedures. Or perhaps terminology changes after training — the key that an instructor referred to as the Return key appears on the user's keyboard as the Enter key. Users also may remember information in a way that makes it difficult to recall, or they confuse similar procedures within or among software packages.

Training problems. Users often call for support upon encountering a detail not included in their training. This might be a feature introduced since the training took place, something taught on a day the user was absent, or simply an inadvertent omission on the trainer's part.

Job-related problems. Users may understand how to perform a particular computer function but not how to apply it appropriately to a given job task. For example, someone might know how to change a client's status to inactive but need clarification of corporate policy for carrying out that function. What these users really need is computer-oriented job support.

Connectivity problems. Users attempting to access an interface between two programs or computers may not know the necessary commands, formats, or other details.

Designated support tasks. Sometimes users' access to a system is restricted for reasons of security or other management-related concerns. A company may not want its users formatting their own hard disks, for example. Users in this company will depend on support for these functions.

The Four Stages of Confusion

Whatever the nature of the computer-related problem, the underlying reason for support calls is confusion. But confusion comes in many forms. In fact, the learning process can be divided into four stages of confusion, each different from the others and requiring a specific type of help. These four stages are *unconscious incompetence, conscious incompetence, conscious competence,* and *unconscious competence,* as illustrated in this account of learning to drive a standard-transmission car.

Imagine going to pick up a new car you'd ordered weeks earlier. When you arrive at the dealership, the car turns out to have a standard transmission, although you ordered an automatic. You've never driven a standard-transmission car before and are somewhat concerned, but you've already paid for the car and don't want to wait any longer for another one.

You get into the car, turn the key in the ignition, and experiment with pressing the gas and clutch pedals. The car groans, bucks, and dies. You've entered the first stage of confusion — unconscious incompetence. You know that you don't know what you need to know, but you don't know exactly what that is.

You put in an SOS call to a friend. Your friend arrives, sits in the passenger seat, and talks you through the shifting procedure as you drive home. By the end of the trip, you've begun to get the hang of it. You can shift from first gear into second and from second into third quite smoothly. You have trouble shifting from neutral into first and knowing when to switch from third into fourth, however, and sometimes you hit fifth instead of third. You recognize these problem areas when they occur, meaning you've reached the second stage of confusion — conscious incompetence. You now have a much better idea of what you don't know.

In continuing to practice, you make your way slowly to the third stage, conscious competence. At that stage, you've mastered the basic rules of standard-transmission driving and are aware of following them. You talk yourself through each step of the shifting procedure, don't let other drivers disturb you, and are reassured when your actions produce the expected results.

Eventually, you realize you aren't mouthing the steps anymore or waiting to find out if you've done things right. You're hardly aware of what you're doing, but it's working. You've become unconsciously competent.

Anyone learning a new skill goes through these four stages. Progress isn't always steady, and sometimes the learner falls back to a previous stage upon encountering a particularly difficult situation. But just as you needed different degrees and kinds of help while moving from one stage to another, computer users require different kinds of support, depending on their stages of confusion.

Unconsciously incompetent users are often those who've had no training but have been asked to do something on the computer. This is a completely alien world to them, and they have almost no vocabulary for asking questions or understanding help that's offered. Those providing support to these users must avoid jargon at all costs, keep their help at the simplest procedural level, and be extremely patient.

Users at the next stage — those who know what they don't know — need less intensive help. In fact, they often just need time to experiment or practice, to get used to certain keystroke sequences, or to commit certain commands to memory. Consciously competent users have usually figured out what's wrong by the time they seek support but want their hunches confirmed before pressing the Enter key.

Providing support for unconsciously competent users can be more complicated. So familiar are they with the procedures that they no longer stop to verify their actions. Consequently, they sometimes make serious mistakes without realizing it, then blame the system for their problems. Support providers must try to help these users shift into a higher level of awareness, then establish a precise common understanding of where things went wrong.

Supporting the Two Types of Users

The nature of support calls and the kinds of help required also vary depending on whether users are of the procedural or navigational type. Procedural users require explicit, keystroke-by-keystroke help. Not only might they panic when given navigational advice — such as a suggestion to try different print options — they probably won't be able to follow it.

Navigational users, on the other hand, don't want to know the appropriate keystrokes for fixing the problem. At least at first, they want an educated guess about what went wrong so they can try to correct the problem themselves.

Support and Thinking Styles

Users request and receive support differently depending on how they think and learn. The approaches to learning and using information can be categorized into four styles — reflective, conceptual, practical, and creative. Most people shift back and forth between two or more of these styles but tend to use one predominantly. This predominant style determines the kinds of questions users ask, how they experience and express confusion, and the kind of support they find most helpful.

Reflective thinkers look at things subjectively. They constantly relate new information to their own experiences and consider how they feel about what they are doing. Their support calls are usually long, involved stories about the job they were doing when the problem arose, the disastrous results, their calls for advice to friends and relatives, and so on — with a description of the problem hidden somewhere in the middle. Support providers can best help them by explaining why they are having the problem and perhaps telling a story about the same thing happening to someone else.

Conceptual thinkers want the whole picture. Not satisfied by screen-level information, they want to understand what's going on behind the screen. When calling for support, they provide more detailed, technical information about the problem than the support staff can possibly use. Support presented in terms of the whole system and referencing a system map (if available) or the manual is most helpful to them.

Practical thinkers just want the facts. Uninterested in extra information, they are constantly on the lookout for shortcuts, macros, and other ways to simplify their computer work. When calling for support, they usually express some anxiety about "fixing the problem" and are most responsive to help provided toward that end.

Creative thinkers love to play. These users tend to learn about the limits of systems and software by testing them. By the time they call for support, they're often in serious trouble, yet they mask their problems by requesting "suggestions." They are most receptive to help that provides innovative, out-of-the-ordinary solutions to their problems.

Other Support Patterns

Understanding the support process begins with understanding the different types of support, levels of confusion, and styles of learning. These elements help build a framework for establishing a support system, but that framework is incomplete without considering other patterns in the way users rely on support. A closer look at these patterns is essential for making the support process more efficient and effective, eliminating unnecessary support calls, and forging a more productive relationship between training and support.

To begin with, the use of support is very uneven. In most organizations, approximately 15 to 20 percent of the users are responsible for 80 to 100 percent of the support demand. And most organizations report that 2 to 5 percent of their users rely on support with a particularly high frequency. These dependent users never internalize procedures; instead, they call and ask a support provider to walk them through even the most routine procedures.

For 70 to 80 percent of all procedural calls, however, the solution to the users' problem is either present on the screen or just one keystroke away. If these users were better trained to read the screen or to access on-line help, their support calls — and the accompanying costs — could be prevented.

In organizations without a formal, designated support function, support is provided exclusively by peers. But even where there are formal support groups, as much of 80 percent of the total support received is *still* given by peers. The minichapter "On-the-Job Learning and Training" discusses the importance of monitoring informal peer training.

Informal support should be monitored and managed to ensure its accuracy and consistency with organizational standards. It also should be empowering; users should learn enough from their departments' resident computer wizards to become independent instead of remaining reliant on them. This helps prevent support from taking up too much of the wizards' time but requires that wizards be provided with appropriate documentation to give to users. Wizards also need support of their own for user problems they can't handle.

Cheat sheets and documentation for mainframe systems and locally developed microcomputer programs often lag behind what's on the screen. Until these materials have been brought up to date, any system change will mean a short-term increase in support requirements.

Training Solutions

Training is one obvious avenue for handling excessive support demands and inefficient or ineffective response to those demands. The following six training measures help users learn to use support appropriately, thereby keeping support costs down and making sure those dollars are well spent.

■ Most important is the premise that all available forms of support are peripherals — just like terminals, keyboards, disk drives, and printers — and should be treated accordingly in training. Users should be taught to use not only hardware and software, but also on- and off-line support and documentation as aids to more competent computer use.

■ Training has a responsibility to convey the organization's policies and procedures for support use. If this is done carefully, users' expectations about support are less likely to clash with reality. Users who are told, "Just call 474-HELP whenever you have a problem," will have different expectations and develop different habits than those who are told, "Print out the problem screen and make a few notes on the printout about what happened. The help desk will probably tell you they'll call back in a few hours, and you should have your manual ready when they call."

■ Training should help users develop the vocabulary and skills needed to describe their problems to a support provider. Many users have no ability to describe their problems, unless they're stuck in limited procedural situations and say something like, "I forgot what key to press to close a window." Users' increased skill in defining problems makes it easier for the support staff to help them, and it might lead to a deeper understanding of the system that would make some support calls unnecessary.

■ Training should include practice in asking for support, with learners posing questions to each other or the instructor. Questions that arise in training also can be turned into actual support calls. Instead of answering a question, the instructor can direct the learner to telephone the support center. If this is not feasible, the trainer can role-play a support provider, facing away from the learner's terminal so that the learner must provide a clear verbal description of the problem. Distributing copies of the support center's log sheet gives users a clear idea of how their calls will be handled and what kind of information the support staff will need.

■ Training should incorporate up-front managerial decisions about whether users should be navigational or procedural. This will ensure that people learn to use computers in the expected fashion.

■ Training must include guided or unguided practice if users are expected to reach the conscious competence stage. Cooperative learning and rebooting activities are other good training vehicles for increasing users' independence and ability to provide and benefit from informal support on the job. Helping each other in class gives users a more confident and thorough understanding of the support process from both sides.

Organizational Solutions

Top-level managers of organizations play an important role in ensuring the efficiency of the training-support cycle. Following are some recommended policies and requirements concerning users and the support function.

■ Organizations can clarify their policies and expectations for support in a written "service level agreement," which delineates processes and responsibilities in a statement such as this:

"We will support all users of ABC software, provided they have completed our class or passed a competency test. Telephone support will be provided between 9 a.m. and 5 p.m. A detailed diagnosis of the problem will be made at the time of the call. In most instances, help also will be provided at that time; however, in some instances, support will not be provided or completed in less than four hours. Requests for system changes will be handled on a quarterly basis."

■ Organizations can require that users have manuals at hand when calling for support. Support staff will ask, "Which manual are you looking at? What page?" and refer to that manual in providing help.

■ Organizations might require that users be registered to be eligible for support-facility use. A registered user is one sanctioned by management — who has a legal copy of the software in question, has been to training, and often, has passed a competency test. This practice makes it much easier to monitor computer, and support, use.

■ "Triage support" is an efficient alternative to immediate, real-time support. With this emergency-room model, users may have to wait for help, depending on the urgency of their problems and the number of other users waiting. One large company has done away with real-time support altogether. All calls are logged and dealt with in order of their apparent urgency. At another company, users are encouraged to use electronic mail instead of phone calls to request help.

Even if policies like these aren't outlined formally, they usually take shape implicitly. However, clearly delineated support policies help keep user frustration and antagonism to a minimum. And if users know what to expect from support, they can plan their time better and use their computers more efficiently.

Finally, when the training and support functions originate in the same department, their distinct duties and responsibilities must be clear. For instance, trainers who also provide support may be tempted to turn every support call into an ad-hoc, telephone-based training session. But that wouldn't be necessary or appropriate for every caller, and unless standards are in place for providing training this way, the training is unlikely to be consistent with what's being done throughout the rest of the organization.

Conversely, problems may arise when training is provided by support staff, since the two functions are based on very different ways of looking at computer systems. Based on a positive view of the system, training gives users a developmental exposure to its possibilities. Support, on the other hand, focuses on system problems. Training influenced by the support point of view tends to be preventive rather than developmental. While users trained this way have a minimal need for support (they've learned how to avoid the common problems), their competence is fairly limited in scope, and they are unlikely to be navigational users.

Joint Responsibilities

Although we have stressed the differences between training and support, they are quite interdependent. Together (and sometimes with management as well), the two functions can look at the vocabulary, concepts, and procedures analyses for the hardware and software used in their organization, deciding what should be taught to which users and what support should deal with afterwards. Even if this process is not cooperative, the support function can do a better job of helping users if it is aware of how they were trained.

Studying the vocabulary, concepts, and procedures analyses on which training is based or sitting in on training sessions enables support providers to talk to users with familiar vocabulary and metaphors. These measures also inform the support staff of the features that have and haven't been taught so they know what level of knowledge to expect from users. Similarly, awareness of its organization's training options enables support staff to make appropriate recommendations to users whose repetitive calls indicate a need for further training.

Support is also a vehicle for controlling an organization's quality of training and overall computer use. The support area receives an enormous amount of information that reflects the effectiveness of training. Suppose, for example, that a trainer conducted a vocabulary, concepts, and procedures analysis for a word-processing course and decided to omit printer-code reformatting. If the support center logged all calls from those who took the class and found out they were all asking how to reformat printer codes, the instructor could adjust the course to better meet learners' needs next time around. Without support's feedback, the course might continue to omit useful material that trainers incorrectly assumed participants were learning.

Unfortunately, organizations rarely take advantage of the quality-control potential of the support function. Because most support staffs are overworked, dealing with an extremely high volume of calls, they rarely have access to on-line tracking systems. If they do any tracking, it's usually limited to monitoring the number and frequency of calls.

For a variety of reasons, the interdependence between training and support is not yet fully appreciated or activated. Sometimes, the two function independently, responding to different pressures and funded by different budgets. Plus, the whole process of computer support is relatively new. Organizations have not yet mastered the management and monitoring of these separate functions, let alone the coordination of them. Yet training and support are so fundamentally related that coordination is extremely important — in communication if not on the organizational chart.

44

Ten Simple Thoughts About Computer Training

1. **Teach learners to work.** Make sure that every moment of computer training brings learners closer to doing their work better, faster, or more easily.

2. **Focus on learning.** Remember that users are learners. If we can spark their curiosity and direct them to resources, we'll have taught them how to be much better learners and users.

3. **Remember that everyone learns differently.** Don't teach as you'd like to learn. Assume that most learners are different from you in their learning styles. Teach in multiple styles.

4. **Teach "just in time" and "just enough."** Cut down on the amount taught and focus on what learners need to do tomorrow.

5. **Don't touch learners' keyboards.** Learners learn by doing, not by watching. The greatest gift you can give a learner is the moment of learning by attempting.

6. **Bring managers into the loop.** The role of the learner's manager is key. Make sure that the manager is involved, engaged, and in the loop for all communications.

7. **Get wired.** Effective, up-to-date trainers are active users of electronic mail, newsgroups, and the Internet. Start by sending a note to: info@masie.com to request a list of on-line resources for computer-training professionals.

8. **Be a learner.** A trainer's single most important activity is to keep learning. By taking ourselves back into the classroom, we keep our own skills current and stay in touch with the challenge of being a learner.

9. **Evaluate learner performance, not your performance.** The focus of evaluation must be on the learners' ability to perform work tasks, not on the trainer's ability to conduct a good class. Evaluate the real return on investment.

10. **Reinforce the training-support connection.** Every learner needs postclass support. Make sure there is a seamless handoff of learners from the training department to the support group. Prevent learner dependency by focusing on learner competency.

Index

Accounting software, 116, 134, 136
Adult learners. *See also* Computer
  users
    andragogy vs. pedagogy, 27-29
    bridging trainers and learners,
      61-63
    characteristics of, 26-28
    computer technology and, 19
    conceptual thinking and, 55-57,
      290
    confusion and, 287-89
    and context setting, 98
    and control, 111
    creative thinking and, 58-60,
      290
    delivery of course content and,
      115-16
    differences in, 26-28, 64-65
    evaluation of, 221-23
    expectations about training, 64-65
    focus on data and function, 32
    and lecture, 127
    Masie Model of Indexing and,
      30-38
    mathematics skills of, 64
    memorization and, 27, 50, 93,
      169, 181
    motivation of, 27, 29
    needs assessment of, 69-71, 74-77
    non-native English speakers, 64,
      124, 157
    note taking and, 111
    organizational roles of, 65
    practical thinking and, 57-58, 290
    reading skills of, 64, 124
    reflective thinking and, 53-55,
      289-90

Adult learners, cont.
    resistance and learner
      expectations, 64-65
    resistance due to lack of
      information, 44-45
    resistance to change, 45
    resistance to in-class reading,
      123, 125, 160, 174
    resistance to learning, 41-43
    resistance to using computer
      system, 43-44
    self-directed, 27-28
    and the set, 97
    thinking-styles theory, 52-65,
      289-90
    tools for creating competent
      users, 23
Adult Learning Theory, 175
America Online, 162. *See also* On-
  line/Internet-based learning
Andragogy, 27-28
Approach, 37
Artificial intelligence, 171
At-your-desk training. *See* Computer
  training
Audience for this book, 14
Audio learning
    advantages of, 159
    audiotape, 229
    benefit selling and, 157
    cost of, 158
    disadvantages of, 160
    history of, 156
    self-study and, 157
    support and, 158
    tips, 161
Audio teleconferencing, 206

Audiovisual media. See names of specific media, such as audio
Authorized Training Centers, 2

BBS. See Bulletin board services
Bellanca, Jim, 52, 95
Benefit selling
    audio learning and, 157
    overview and, 132
    the set and, 98
    slides and, 202
    video learning and, 212, 214
    video teleconferencing and, 206
Berliner, David, 13, 128
Blackboards, 177-79
Breakout groups. See Cooperative learning
Breaks, 91, 112
Bulletin board services. See also On-line/Internet-based learning
    bulletin board models, 163
    E-mail broadcast list models, 164-65
Bundled models, 9
"Bundles" of support. See Support
Burnout, 236. See also Management of computer training
Buzz groups. See Cooperative learning

CAD/CAM systems, 185
CAI. See Computer-based training
Case studies. See Simulation
Cassettes. See Audio learning
CBE. See Computer-based training
CBT. See Computer-based training
CD-ROM technology, 6, 60, 161, 175, 180, 184, 192
Certification
    as evaluation tool, 235-36
    CNE, 9
    employee contributions to, 8
    exams, 266
    IBM, 236
    Lotus, 236
    Microsoft, 236
    Novell, 236
    testing program and, 3-4

Certified Novell Engineer. See CNE/CNA programs
Change, resistance to, 45
Chargeback, 8, 22, 254, 258-59
Cheat sheets. See also Job aids
    advantages of, 169
    definition of, 168
    disadvantages of, 169-70
    practical trainers and, 61
    as print documentation, 283
    quick-reference guides, 281
    support and, 291
    tips, 170
Chunks, 99, 132
Classroom environment
    distractions, 109
    lighting, 107-108, 194
    noise, 108
    seating arrangements, 106-107, 194
    seating plans, 107
    temperature, 108
    ventilation, 108
Classroom management
    breaks, 112
    greetings, 110-11
    house rules, 111
    introductions, 112
    jargon, 112
    on-the-spot decisions, 113
Client-server models, 165
Climate-setting. See Classroom management
CNE/CNA programs, 235-36
CompuServe, 162. See also On-line/Internet-based learning
Computer-based training, trends in, 6. See also Computer training
Computer learning
    cost of, 4
    definition of, 12
    types of, 21
Computer literacy training, 292
Computer programmers. See Programmers
Computer resistance, 40-41, 43-44

Computer systems
  benefit-selling words
    concerning, 44
  evaluation of, 190-91
Computer trainers. *See also*
  Outsourcing
    advice for, 252
    as facilitators/coaches, 29
    "borrowed," 24
    bridging trainers and learners,
      61-63
    burnout and, 250-51, 236
    career paths, 249-50
    characteristics of the best, 39
    contract, 264
    course-development function,
      244-45
    evaluation of, 224-26
    freelance, 24
    full-time, 24
    hiring of, 245-47
    job descriptions for, 244
    management function, 245
    marketing function, 245
    needs assessment for, 73-74
    part-time, 244
    patience of, 247
    profession of, 243-53
    retired employees as, 268
    salaries, 248
    senior trainers, 244
    skills required of, 9, 16, 247
    styles/affinities, 247
    thinking styles of, 60-61
    wandering, 6
Computer training
  at-your-desk training, 206, 255
  benefit-selling words and, 44
  bringing in training, 268-69
  budgeting for, 4
  bundled models, 9
  characteristics of good training,
    22-23
  classroom environment, 106-
    109
  classroom management, 110-13

Computer training, cont.
  comprehensive overview of
    material, 87
  conceptual thinking and, 55-57
  consortium training, 271
  contracting, 24
  cooperative learning, 114-21
  in corporate setting, 156, 249
  costs associated with lack of
    training, 22
  costs of, 4, 18
  courseware, 5, 271
  creative thinking and, 58-60
  decision making and, 13
  definition of, 12-13
  design process for, 67-77
  determination of content for, 80-
    81
  developing and delivering, 18
  development of the profession,
    243-53
  excluded workers, 5
  external, 264
  full-service classroom, 3
  "get-'em-started" approach, 87
  goal of, 22-23, 26
  government support of, 8
  growth of, 156
  history of, 12, 23-24
  humor in, 155
  the ideal, 246
  in the workplace, 6
  in-class reading, 122-25
  interdependence of training and
    support, 295-96
  job training and, 5
  just-in-time, 5, 17, 206
  lecture, 126-36
  location of, 5
  management of, 238-42
  motivation, 5
  navigational users, 47-50, 89,
    93, 149, 168, 289, 293
  need for, 20, 23
  needs assessment for, 66-77
  objectives for, 78-84
  on-line, 163

Computer training, cont.
  on-the-job learning/training,
    137-42
  organizational approach to, 25
  organizational structure for, 24
  overview, 5
  personnel responsible for, 14-19
  planning, 67
  practical thinking and, 57-58,
    60-61
  procedural users, 47-50, 131,
    142, 169, 212, 273-74, 289,
    293
  purchasing training, 8-9, 264-72
  purpose of, 241
  rebooting learners, 143-47
  reflective thinking and, 54
  related to hardware/software use,
    25
  resources for purchasing
    training, 264-72
  review of old material, 103
  Sagamore Design Model, 62-63,
    95-103
  in same department as support
    services, 294-96
  scheduled help-desk-based, 6
  scheduling of, 241, 242
  scheduling of external trainers,
    270
  self-study, 148-51
  sequencing course content, 102,
    103
  simulation, 152-55
  skills required for, 14
  support and, 240
  teaching of procedures, 103
  technology advancements and,
    2, 24
  ten simple thoughts about, 297-
    98
  timing of, 4
  tools for creating competent
    users, 23
  use of support services and,
    284-96
  user-friendliness and, 21

Computer training, cont.
  user requests for, 6-7
  versus computer support, 25
Computer training. See also Design
  process; Computer learning;
  Management of computer training
Computer users. See also Adult
  learners
  navigational users, 47-50, 89,
    93, 149, 168, 289, 293
  procedural users, 47-50, 131,
    142, 169, 212, 273-74, 289,
    293
Computer-assisted instruction. See
  Computer-based training
Computer-based training
  advantages of, 173-74
  bundling with applications, 6
  CD-ROM technology and, 175
  cost of, 173
  development of, 173
  disadvantages of, 174
  growth of, 6
  interactive video and, 176, 185
  link to classroom learning, 7
  personal learning and, 6
  reflective thinking and, 55
  Sagamore Design Model and,
    173
  skills for CBT development,
    175-76
  thinking styles and, 173
Computer-training staff
  advice for, 252
  burnout and, 236, 250-51
  career opportunities for, 249-50
  characteristics of successful
    trainers, 253
  course-development role, 244-
    45
  description of computer-training
    profession, 243
  hiring advice, 245-46
  management role, 245
  marketing and training
    consultant role, 245
  salaries, 248-49, 252

Computer-training staff, cont.
      skill sets required, 247
      training contract coordinator
            role, 245
      training role, 244
Concepts, 89, 93
Conceptual thinking
      learning style, 55-57
      support services and, 56,
      trainer style, 60
Confusion
      check for, 99-100
      documentation and, 276-77
      stages of, 287-89
Consortium training, 271
Consultants, 268
Context-setting for training, 98
Contract learning. *See* Learning
      contracts
Cooperative learning
      advantages of, 116-17
      costs of, 116
      definition of, 114
      disadvantages of, 114-18
      future trends, 120-21
      group composition, 118-19
      group size, 118
      guided practice and, 100, 116
      in-class reading and, 123
      Johnsons' research on, 114-15,
            117
      lecture and, 116, 136
      objections to, 115
      opportunities for learners, 115-16
      and support, 293
      time allocation, 119
      tips, 118-20, 124
      unguided practice and, 100, 116
      uses of competition, 119
Cooperative-learning-oriented lecture,
      136
Corporate training departments, 3, 14
Costs
      associated with lack of training,
            22, 257
      associated with
            training/learning, 254-59

Costs, cont.
      chargeback models, 258-59
      desktop computer training
            estimate, 254
      equipment, 256
      facilities, 256
      hidden, 18
      materials, 256
      needs assessment and, 68
      payment options, 258-59
      pricing of classes/services, 9
      public seminar, 265-66
      retraining, 257
      salaries of learners, trainer,
            developer, 255
      supervision, 256
      support, 256, 259
      training consultants and
            companies, 268-69
      training/learning vs.
            development, 257
      travel, 256
Courseware
      content decisions, 87
      custom, 5, 264, 269
      customized engines, 271
      design of, 265, 270
      development of, 244-45, 247,
            251, 255, 257, 271
      generic, 271
      VCP Inventory and, 271
Creative thinking
      learning style, 58-60
      support services and, 58
      trainer style, 61

Data collection, 74-75
dBASE, 37
Decisions
      about computer training, 13
      content, 87
Default styles. *See* Thinking styles
Demonstration, 132-33
Dependent users. *See* Support
Design
      assessing the learner, 69-71

Design, cont.
  assessing the system or software, 71-72
  assessing the work context, 72-73
  assessing trainer needs, 73-74
  custom, 265
  data collection, 74-75
  decision making involved in, 67-68
  design tips, 102-103
  needs assessment, 66-77
  objectives, 83-84
  purchased training, 264-72
  review of old material, 103
  Sagamore Design Model, 62-63, 95, 103
  sequencing course content, 102-103
  using needs-assessment data, 76-77
  validation of needs-assessment data, 76
  VCP Analysis and, 92-93
  VCP Inventory and, 88-92
  Video teleconferencing and, 7-8
Desktop video teleconferencing. See Video teleconferencing
Development
  of applications, 18
  local customization, 7
Distractions, 109
Documentation
  conceptual thinking and, 56
  confusion associated with, 274, 276-77
  cost-effectiveness of, 274
  creative thinking and, 59
  customizing, 283
  design of, 279-80
  evolution of, 275-76
  examples of, 280
  heavy referencing, 277-78
  industry standards and, 276
  light referencing, 278
  modifications to, 274, 277, 280, 281
  need for, 273

Documentation, cont.
  on-line, 281-82
  practical thinking and, 58
  print, 282-83
  quality of, 276
  reflective thinking and, 55
  for self-study, 148-49
  Sagamore Design Model and, 278-79
  standard conventions in, 280
  as a system feature or peripheral, 274
  thinking styles and, 63-64
  third-party, 275
  trainers' attitudes about, 279
  training with, 274, 277
  types of, 281-83
  user expectations of, 274-76
  VCP Inventory and, 88
  vendor-supplied, 275
  volume of, 281
  ways to use, 278-79

E-mail, 164, 165, 167, 236. See also Bulletin board services
Electronic performance-support systems. See Performance-support systems
English as a second language, 64, 124, 157
Evaluation
  clients for, 230
  certification and, 235-36
  competency test, 222
  complicated nature of, 220-21
  computer-training standards and, 242
  course, 226
  courseware, 271
  during training, 221-22
  environmental factors, 227-29
  of external courseware, 272
  focus of, 230-31
  focus on performance, 221-22
  forms and questionnaires, 229
  instructor performance, 224-26
  interviews, 230

Evaluation, cont.
    learner performance, 221
    management of computer
        training, 238-42
    observation, 229
    postcourse, 222
    postcourse telephone survey, 223
    process of, 230-31
    smile sheets, 231-35
    software or system, 226-27
    technology for, 236
    tips on evaluation methods,
        229-30
Expert users/"wizards"
    OJL and, 140
    as support providers, 285, 291
    as trainers, 244, 254
    training responsibilities of, 14, 17
    as user-group members, 210
External training centers/trainers. *See*
    Outsourcing; Purchased training
Evaluation
    certification, 235-36
    of course, 226
    difficulty of, 220, 236-37
    of environmental factors after
        training, 228
    of environmental factors during
        training, 227-28
    five factors in, 221
    handouts and, 225, 226
    of instructor performance, 224-26
    justification of training and, 220
    of learner performance after
        training, 222
    of learner performance during
        training, 221-22
    process of, 230-31
    sample list of observation
        criteria, 225
    sample postcourse telephone
        survey, 223
    smile sheets, 231-35, 236
    of software or system, 226-29
    technology for, 236
    tips on methods, 229-30
    trainer burnout and, 236, 250-51

Films. *See* Video
Flipcharts, 98, 177-79
Frankston, Bob, 216
Freenet, 167
Functional illiteracy, 64
Future trends, 120, 142, 187, 198,
    215

Games, 155. *See also* Simulation
Gery, Gloria, 217
Goodman, Joel, 155
Grapevine, and needs assessment, 75
Greetings, 110-11
Groupware, 28, 121, 217, 236
Guided practice, 100-101, 107, 116,
    158, 212-13, 279, 293

Handouts
    advantages of, 181
    disadvantages of, 181
    documentation and, 182
    evaluation and, 225, 226
    memorization anxiety and, 27
    peer training and, 182
    tips, 182
    uses of, 98, 116, 122, 125, 134,
        179, 180
"Hands-on" time, myth of, 118
Help desk. *See also* Support
    assistance, 198
    relationship with computer-
        training function, 240
    support for navigational users, 50
    support for procedural users, 50
    as tutor, 2
House rules, 111
Humor and games in training, 155.
    See also Simulation
HUMOR Project, The, 155
Hunter, Madeline, 95-96

Illinois Renewal Institute, 52
Illiteracy, 64
In-class reading
    advantages of, 123-24
    aversion to, 160
    disadvantages of, 124

In-class reading, cont.
    thinking styles and, 123
    tips, 124-25
Independent learning. *See* Self-study
Indexing, 37-39, 71. *See also* Masie
    Model of Indexing
Individual learning. *See* Self-study
Information transfer, 99, 279
Instructors. *See* Computer trainers
Interactive on-line help. *See* Bulletin
    board services
Interactive tutorials. *See* Computer-
    based training
Interactive TV, 184
Interactive video, 156, 176, 183-87
Internet, 6, 7, 18, 93, 121, 162, 164-
    67, 298. *See also* On-line/Internet-
    based learning
Internet-based learning, 7. *See also*
    On-line/Internet-based learning
Interviews
    evaluation, 222-24
    needs assessment, 75
Introductions, 112
IVI. *See* Interactive video

Jargon, 112
Job aids. *See also* Cheat sheets
    audio learning and, 158
    creative thinkers and, 59
    as print documentation, 283
    rebooting and, 145
Johnson, David, 114, 117, 118
Johnson, Roger, 114, 117, 118
Just-in-time training. *See* Computer
    training

Keyboard templates. *See* Cheat sheets
Keystroke guides. *See* Cheat sheets
Knowles, Malcolm, 27-28

LAN, 162, 184
Large-screen projection
    advantages of, 189-90
    choosing a projection
      technology, 191-95
    disadvantages, of, 190

Large-screen projection, cont.
    LCD projection panels, 191-93
    lighting and, 108
    mirroring and, 196
    television, 194-95
    tips for, 190-91
    video-projection devices, 193-94
Laser discs, 175, 183-87
LCD projection panels, 191-92
Learner tests
    Indexing Test, 37-38
    Truth Test, 35-56
    Value Test, 36-37
Learners. *See* Adult learners
Learning ability, 37-38
Learning by observation. *See* On-the-
    job learning; On-the-job-training
Learning contracts, 45-46, 59
Learning differences
    thinking styles and, 51-64
    other, 64-65
Learning resistance, 41-43
Learning shells. *See* Performance-
    support systems
Lecture
    advantages of, 129-30
    and audiovisual aids, 128
    benefit selling and, 132
    cautions concerning, 126-27
    cooperative-learning-oriented
      lecture, 136
    cost-effectiveness of, 128
    definition of, 126
    demonstration, 132-33
    disadvantages of, 130-31
    in-class reading and, 123, 124
    learner participation and, 128,
      130, 133-36
    overview, 132
    random-access lecture, 134
    short explanation, 132
    Socratic method, 136
    solicited participation, 134
    theory session, 133
    thinking styles and, 128-29
    tips, 131-32
    uses of, 126-29

Lecture, cont.
    variations on, 132-33
    voluntary participation, 133-36
Lighting, 107-108
Liquid-crystal display panels. *See* LCD
  projection panels
Literacy, 64
Lotus 1-2-3, 5, 37

Mager, Robert, 83
Management of computer training
    applicability and emphasis on
      performance, 221
    appropriate staffing, 239
    avoiding burnout, 250-52
    career paths of trainers, 249-50
    centralization of, 238-39
    chargeback models, 258-59
    cooperation with other organiza-
      tional functions, 239-41
    costs of training, 254-59
    evaluation of, 230-31, 265
    external training and, 267-68
    hidden cost of poorly managed
      training, 18
    hiring of trainers, 245-47
    job descriptions for computer
      trainers, 244
    marketing of training, 245
    outsourcing of training, 239
    planning for training, 20-21
    providing structured learning,
      21
    purchased training and, 265,
      267-68
    salaries of trainers, 248
    standards, 242
    support of user groups, 210
    understanding training role vs.
      hardware/software use, 25
Managers
    computer training and, 14, 17-
      18
    public seminars and, 265-66
    support services and, 293-95
Manuals, as learning aid, 2. *See also*
  Documentation

Marketing
    comprehensive approach to,
      261-62
    for-profit approach to, 261
    mistakes in, 261
    responsibilities for, 260-63
    techniques, 261-62
    tips/tricks, 262-63
    and training consultation, 245
    truth in, 262
MASIE Center, The, 142, 205, 227,
  243, 245, 248, 315
Masie Model of Indexing, 29, 30-39
Mathematics skills, 64
Media programs. See names of specific
  media, such as audio
Memorization, 27, 50, 93, 169, 181, 277
Microsoft Excel, 5, 37, 86
Microsoft Publisher Newsletter
  Wizard, 217
Microsoft Wizards, 217
Mirroring
    advantages of, 197
    disadvantages of, 198
    future trends, 198
    large-screen projection and, 196
MIS departments
    responsibility for training costs,
      258
    training/support role, 18, 24, 275
MIS management
    development/delivery of compu-
      ter training and, 18, 24
    training responsibilities, 18, 245
Motivation, 27, 29

Navigational users, 47-50, 89, 93,
  149, 168, 289, 293
Needs assessment
    around coffeepot/in restroom, 77
    assessing the learner, 69-71
    assessing the system or software,
      71-72
    assessing the work context, 72-73
    assessing trainer needs, 73-74
    computer-training standards
      and, 242

Needs assessment, cont.
  data collection, 74-75
  importance of, 66-68
  last-minute assessment, 75
  surveys for, 74
  use of data, 76-77
  validation of data, 76
  and VCP analysis, 92
  vendors and, 267
Network. *See* Mirroring
Network Interactive Forms, 236
Network learning, 7. *See also* On-line/Internet-based learning
Neuro Linguistic Programming, 52
New employee orientation, 92
Noise, 108
Non-native English speakers, 64, 124, 157
Nonprint media. See names of specific media, such as audio
Novell Coaches, 217

Objectives, 78-84, 92, 242
Objective setting, 27
Observation, for evaluation, 224-26, 229
OJL. *See* On-the-job learning
OJT. *See* On-the-job training
On-line conferencing. *See* Bulletin board services
On-line documentation, 281-82 . *See also* Documentation
On-line/Internet-based learning
  advantages of, 166
  agents/newsgroups (filters), 165
  bandwidth, 165
  bulletin board models, 163
  definitions of terms related to, 162
  disadvantages of, 166-67
  E-mail broadcast list models, 164-65
On-the-job learning
  advantages of, 139-40
  costs of, 138-39
  definition of, 137
  disadvantages of, 140-42

distractions and, 109
On-the-job learning, cont.
  expert users and, 140
  future trends, 142
  legitimization of, 138-39
  peer training, 140
  temps as trainers, 142
  versus on-the-job training, 137
On-the-job training
  "covert coaches," 241
  definition of, 137
  handouts and, 182
  history of, 137-38
  peer training and, 182
  uses of, 137
  versus on-the-job learning, 137
On-the-spot decisions, 113
Oracle, 165
Overhead projectors
  advantages of, 200
  disadvantages of, 200-201
  LCD panel and, 199
  lighting and, 108
  tips for, 200-201
  uses of, 199
Outsourcing. *See also* Purchased training
  support and, 3
  of training, 24
  trends in, 3
Overview, 87, 132. *See also* Lecture

"Packaged" courses, 268
Pedagogy, 27-28
Peer support. *See* Support
Peer training. *See* On-the-job learning; On-the-job training
Performance shells. *See* Performance-support systems
Performance-support models. *See* Support
Performance-support systems
  costs associated with, 218
  definition of, 216
  examples of, 217-18
  Gloria Gery and, 217
  new marketing angle and, 218
  systems and features of, 217

Pike, Bob, 155, 201

Powersoft, 165

Practical thinking
learner style, 57-58
support services and, 58
trainer style, 60-61

Practice
arrangement of terminals for, 107
documentation and, 279
guided practice, 63, 100-01,
168, 173, 212, 271
support services and, 293
unguided practice, 59, 101, 168,
173, 271

Pricing. *See* Costs

Presentation code/software, 172-73

Procedural users, 47-50, 131, 142,
169, 212, 273-74, 289, 293

Procedures, 89-90, 93, 103

Prodigy, 162. *See also* On-line/
Internet-based learning

PROFS, 2

Programmers, 14, 216, 275

Prompt cards. *See* Cheat sheets

PSS. *See* Performance-support systems

Public seminars, 264, 265-66, 268,
269, 271

Purchased training
bringing in training, 268-69
consortium training, 271
costs of, 265, 268-69
courseware and, 271
design process and, 264-65,
268-69
evaluation of, 272
expectations of, 267
forms of, 264-65
management involvement in,
267-68
need for, 264
public seminars and, 265-66
resources for, 268
scheduling of, 270
selection of training vendor,
266-67
sneaker-based training, 270

Purkey, William, 134

Questionnaires, for evaluation, 229

Questions during training, 62, 63, 99-
100, 133-36, 267

Quick-reference cards. *See* Cheat
sheets

Random-access lecture, 113

Reading. *See* In-class reading

Reading assignments, in-class, 122-25

Reading skills, 64

Rebooting
advantages of, 145-46
sample list, 146-47
and support, 293
tips, 146
of trainers, 147

Reference manual, 282

Reflective thinking. *See also* Thinking
styles
learner style, 53-55
support services and, 54
trainer style, 60

Remediation, 123, 128, 138, 142, 184,
226, 281

Resistance. *See* Adult learners

Retraining, need for, 22

Review of old material, 103, 145

Role plays. *See* Simulation

Sagamore Design Model
CBT and, 173
check for confusion, 99-100
check for understanding, 101-
102
classroom-based training and,
96
context, 98
design tips, 102-103
documentation and, 278-79
evaluation and, 221
guided practice, 100-101
information transfer, 99
as link between study of school
learning/computer training,
95
motivation, 98-99

Sagamore Design Model, cont.
    non-classroom-based training
        and, 96
    objectives, 98
    OJL and, 138
    the set, 97-99
    simulation and, 153
    thinking styles and, 62-63, 102
    unguided practice, 101
    uses of, 96-97
    video learning and, 212
    video teleconferencing and, 206
Salaries, trainers', 248
Scheduling of external trainers, 270
Scriptsit, 156
Seating arrangements, 106-107, 135
Self-paced learning. See Self-study
Self-study
    advantages of, 150
    CBT and, 148-51, 172
    disadvantages of, 150-51
    tips, 151
    use of audio for, 157
Seminars. See Public seminars
Short explanation, 132
SIGS. See User groups
Simon, Sid, 226
Simulation. See also Games
    advantages of, 153-54
    CBT and, 174
    creative trainers and, 61
    definition of, 152
    disadvantages of, 154
    humor and games in training,
        155
    role plays, 293
Slave systems. See Mirroring
Slides
    advantages of, 203
    benefit selling and, 202
    disadvantage of, 203
    lighting and, 108
Small-group discussion. See
    Cooperative learning
SMART system, 236
Smile sheets, 231-35
Sneaker-based training, 6, 142

Socratic method, 136
Softbank Institute, 218
Software
    needs assessment and, 71-72
    evaluation of, 226-27
    locally developed, 271
    VCP Inventory and, 88-92
Solicited participation, 134
Special-interest groups. See User
    groups
Statistical software, 86
"Stupidity check," 100
Support groups. See User groups
Support
    availability of resources, 23
    "bundles" of, 259
    computer training and, 284-96
    conceptual thinking and, 290
    cooperative learning and, 293
    costs of, 240, 255-59, 285, 291
    creative thinking and, 290
    dependency on, 251, 257, 259,
        260-61, 291
    help-desk staff, 17
    help-desk-based training, 6
    informal, 291
    interdependence of training and,
        295-96
    manual use, 285
    navigational users and, 50
    needs for, 284-85
    on-line, 163
    organizational solutions
        pertaining to, 293
    outsourcing of, 268
    peer support, 115-16, 198, 291
    policies and procedures
        pertaining to, 293-95
    practical thinking and, 290
    procedural users and, 50
    quality-control potential, 295-96
    rebooting and, 293
    reflective thinking and, 289-90
    responsibilities shared with
        training function, 295-96
    in same department as training,
        294-96

Support, cont.
stages of confusion and, 287-89
thinking styles and, 289-90
training and, 240
training solutions for excessive support demands, 292-93
types of, 286-87
types of users and, 289
use of, 284-85
Surveys for needs assessment, 74
Sylvan learning, 236
System modifications, 22

Tapes. *See* Audio learning
TDI. *See* Computer-based training
Teachable items, 86-94
Teaching model, 28
Technical experts, as computer trainers, 15
Technical reference manual, 283
Technologies. See names of specific media, such as audio
Technology
articles about, 1
evolution of, 2, 24
Teleconferencing. *See* Video teleconferencing
Television, 194-95
Temperature, 108
Temps as trainers, 142
Terminals
arrangement for practice, 107
arrangement for training session, 107
noise of, 108
Theory session, 133
Thinking styles
audio learning and, 157
conceptual thinking, 55-57, 64, 123, 128, 136, 157, 170, 173
creative thinking, 58-60, 64, 115, 123
default styles, 53
documentation and, 63-64
in-class reading and, 123
practical thinking, 57-58, 63, 64, 98, 103, 115, 123, 173

Thinking styles, cont.
reflective thinking, 53-55, 64, 115, 123, 153, 157, 289
resistance and, 63
Sagamore Design Model and, 62-64, 102
support services and, 63-64, 289-90
theory of, 52-65
trainers', 60-61, 73
Third-party trainers. *See* Outsourcing
Trainers and computer training. *See* Computer trainers
Training. *See* Computer training
Training departments. *See* Corporate training departments
Training vendors. *See* Vendors
"Triage support," 294
Tutorials, 283

Understanding, check for, 101-102
Unguided practice, 101, 107, 116, 158, 213, 279, 293
User-friendliness
myth of, 21, 241
relative to user skills, 21
User groups
advantage of, 209
bulletin boards and, 164
disadvantages of, 209
management support of, 210
sponsorship/administration of, 208-209
tip, 210
training and support and, 210
User's guide, 283
Users. *See* Adult learners; Computer users; Expert users

VCP Analysis, 92-93, 262, 270, 295
VCP applications
evaluation tool, 94
random-access agenda, 94
VCP Inventory
business VCP, 91
concepts, 89
conducting the inventory, 88-91

VCP Inventory, cont.
    deciding what to teach, 86-87
    example of VCP listing, 91
    new employee orientation and,
        91
    preparation of comprehensive
        VCP list, 90-91
    procedures, 89-90
    as skills-assessment technique,
        92
    types of content, 86
    and vendors, 265
    vocabulary, 88
VCP Model of Evaluation Survey, 94,
    234-35
Vendors, 164, 255, 266-67, 269
Ventilation, 108
Video learning. *See also* Interactive
    video
    advantages of, 214
    benefit selling and, 212-14
    costs associated with, 212
    disadvantages of, 212, 214
    formats of, 213
    future trends, 215
    production of, 158
    Sagamore Design Model and,
        212
    tip, 215
    videotape, 229
Video-projection devices, 193-94

Video server, 184, 187
Video teleconferencing
    advantages of, 206-207
    audio teleconferencing, 206
    benefit selling and, 206
    challenges of, 205
    cost of, 204
    description of, 204
    disadvantages of, 207
    Sagamore Design Model and,
        206
    satellite-delivered, 205-206
    uses of, 204-206
Visual Basic, 172
Visual Macro Scripting, 37
Vocabulary
    support services and, 292
    training and, 88, 92-93
Vocabulary, Concepts, and Procedures
    Inventory, 85-94. *See also* VCP
    Inventory
Voluntary participation, 135-36

WAN, 13, 163
Wandering trainers. *See* Sneaker-based
    training
Whiteboards, 177-79
"Wizards." *See* Expert users
Word-processing software, 86, 156
Workstations, 108

The MASIE Center

The MASIE Center is an international think tank dedicated to the intersection of technology and learning. The center provides research, publications, resources, training, networking, and consulting to organizations throughout the world.

The MASIE Center services include:

■ The MASIE Forum: A membership subscription service for organizations interested in the fields of technology and learning, and technical education. Forum membership includes:

– Monthly telephone broadcasts hosted by Elliott Masie
– Monthly faxed updates
– Quarterly research reports
– Quarterly professional-development videotapes
– Weekly E-mail networking digests

Subscriptions are $950 per site for a 12-month membership.

■ Consultation and training: The center provides targeted training in the development of technical skills for training professionals and the reengineering of corporate learning departments.

■ Keynote presentations: Elliott Masie gives keynote presentations at major international and national conferences on a range of technology and learning topics.

For more information about MASIE Center services, contact:

The MASIE Center
75 Cambridge Parkway, Suite PH3
Cambridge, MA 02142
Phone: 1-800-98-MASIE
Fax: 1-800-96-MASIE
International telephone: 617-252-0845
E-mail: info@masie.com

WANT MORE COPIES?

This and most other Lakewood books are available at special quantity discounts when purchased in bulk. For details, write: Lakewood Books, 50 South Ninth Street, Minneapolis, MN 55402. Phone: (800) 328-4329 or (612) 333-0471. Fax: (612) 333-6526.

OTHER LAKEWOOD PUBLICATIONS

Dynamic Openers & Energizers: 101 Tips and Tactics
for Enlivening Your Training Classroom $14.95

Powerful Audiovisual Techniques: 101 Ideas to Increase
the Impact and Effectiveness of Your Training $14.95

Optimizing Training Transfer: 101 Techniques for Improving
Training Retention and Application $14.95

Motivating Your Trainees: 101 Proven Ways to Get Them
to Really Want to Learn $14.95

Managing the Front-End of Training: 101 Ways to Analyze
Training Needs — and Get Results! $14.95

Creative Training Tools: 101 Easy-to-Use Ideas for
Increasing Trainee Participation $14.95

THE COMPLETE SET: 6-PACK OF "101" BOOKS $59.95

THE COMPLETE SET: The HRD Library $139.95

Creative Training Techniques Handbook, Second Edition $49.95

Designing and Delivering Cost-Effective Training —
and Measuring the Results, Second Edition $39.95

What Works at Work: Lessons from the Masters $29.95

"Customers From Hell Are Customers, Too" T-Shirt $12.00

TRAINING Magazine "The Human Side of Business" T-Shirt $12.00

TRAINING Magazine (12 issues per year) $68.00

Creative Training Techniques Newsletter (12 issues per year) $99.00

Training Directors' Forum Newsletter (12 issues per year) $118.00

TO ORDER ANY OF THE ABOVE, OR TO REQUEST A FULL CATALOG ON TECHNOLOGY AND LEARNING PRODUCTS AND SERVICES, CONTACT:
Lakewood Books, 50 South Ninth Street, Minneapolis, MN 55402.
Phone: (800) 328-4329 or (612) 333-0471. Fax: (612) 333-6526.

UNCONDITIONAL GUARANTEE

Examine and use any of the resources on this page for a full 30 days. If you are not completely satisfied, for any reason whatsoever, simply return them and receive a full refund of the purchase price.